W9-BVB-414

AN AMERICAN CHRISTMAS

An AMERICAN CHRISTMAS

A SAMPLER OF CONTEMPORARY STORIES & POEMS

EDITED BY JANE B. HILL

Peachtree Publishers, Ltd.

Published by
PEACHTREE PUBLISHERS, LTD.
494 Armour Circle, N.E.
Atlanta, Georgia 30324

Manufactured in the United States of America

Library of Congress Cataloging-in-Publication Data

An American Christmas.

1. Christmas--Literary collections. 2. American literature--20th century. I. Hill, Jane B.
PS509.C56A43 1986 810'.8'033 86-21268
ISBN 0-934601-00-3

1st printing

For Betsy and for Bob

CONTENTS

An
AMERICAN CHRISTMAS

DAVID BOTTOMS

The Boy Shepherds' Simile

Wind rose cold
under our robes, and straw blew loose
from the stable roof.
We loved the cow tied to the oak, her breath rising
in the black air, and the two goats trucked
from the Snelling farm, the gray dog shaking with age
and weather.
                    Over our scene a great star hung
its light, and we could see in the bleached night
a crowd of overcoats peopling the chairs.
A coat of black ice glazed the street.

This was not a child or a king,
but Mary Sosebee's Christmas doll of a year ago.

We knelt in that knowledge on the wide front lawn
of the First Baptist Church
while flashbulbs went off all around us
and a choir of angels caroled from their risers.
This was not a child wrapped in the straw
and the ragged sheet, but since believing was an easy thing
we believed it was like a child,
a king who lived in the stories we were told.
For this we shivered in adoration. We bore the cold.

GARRISON KEILLOR

from *Lake Wobegon Days*

When I was fifteen, a girl I wrote three poems for invited me to Christmas Eve so her parents could see that I wasn't as bad as many people said, and after a big meatball supper and a long thoughtful period between her dad and me as she and her mom cleared the dishes when he asked me what I intended to do with myself, we went to the ten o'clock candlelight service at Lake Wobegon Lutheran. My mind wasn't on Christmas. I was thinking about her. She had never seen the poems because they were too personal, so she didn't know how much I loved her.

The lights went out, and the children's choir began its slow march up the aisle, holding candles and singing *"Hjemmet paa Prairien"* ("Home on the Prairie") — "To our home on the prairie, sweet Jesus has come. Born in a stable, he blesses his own. Though humble our houses and fortunes may be, I love my dear Savior who smiles on me" — and in the dark, the thin sweet voices and illuminated faces passing by, people began to weep. The song, the smell of pine boughs, the darkness, released the tears they evidently had held back for a very long time. Her mother wept, her father who had given me stony looks for hours bent down and put his face in his hands, her lovely self drew out a hanky and held it to her eyes, and I too tried to cry — I wanted to cry right along with her and maybe slip my arm around her shoulders — and I couldn't. I took out my handkerchief, thinking it would get me started, and blew my nose, but there was nothing there.

I only cried later, after I walked her home. We stood on her steps, she opened the door, I leaned toward her for one kiss, and she turned and said, "I hate to say this but you are one of the coldest people I ever met." I cried at home, in bed, in the dark. Turned my face to the wall and felt hot tears trickle down my face. Then woke up and it was Christmas morning.

Now an older guy, I've gotten more moist and when the decorations go up over Main Street from Ralph's north to the mercantile, I walk down alone to look at them, they are so beautiful — even old guys stand in wonder and are transported back to childhood, though of course these are the same decorations as when we were kids so it doesn't take much imagination. The six-foot plywood star with one hundred Christmas bulbs, twenty on each point, was built by Mr. Scheffelmacher's shop class in 1956; I flunked the quiz on electricity and didn't get to work on it. I sanded the edges a little, though I had flunked wood too. Later, I flunked the ballpeen hammer and was kicked out of shop and into speech class — Mr. Scheffelmacher said, "All you do is talk, talk, talk, so you might as well learn how." I begged him to let me stay in shop, which was getting into sheet metal and about to make flour scoops, but he said, "You couldn't even pass wood. You couldn't even make a decent birdhouse!" and he was right. My birdhouse leaked, and the birds were so mad about it, when I tried to caulk the roof, they attacked me, Mr. and Mrs. Bluebird. So I dragged myself into speech and had to make up the work I had missed: five speeches in one week: humorous, persuasive, extemporaneous, impromptu, and reflective, and suddenly, talking, which had been easy for me at the shop bench, became impossible. I dragged my feet to the front of the room, afraid my loafers would flap (they had been my brother's), and stood there, a ridiculous person six-feet-three and a hundred fifty pounds, trying to keep my jaw slack as I had practiced in a mirror to make up for a small chin, and mumbled and got hot across the eyes and had to say, "Anyway, as I started to say. . . ." which Miss Ferkovich marked you down for three points for because "Anyway" showed disorganization, so I failed speech, too, but speech was the end of the line — if you couldn't speak, where could you go? To reading? I sat in speech and drew stick men hanging on the gallows, listening to Chip Ingqvist's reflective, entitled "A Christmas Memory," which was about his dear old aunt whom he visited every Christmas, bringing sugar cookies, and was so good he did it twice in class and again for school assembly two weeks after Christmas and then in the district speech tournament, the regional, and the state, and finished first runner-up in the reflective division, and yet it always sounded so sincere as if he had just thought of it — for example, when he said, "And oh! the light in her eyes was worth far more to me than anything money could buy," a tear came to his voice, his eyes lit up like vacuum tubes and his right hand made a nice clutching gesture over his heart on his terrific brown V-neck sweater, which I mention because I felt that good clothes gave him self-confidence, just as the clothing ads said and that I might be sincere like him if instead of an annual Christmas sweater I got a regular supply. Anyway, Christmas decorations sure bring back a lot of memories for me.

Depending on your angle, the stars seem to lead the traveler toward the Sidetrack Tap, where the old guys sit and lose some memory capacity with a glass of peppermint schnapps, which Wally knows how to keep adding to so they can tell the old lady they only had one. After one of those continuous drinks, they try not to look at the bubble lights on the little aluminum tree on the back bar. Bud is there, who gets a twinge in his thighs around Christmas, remembering the year the ladder went out from under him as he was hanging decorations, and he slid down the telephone pole, which was somewhat smoother after he slid down than before. In addition to the large star, you see smaller ones that look like starfish, and stubby candles, and three wise men who in their wonder and adoration appear a little stupid, all made by shop classes on a jigsaw, and angels that, if you look at them a certain way, look like clouds. The manger stands in front of Our Lady church, the figures (imported from Chicago) so lifelike it gives you the chills to see them outdoors — it's so cold, they should take their flight to Egypt! The municipal Christmas tree stands in front of the Statue of the Unknown Norwegian who seems to be reaching out to straighten it. It leans slightly toward the south, away from the wind.

One bitter cold night, a certain person stepped out of the Sidetrack Tap and crossed the street under the clear starry sky toward the gay lights of the municipal tree and noticed that he needed to take a leak. It was three blocks to home, and the cold had suddenly shrunk his bladder, so he danced over toward the Unknown and picked out a spot in the snow in the dark behind the tree where nobody would see him.

It was an enormous relief at first, of course, like coming up for air after a long submersion, but it also made him leery to be so exposed right out on Main Street. So many dark windows where someone could be watching, and what if a car came along? They'd know what was up. Him, profaning a monument to the Norwegian people. "I should stop — right now!" he thought. His capacity, though: it was amazing! Like a horse. Gallons, already, and it didn't feel like he could put the cork back in. Then he saw the headlights. Only for a moment, then the car turned the other way, but in that moment he hopped six feet to one side and stood in shock until the taillights disappeared, and only then did he hear the hiss of liquid on the hot bulb and look and see what he was doing. He was peeing on the tree! Pissing on Christmas! Then the bulb burst. Pop!

"Oh God, what a pig I am!" he thought. He expected the big spruce to fall on him and crush him. Pinned under the tree, found the next morning, frozen to death with his thing in his hand. The shame to his family. The degradation of it. Finally he was done *(you pig!)*. There was a stain in the snow as big as a bathtub, and another one where he had stood before. He dumped handfuls of clean snow on them, but it turned yellow. Then he walked home, got a snow shovel, came back, and carried his mess, shovel by shovel, across the street to the side of the Sidetrack Tap, and brought back shovels of clean snow to fill in. He smoothed it over and went home to bed.

It was not such a happy holiday for him for the recollection of what he had done *(pig)*, which if any of his children had done it he would have given them holy hell. He bought them wonderful presents that year and a gold watch for his wife, and burned when they said what a great guy he was, and it wasn't until January after the tree came down that he started to feel like he could drop in at the Sidetrack and relax with a couple of beers.

We get a little snow, then a few inches, then another inch or two, and sometimes we get a ton. The official snow gauge is a Sherwin-Williams paint can stuck to the table behind the town garage, with the famous Sherwin-Williams globe and red paint spilling over the Arctic icecap. When snow is up to the top of the world, then there is a ton of snow. Bud doesn't keep track of the amount beyond that point because once there is that much snow, more doesn't matter a lot. After the ton falls, we build a sled run on Adams Hill, behind the school, with high snow embankments on the turns to keep our sleds on the track at the thrilling high speeds we reach once the track is sprayed with water and freezes. Everyone goes at least once, even Muriel. Up at the Pee Tree, you flop on your belly on the sled and push off, down an almost straight drop of twenty feet and *fast* into a right-hand turn, then hard left, then you see the tree. It is in the middle of the track and will bash your brains out unless you do something. Before you can, you're in the third turn, centrifugal force having carried you safely around the tree, and then you come to the jump where some cookies are lost, and the long swooping curve under the swings, and you coast to a stop. You stand up and look down and see that you've almost worn the toes of your boots. You had the brakes on and you didn't notice.

At the swimming beach, the volunteer firemen have flooded the ice to make a glass sheet and hung colored lights in a V from the warming house to the pole on the diving dock. The warming house is open, the ancient former chickenhouse towed across the ice in 1937 from Jensens' when he gave up poultry after some exploded from a rich diet that made their eggs too big. When Bud fires up the cast-iron Providence wood stove, a faint recollection of chickens emanates from the floor. The stove stands in the middle, the floor chopped up around it where decades of skaters stepped up and down to get feeling back in their feet, and the benches run around the walls, which are inscribed with old thoughts of romance, some of them shocking to a child: news that Mother or Dad, instead of getting down to business and having you, was skylarking around, planting big wet smackers *(XXXXX)* on a stranger who if he or she had hooked up with her or him you would not be yourself but some other kid. This dismal prospect from the past makes a child stop and think, but then — what can you do? — you lace up and teeter down the plywood ramp and take your first glide of the season. It's a clear night, the sky is full of stars and the brilliant V points you out toward the dark, the very place your parents went, eventually, holding hands, arms crossed, skating to the Latin rhythms of Cully Culbertson and His Happy

Wurlitzer from the *Rexall Fun Time* album played through a mighty Zenith console put out on the ice, where some of the oldsters still cut a nice figure. Clarence and Arlene Bunsen, for two: to see him on the street, you'd know he has a sore back, but on the ice, some of his old form returns and when they take a turn around the rink in tandem, you might see why she was attracted to him, the old smoothie. Once two people have mastered skating the samba together, it isn't that much harder to just get married, says Clarence. She has bought a new pair of glasses, bifocals, that, when she looks at him, bring his ankles into sharp focus, slightly magnified.

In some homes, decorations don't appear until Christmas Eve afternoon, except for the Advent wreath on the supper table, its candles lit every night during supper. Catholics believe in abstaining before a feast — it sharpens the appetite — so Father Emil gives up his 9 P.M. finger of brandy for weeks so that his Christmas Eve brandy will taste more wonderful, even when Clarence brought him a bottle of Napoleon brandy far more wonderful than the Dominican DeLuxe Father buys for himself. "None for me," he said. "Oh, come on," Clarence said, "you only live once." Clarence is Lutheran but he sometimes drops in at the rectory for a second opinion. It is Father's opinion, however, that a person does not only live once, so he put the Napoleon on his bookshelf behind *War and Peace* where he would remember it. Even on Christmas Eve, one finger is the correct portion, by him, and it's a miserable mistake to think that two would be twice as good, and three even better, or putting both hands around the bottle and climbing into it. That's no Christmas. The true Christmas bathes every little thing in light and makes one cookie a token, one candle, one simple pageant more wonderful than anything seen on stage or screen.

The Kruegers ask him over to watch the Perry Como Christmas special and out of respect for their tremendous contributions over the years, he goes, and sits in glum silence watching tanned, relaxed people sing "O Little Town of Bethlehem" on a small-town street like none he's ever seen. A man appears on the screen to talk about Triumph television sets as the perfect Christmas gift, as behind him a viewing couple turn and beam at each other as if TV had saved their marriage. The Kruegers enjoy martinis, a vicious drink that makes them sad and exhausted, and the Mister gets up during commercials to adjust the picture, making it more lurid — greenish faces like corpses of the drowned, then orange, the victims of fire — and then the Krueger boy says, "Oh, *Dad*," and fixes it to normal, but even that looks lurid, like a cheap postcard. They sit, enraptured by it, but what dull rapture: not fifteen words spoken between them in the whole hour until, in the middle of "Chestnuts," the phone rings — it's Milly's sister in Dallas — and though it's only a commercial, Milly doesn't take her eyes off the screen, doesn't make a complete sentence, just says "uh-huh" and "oh" and "all right, I guess" as if the lady demonstrating the dish soap is her sister and her sister is a telephone salesman. A dismal scene compared to church, people leaning forward to catch the words coming from their children's mouths, their own flesh and blood, once babes in arms, now speaking the Gospel. What would the Kruegers do if during Perry's solo the doorbell rang and they heard children singing a carol on the porch? — would they curse them?

The German club from high school goes caroling, most of them Catholic kids but it's Luther they sing: *Vom Himmel hoch da komm ich her, Ich bring euch gute neue mar.* Luther League goes out, Catholic youth, Lutheran choir, Miss Falconer's high school choir, the Thanatopsians troop around and warble in their courageous ruined voices, Spanish Club, G.A.A., 4-H, even Boy Scouts sidle up to a few doors and whisper a carol or two. *O Christmas tree, O Christmas tree/How brightly shine thy candles.* The Scouts carry candles, which drip onto their jackets. Jimmy Buehler, Second Class, whose mother confiscated his phonograph because AC/DC's song "Highway to Hell" made her nervous, is their best singer; his sweet tenor leads the others. *And from each bough, a tiny light/Adds to the splendor of the sight.*

The carols that Miss Falconer's choir sings along Elm Street are a relief from the *Hodie* they practiced so hard for the Christmas assembly. Day after day, they sat and looked at the floor, which reeked of disinfectant, and breathed quietly through their mouths as she stood over them, still as a statue, and said, "Well, maybe we should cancel the whole concert. I'm not getting one bit of cooperation from you." She sighs at the shame of it and folds her arms. In a school this small, you don't get to specialize: one day Coach Magendanz is trying to bring out the animal in you, and then you are Ernest in *The Importance of Being,* and then you are defending the negative in the question of capital punishment, and the next day you're attempting sixteenth-century polyphony. "Tenors, open your mouth, you can't sing with your mouths shut. Basses, read the notes. They're right in front of you."

So great is the town's demand for Christmas music, some of them are going straight from this practice to Mrs. Hoglund's at the Lutheran church or to Our Lady choir practice and a different *Hodie* under Sister Edicta, a rehearsal in parkas in the cold choir loft, Father Emil having blanched at the latest fuel bill and turned the thermostat down to fifty-five. A cold Advent for Catholics, thanks to Emile Bebeau, the itinerant architect who designed this pile in 1878, no doubt intending the soaring vaulted ceiling to draw the hearts of the faithful upward; it also draws heat upward, and the parish is in hock to a Lutheran fuel-oil supplier. Father is dreaming of a letter from Publishers' Sweepstakes: "Dear Mr. Emil: It's our great pleasure to inform you —" or an emergency check from Bishop Kluecker, though Our Lady is not a diocesan parish but a mission of the Benedictines and Father reports to an abbot in Pennsylvania who observes the rule of silence, at least in financial matters.

The Sons of Knute don't carol in person, God having given them voices less suitable for carols than for wallies and elmers, but they do sponsor a choir of fourth-graders who learn two Norwegian carols well enough to sing them in dim light and make the rounds in the snow after supper, alternating carols house to house. One is usually enough to make any Knute wipe his eyes and blow his nose — *Jeg er så glad hver julekveld, Da synger vi hans pris; Da åpner han for alle små, Sitt søte paradis.* ("I am so glad on Christmas Eve, His praises then I sing; He opens then for every child The palace of the King") — and two might finish him off for good. Even Hjalmar, who sat like a fencepost through little Tommy's rare blood disease on "The Parkers" while Virginia put her head down and bawled, even Hjalmar hears

Jeg er så glad hver julekveld; his pale eyes glisten, and he turns away, hearing his mother's voice and smelling her *julekake,* the Christmas pudding, Mother sitting in a chair and working on her *broderi,* a pillowcase with two *engler* hovering over the *krybbe* where Jesus lies, the bright *stjerne* in the sky. *"Glade Jul!"* the fourth-graders cry, and back come Hjalmar's own boyhood chums in fragrant memory to greet him. "Hjally! Hjally!" they call, standing in the frame of bright windowlight on the brilliant snow of 1934.

Custom dictates that carolers be asked in and offered a cookie, a piece of cake, something to nibble, and so must every person who comes to your door, otherwise the spirit of Christmas will leave your house, and even if you be rich as Midas, your holiday will be sad and mean. That is half of the custom; the other half is that you must yourself go visiting. Everyone must get at least one unexpected visitor, otherwise they'll have no chance to invite one in and Christmas will be poorer for them. So, even if when they open the door, their thin smile tells you that you have arrived at the height of an argument, and even if, as you sit and visit, sulfurous looks are exchanged and innuendos drop like size-12 shoes, you are still performing a service, allowing them to try to be pleasant, even if they don't do it well.

Baking begins in earnest weeks ahead. Waves of cookies, enough to feed an army, enough to render an army defenseless, including powerful rumballs and fruitcakes soaked with spirits (if the alcohol burns off in the baking, as they say, then why does Arlene hide them from her mother?). And tubs of *lutefisk* appear at Ralph's meat counter, the dried cod soaked in lye solution for weeks to make a pale gelatinous substance beloved by all Norwegians, who nonetheless eat it only once a year. The soaking is done in a shed behind the store, and Ralph has a separate set of *lutefisk* clothes he keeps in the trunk of his Ford Galaxie. No dogs chase his car, and if he forgets to change his *lutefisk* socks, his wife barks at him. Ralph feels that the dish is a great delicacy and he doesn't find *lutefisk* jokes funny. "Don't knock it if you haven't tried it," he says. Nevertheless, he doesn't offer it to carolers who come by his house because he knows it could kill them. You have to be ready for *lutefisk.*

Father Emil doesn't knock *lutefisk;* he thinks it may be the Lutherans' penance, a form of self-denial. His homily the Sunday before: we believe that we really don't know what's best for us, so we give up some things we like in the faith that something better might come, a good we were not aware of, a part of ourselves we didn't know was there. We really don't know ourselves, our own life is hidden from us. God knows us. We obey His teaching, even though painful, entrusting our life to Him who knows best.

The faithful squirm when he says it. What comes next? they wonder. No Christmas this year? Just soup and crackers? Catholic children see Lutheran children eating candy that the nuns tell them they should give up until Christmas and think, "Ha! Easy for nuns to talk about giving up things. That's what nuns do for a living. But I'm twelve — things are just starting to go right for me!"

Lutherans also get a sermon about sacrifice, which the late Pastor Tommerdahl did so well every year, entitling it, "The True Meaning of Christmas," and if you went to church with visions of sugarplums dancing in your head, he stopped the music. Santa Claus was not prominent in his theology. He had a gift of making you feel you'd better go home and give all the presents to the poor and spend

Christmas with a bowl of soup, and not too many noodles in it either. He preached the straight gospel, and as he said, the gospel is meant to comfort the afflicted and afflict the comfortable. He certainly afflicted the Lutherans.

I only heard his sermon one year, and I liked it, being afflicted by Christmas, knowing how much I was about to receive and how little I had to give. I was ten, my assets came to eight bucks, I had twelve people on my list and had already spent three dollars on one of them: my father, who would receive a Swank toiletries kit with Swank shaving lotion, Swank deodorant, Swank cologne, Swank bath soap on a rope, and Swank hair tonic, an inspired gift. I walked into Detwiler's Drugstore and there it was, the exotic Swank aroma that would complete his life and bring out the Charles Boyer in him, so I said, "Wrap it up," and was happy to be bringing romance into his life until the cash register rang and I realized I have five bucks left and eleven people to go, which came to forty-five cents apiece. Even back then forty-five cents was small change.

I imagined a man walking up and giving me fifty dollars. He was fat and old and had a kind face. "Here," he said, and made me promise I wouldn't tell anyone. I promised. He gave me two crisp new twenty-five-dollar bills, a rarity in themselves and probably worth thousands. A Brink's truck raced through town, hit a bump, and a bag fell out at my feet. I called the Brink's office, and they said, "Nope. No money missing here. Guess it's your lucky day, son." Crystal Sugar called and said that the "Name the Lake Home" contest winner was me, and would I like the lake home (named Mallowmarsh) or the cash equivalent, fifteen grand?

But there's nothing like a sermon against materialism to make a person feel better about having less. God watches over us and loves us no less for knowing what we can't afford. I took the five dollars and bought small bottles of Swank lotion for the others, which smelled as wonderful as his. If you splashed a few drops on your face, you left a trail through the house, and when you came to a room, they knew you were coming. It announced you, like Milton Cross announced the opera.

Dad was so moved by his gift, he put it away for safekeeping, and thanks to careful rationing over the years, still has most of his Swank left.

Father Emil still has the bottle of Napoleon brandy.

I still have wax drippings on the front of my blue peacoat.

The *Herald-Star* still prints the photo of Main Street at night, snowy, the decorations lit, and underneath, the caption "O little town of Wobegon, how still we see thee lie" — the same photo I saw in the paper when I was a boy. That's Carl's old Chevy in front of Skoglund's, the one he traded in on the Chevy before the Chevy he's got now. He's sorry he traded it in because the new one is nothing but heartache. The one in the photo ran like a dream.

The Christmas pageant at Our Lady has changed a little since Sister Arvonne took the helm. Under Sister Brunnhilde, it was as formal as a waltz, but it had a flaw in that the speaking parts were awarded to the quietest, best-behaved children, while the rambunctious were assigned to stand in silent adoration, which often meant that the speakers of glad tidings were stricken with terror and had to be hissed at from the wings while a heavenly multitude stood by and smirked and poked each other.

Sister Arvonne is a reverent woman, like Sister Brunnhilde, but is much smaller and light on her feet, so her reverence takes other forms than kneeling, such as reform, for example. It was Arvonne who took the pruning shears and whacked the convent lilacs into shape; overgrown bushes that had been sloughing off for years she cut back and the next spring they got down to the business of blooming. So did she when the new edict came down on nun dress. She put her wimple on the bust of Newman and developed a taste for pants suits. Some old *Catholische* thought it was the end of the world, but looking at her, they could see it wasn't. She zipped around like it was eight o'clock in the morning. Around the same time, the new liturgy was greeted with a long low moan from the faithful and even from the unfaithful — Arvonne's sister Rosalie who had not uttered a Pater Noster since the early days of the Eisenhower administration nevertheless mourned the Latin mass as if it were her dear departed mother — but Arvonne didn't pause for a moment. "English," she told Rosalie, "is an excellent language. Look at Shakespeare. Look at Milton — hell, if a Congregationalist could write like that, think what you could do if you actually knew something."

Sister Brunnhilde had directed the pageant forever, and, massive woman that she was, seemed permanently in place, like a living pulpit, but Sister Arvonne bided her time, lispened to Sister complain about how unappreciated and unacknowledged this annual burden was, sympathized with her, drew her out, and when she had drawn Sister so far out that she couldn't go back, Sister Arvonne sweetly sliced off the limb and took over.

She set out to cut down on smirking by creating more speaking roles. She brought in Zacharias and Elizabeth and tried to write some lines for Joseph:

> No room?? But my wife is great with child!
> Here, Mary. You lie down and I'll get the swaddling clothes.
> Should we put the baby in the manger?
> Is it a boy or a girl?

The last one appealed to her in a way, but all of them struck her as *forced* somehow and she gave up on him. She had never been clear about Joseph. The shepherds, too, were a problem. They had only one line, and as she well knew from her own acting experience, one line is harder than a hundred. You practice "Let us go to Bethlehem and see this thing which is come to pass, which the Lord has made known unto us" a hundred times, and yet there's no telling what will come out when it's your turn to shine. Intense rehearsal of one line may drive it deeper into the brain, to where you can't remember it that night and can't forget it for the rest of your life. She gave the shepherds a good speech from the Book of Isaiah.

"They'll never remember it," said Sister Brunnhilde who came to rehearsal one day to help out. "It's too complicated. They're all mumbling. Nobody will hear a word they're saying."

"It'll be beautiful. Besides, everybody knows the story anyway," said Sister Arvonne, and she was right, of course. A cloud of incense drifted down the center aisle behind Zacharias as he marched forward, praising God, his short arms upraised, swinging the censer like a bell, and the cloud enveloped him where he knelt at the steps to the altar, when the angel Gabriel jumped out and shouted, "Fear not!" Gabriel, exceedingly well dressed, announced that Z. would have a son, named John, who would be great in the sight of the Lord. "I am an old man!" cried Zacharias. And Gabriel struck him dumb, for his unbelief. His wife, Elizabeth, also old, helped him away, and you could tell that she believed they'd have a baby, she was counting the days. When the Blessed Virgin came in to grind corn, you could see that she was very shy, and you hoped the angel would speak softly. He waited in the shadows, adjusting his magnificent wings, grooming himself, and then walked up behind her. "Hail Mary, full of grace, the Lord is with thee. Blessed are thou among women." She fell down. He told her, "And behold thou shalt conceive in thy womb, and bring forth a son, and shalt call his name Jesus." He told her about Elizabeth, which seemed to make her feel better. She said, still lying on the floor, "Behold the handmaid of the Lord; let it be according to thy word."

Elizabeth helped her up, and they hugged each other. Mary said the Magnificat. John was born and Zacharias recovered his tongue and gave a speech about the tender mercy of God who had visited his people, to give light to them who sit in darkness in the shadow of death, to guide our feet into the way of peace. And then the lights went out for a spooky minute or two, during which you knew something had gone wrong and everything was about to come to a big crashing halt, but the lights came on and there was the manger and Mary and Joseph. Shepherds were lounging a little way away, where the angel made his third appearance, illumined by powerful beams, and cried, "Fear not!" and they all fell down. A heavenly choir joined him in song.

Wise men appeared, coming up the aisle, uncertain whether they were doing the right thing. "Where is he that is born King of the Jews? For we have seen his star in the east and are come to worship him." They met the gang of shepherds going west and all went in together and knelt down at the manger. Gifts were given, prayers said, and some of the shepherds remembered most of the long prophetic passage from Isaiah. "Behold the Lamb of God who taketh away the sins of the world," one said.

And then silence. The children huddled together on their knees, heads bowed, such a peaceful sight and yet you wondered if it was the end or what came next — nobody moved, Mary and Joseph knelt like statues, nobody said a word. They remained in perfect adoration until the organ began to play and then, remembering that it was time to go, they got up and left, and the pageant was over.*

---

*L. W. Lutheran once bought (by mistake) twenty copies of (rehearsed for almost a week) a Christmas pageant entitled "The New Christmas," in which, on page four, they found:

> And the spirit of truth came upon them, and it gave them a great brightness, and naturally they were worried. And the spirit of truth said, "Don't worry. I've come with good news that should make you really happy, for there is born today a child who shall be a symbol of new beginnings and possibilities. And suddenly there was the spirit of truth a multitude of truths, praising goodness and saying, "It's wonderful! Peace on earth and real understanding among people."

The purchase price was nonrefundable.

The tree enters a few days before Christmas, a fresh one bought from Mr. Fjerde or Mr. Munch, two adjoining bachelor farmers who share a small forest of evergreens where you can cut one for yourself. Mr. Fjerde is a silent man, and when you bang on his door, your tree in hand, he won't even tell you the price; he waits to hear your offer and then nods or looks studious until you come up a dollar. But Mr. Munch will talk your ear off, and to hear him tell it, he never meant to raise Christmas trees, they simply snuck into his property one day, and if he ever has the time he'll clean them out with a backhoe.

"They grow like goddam weeds, you know," he says, "and they eat the hell out of your soil — that's good soil there, a guy oughta be doing something with it, it's a shame to let it go like I have. Goddam, I think next spring I maybe oughta get in there with some herbicide, get them cleaned out. Or I could burn them. *Ja,* I think maybe I'll burn them."

Mother can't bear to hear swearing, so she sits in the car with the windows rolled up and a choir singing on the radio. "You stay here," she tells me, but I go with Dad up to Mr. Munch's back door for the thrill of it. Bachelor farmers disobey almost every rule my parents ever laid down; the yard is full of junk under the snow, including a broken-down sofa, a washing machine, an old icebox leaning against a tree with its doors hanging open and more junk inside it. A hill of old tin cans sits about a can's throw from the back door. Mr. Munch is unshaven, a cloud of white hair on his head; his clothes are dirty, brown juice runs down his chin, his breath smells of liquor. "He's not fit to live with decent people," Mother told me when I asked why he lived alone. And yet he seems to have gotten away with it; he is as old as my grandpa. God hasn't struck him with lightning, the way you might think.

He ducks into his little house to get two dollars' change from his cigar box, and I see that he does not clean his room either. Old breakfast scraps on the plate on the table — what a luxury to get up and walk away from a meal! He carefully counts out the two dollars into Dad's hand, and says, "You be careful with that tree now. Those things are like explosives, you know. I sold these people a tree, I think it was last year, and two days later they was all dead. It blew up one night and burned them all so you couldn't tell one from the other. I tell you I wouldn't have one if you paid me. Even fresh — they can go off like a bomb, you know. *Boom!* Just like that."

"Merry Christmas," Dad said.

"God help you," said Mr. Munch.

News of incendiary Christmas trees was no news to Mother. She knew all about fire hazards. Oily rags never spent a night in our house. A paintbrush in a can of thinner was allowed half an hour to get clean, and then the thinner went down the drain with fifty gallons of water behind it. Extension cords that looked frayed or suspicious were bound up in Scotch cellophane tape. A jar of flour sat on the counter by the stove, ready in case of fire; once, the gas flame under the spaghetti sauce flared up and Mother went for her flour, but we ate the sauce anyway — "It's only flour," she said, "same as in the noodles" — though it stuck to the roofs of our mouths like Elmer's glue. Any unusual sound from the furnace, a wheeze or sigh, and she could see (1) fuel oil leaking on the floor and making an immense dark pool creeping closer and closer to the pilot, or (2) carbon monoxide drifting up the ducts and flowing invisibly into our lives. Our fireplace was used only under supervision, and even after she had doused the coals with water, she often couldn't sleep and tiptoed down and laid on another quart or two.

As a result, I grew up with a passion for fire and sometimes lit a few farmer matches in my room for the sheer pleasure of it, and one year, two days before Christmas, when the Mortensons' house burned down (they didn't *know* that the tree caused it, but it could've) when I was staying at Uncle Frank's farm, I felt terrible for having missed it. I also felt bad for wanting to have seen it, because they lost everything in the fire including all their presents, an awful tragedy, but nonetheless one I was sorry to miss.

Dad's fear was that Christmas would throw him into the poorhouse. Mother felt that each of us should get one big present every year in addition to the socks, Rook game, paddleball set, model, ocarina, shirt, miscellaneous gifts: one *big* one, like a printing press or a trike or Lincoln logs. Dad thought the ocarina should be enough for anybody. He for one had never been given a toy as a child but *made* his own toys, as everyone did then, out of blocks of wood and string and whatnot, and was content with them, so the thought that a boy *needed* a large tin garage with gas pumps out front and crank-operated elevator to take the cars up to the parking deck was ridiculous to him and showed lack of imagination. "I don't want to know," he said when Mother walked in with a shopping bag full, but then he had a look, and one look made him miserable. "Twelve dollars? *Twelve dollars?*" He believed that spending was a tendency that easily got out of hand, that only his regular disapproval kept Mother from buying out the store. It all began with Roosevelt who plunged the country into debt and now thrift was out the window and it was "Live for today and forget about tomorrow" with people spending money they didn't have for junk they could do without and Christmas was a symptom of it. He went into the Mercantile to buy a pair of work socks and saw a German music box that made him wonder what the world was coming to. Eight dollars for a piece of junk that played "Silent Night," which was maybe worth seventy-five cents, but there was Florian Krebsbach buying the thing who owed money to a list of people as long as your arm. That was Christmas for you.

The twin perils of the poorhouse and the exploding tree made for a vivid Christmas. Where the poorhouse was, I didn't know, but I imagined it as a gray stone house with cold dank walls where people were sent as punishment for having too much fun. People who spent twelve dollars here and twelve dollars there, thinking there was more where that came from, suddenly had to face facts and go to the house and stay in it and be poor. I might go with Dad or I might be farmed out to relatives, if the relatives wanted me, which probably they wouldn't, so I'd live in a little cell at the poorhouse and think about all the times I had begged for Dad to buy me things. I would eat rutabagas and raw potatoes and have no toys at all, like Little Benny in *The Mysterious Gentleman; or, The Christmas Gruel; A True Story of an Orphan in the East London Slums,* except that Little Benny was patient and never complained or asked anything for himself and was adopted by a kind benefactor and brought into a life of fabulous wealth and luxury in a Belgravia mansion, whereas I, a demanding and rebellious and ungrateful child, was heading in the opposite direction, toward the dim filthy room and the miserable pile of rags for a bed and the racking coughs of our poor parents, dying of consumption from hard labor to earn money to buy the junk I demanded.

On the other hand, the danger of Christmas-tree fire some night killing us all in our beds seemed to point toward a live-for-today philosophy, not that we necessarily should go whole-hog and buy everything in the Monkey Ward catalog, but certainly we could run up a *few* bills, knowing that any morning could find us lying in smoldering ruins, our blackened little bodies like burnt bacon that firemen would remove in small plastic bags. Simple justice demands that a person who dies suddenly, tragically, at a tender age, should have had some fun immediately prior to the catastrophe. If your mother yells at you and you go off on your bike feeling miserable and are crushed by a dump truck — that would be a much worse tragedy than if it had been your birthday and you had gotten nice presents, including the bike, and were killed in a good mood.

Then one Christmas I opened a long red package and found a chemistry set, exactly what I wanted, and sat and stared at it, afraid to look inside. For Mother to buy me one, given her feelings, was more than adventurous, it was sheer recklessness on her part, like a gift of Pall Malls and a bottle of whiskey. The year before, I tried to aim her toward the Wards deluxe woodburning kit, pointing out that I could earn money by making handsome Scripture plaques, but she said it was too dangerous. "You'll burn down the house with it," she said. So, a year later, to get a chemistry set, complete with Bunsen burner, fuel, a little jar marked "Sulphur," and who knew what else, I didn't dare show how happy I was. "Thank you," I said, humbly, and put it aside and tried to look interested in what other people were getting, afraid that if I got too excited about chemistry, she'd want to have a closer look at it.

After a little elaborate politeness, thanking her for the nice socks and wonderful underwear, admiring my sister's dollhouse, I slipped away to the basement and set up my laboratory on a card table next to the laundry tubs. The instruction book told how to make soap and other useful things I didn't need, and omitted things I was interested in, such as gunpowder and aphrodisiacs, so I was on my own. I poured some liquid into a peanut butter jar and dumped some white powder in it — it bubbled. I poured a little bit on the table as an experiment and it hissed and ate a hole in the leather, which made me think, if it had spilled on me it would have eaten my hands off down to the wrists. Would it eat the jar? Would it eat the drain pipe? Had the makers of Junior Scientist included chemicals so deadly they might destroy a house? Upstairs, everybody was enjoying Parcheesi, unaware of the danger. I got out a tube of thin metal strips that I thought must be solder, and lit a match to melt some onto a plastic cowboy to give him a coat of armor, but instead the strip burst into fierce white flame as bright as the sun — I dropped it on the floor and stomped it to bits. My cowboy's face was gone, his head a blackened blob drooped down on his chest — what I would look like if I kept fooling around. I packed away the chemistry set and stuck it on the shelf behind the pickled beets. Eight dollars wasted. My poor father. Little Benny sold matches on the streets of London in bitter weather to buy medicine for his sick father, but I was a boy who played with fire and came close to killing everybody. Poor me, too. My big present was a big joke. What was Mother thinking of?

I went upstairs and moped around in the doorway so they could see me, but they were too busy having a good time. I went up to my room to mope around up there, maybe someone would come and find me and ask what was wrong, but time passed and nobody did. Mother called up the stairs to ask if I was hungry, but when I yelled that I wasn't she didn't come to find out why. I went to the stairs to yell down that maybe I'd just go to bed, and as I was about to yell, I looked in the door to my sister's room and saw the dollhouse.

It was a two-story white house, two bedrooms upstairs, living room, dining room, and kitchen. I had helped her carry it to her bedroom and set it on the floor by her bed and arrange the furniture, and now the Peabodys were about to enjoy their Christmas dinner. Upstairs, their plastic beds were permanently made; downstairs, a perpetual fire glowed in the fireplace, their two tabby cats curled up on the floor.

Minutes later, the big olive-drab B-17 revved up its engines and roared off the flight deck and down the dark hallway. The poor helpless family, Phoebe and Pete Peabody and little Petey and Eloise, sat in their elegant dining room, their movable arms placed politely on the table, their smiling little faces turned toward the turkey, as the hum of the deadly aircraft came closer and closer. Their great protector was miles away, engrossed in Parcheesi. They sat in pathetic dignity as the craft circled overhead and finally came in on its bombing run, dropping tons of deadly Lincoln logs. Pete was the last to die, sitting at the head of the table, a true hero, and then it was all over and Christmas lay in ruins with clouds of smoke rising from it, and the bomber returned to the carrier, its crew jabbering and laughing in Japanese. But little Petey wasn't dead! He rose painfully from under a pile of furniture and limped out of the house. He was badly injured and would have to spend some time in a hospital until his burns healed, but somehow he would get over his frightful loss and grow up and be a normal, happy person.

After Christmas, time drifted awhile; beyond Christmas there was nothing to look forward to. The tree got dry and was finally hauled out half-naked of needles and I set it on fire. New Year's Day was an imitation, Christmas without gifts, and New Year's Eve passed without much notice, Mother and I trying for three years to stay awake by playing Parcheesi until one year we made it over the top to midnight. On the radio at eleven, Ben Grauer came on from Times Square to narrate the amazing descending ball of light that marked the New York New Year, and Guy Lombardo and his Royal Canadians played from the Waldorf, which was exciting to imagine — the elegant Ben in a tuxedo standing on the rooftop watching the meteor fall, the handsome Guy and his band in their scarlet tunics like Sergeant Preston's, playing saxophones on horseback, their faithful huskies lying nearby — but it would have been more exciting to watch it on television, which we didn't have. At midnight our time, nothing happened. Mother and I hoisted a glass of grape Kool-Aid. I said, "Here's mud in your eye," and tossed it back, screwed up my face, and said, "Ha!" "Where'd you get that?" she said. On television, of course. She reminded me that watching television was as bad as going to the movies. The next morning she went next door to the Holmbergs' to borrow sugar and visited awhile and watched some of the Tournament of Roses.

LOUISE SHIVERS

A Privileged Character

The green and red lights on the Christmas tree stood out in the dimness of the room like the traffic lights on Walton Way on a dark rainy night. But I wasn't looking at the tree. I lay sprawled out on the floor, my fingers snapping and unsnapping the metal rings of my school notebook. After almost pinching my finger, I switched to doodling with a pencil on the lined paper, making whirls over and over.

"The Palmer Method for beautiful handwriting," I said in mimicry of my jay-voiced teacher, Miss Minnie Deans. Under my breath I muttered: "Fat chance! Even if I *did*, some brother — or baby — would come along and scribble on it, or drool!"

About that time my longlegged father thumped through

the room and gestured toward the mantel. He said: "Santy Claus won't be bringing much, but if you've got your stockings hung up so they'll stay, you'd better get on to bed so he can come at *all*."

I knew that his side glance was meant for me. At eleven, I was the oldest of six and, like it or not, that made me the leader. I sighed as I pushed myself up on my sharp elbows, reached down to pull up my socks and slowly made the effort to get to bed. As I left the room I looked back over my shoulder at the mantel. Under the little bunches of holly we had arranged across the top, six long brown rayon stockings were hanging limp and empty.

Huh! I thought, Looks like some woman from across the tracks has done her washing and then gone off and left it.

I went on into the bedroom. I was still sleeping in the same room with three of my brothers then. As I sat on the side of the bed and started unbraiding my plaits, I thought of the words I'd said that afternoon. "Why do there have to be so many of us?"

Daddy had been getting into the car at the time, his long arms holding two bulging brown paper bags. I sat there in the front seat like a bump on a log wondering how he was going to get the sacks in the car since all five of the boys were inside crawling all over each other like kittens in a towsack. Even the baby was with us!

Earlier, I had stuck my head into the kitchen to see why we had to take the baby along. When I saw how the kitchen looked, I didn't ask. Mother and Gyp were in there working up a storm on the Christmas dinner. Gyp has always worked for us, money or no money. The strong warm smell of vanilla flavoring came by my nose as I leaned inside. The big high-ceilinged room seemed to be full of white. Mother was standing by one table cracking a coconut with a hammer. I could see she had already cracked and grated one because the white filmy milk stood in a bottle. The pieces of discarded shell lay on the white enamel table top looking like little barges on a frozen lake. A mountain of grated flakes stood ready. I knew that sometimes Daddy's patients paid him in brown eggs so I wondered if this time maybe one had paid him in coconuts.

Mother was saying to Gyp:

"Will said he didn't want to see any pink food coloring in the cake this year." They laughed together and I remembered that this was Daddy's way of telling mother not to grate her fingers.

Gyp was separating egg whites from yolks like she was doing some kind of juggling act. When she saw me she said:

"What you want in here, Callie? Wantin' to get me a Christmas present?" As sour as I'd been feeling, I had to laugh at her, she was talking about our little joke, the one that had started when I was just a baby.

"You're right," she said. "I still want the same thing; 'Sumpin t'eat, Sumpin t'wear and Sumpin t'play with.'"

Mother laughed at us too, and Gyp caught herself just in time as a drop of the yellow egg yolk tried to slip out of the cracked brown shell into the glaze of the white.

* * *

At Christmastime every year the fish market on Broad Street sold candy, bins of all different kinds of hard candy, not to mention tinsies and chocolate drops. Crates of every kind of fruit you could think of were stacked out front. We were sitting parked by the curb waiting for Daddy to make his stop. In spite of all the Christmas flurry, I was feeling out-of-sorts and invisible. I was thinking: *Why can't we be more like other people? Why do there have to be so many of us?*

I glanced up just as a big black sedan double-parked right beside us. Sitting in back was Virginia Dickens, the smartest girl in my class. Of course *she* had the whole back seat to herself.

Wildly embarrassed at being in the car with the rowdy boys clamoring and pulling at each other's aviator caps, I looked quickly down at the floor and didn't glance up again until I heard the Dickens car crank up and pull off.

When Daddy came back, I blurted it out: "Why! Why so many of us?"

He looked over at me, concern in his brown eyes.

"Well," he said, his voice slow and soft as it always was, "Which one would you want to be without?"

Now, as I finished undoing my hair, and pushing it back behind my ears, I reached under the bed for my notebook and ripped a page out. In a big sprawl I wrote across the page: "Don't wake me up, I'm skipping Christmas."

Raider, my ten year-old brother, stuck his head out from underneath his blanket. When he saw my note he said: "What do you think you are, Callie, a privileged character?"

Ben T. echoed from his pillow beside Raider: "P.C., P.C." and then added solemnly, "Callie, you gone get some switches."

I lay there for a while, full of confusion and resentment. Finally, I drifted off to sleep. Just before dawn, I thought I heard the sounds of the milkman. Rattle, jingle, clink. Am I dreaming? I wondered. I seemed to watch the white-uniformed milkman get out of the Sancken's truck with the bottles clanking in his carrier. Then I must have drifted in my sleep. I saw the bottles sitting on our steps where he had left them; the cold air had already frozen the cream at the top and icy crystals had forced the stoppers up until they perched on top like little hats. As I looked at this, my mouth feeling the cold iciness, the milkman stepped out of the mist of dream whiteness and spoke: "I forgot something," he said. Reaching back into the truck he pulled out a big white coconut cake.

I was standing on the front steps then and he put the cake in my hands saying: "Take it Callie, it's your angel coconut cake."

I accepted the huge cake, but since it was so heavy, I put it down on the front porch. As I stood looking, it stopped being a cake and became an angel! The white flakes of the coconut had changed into soft white feathers on beautiful wings!

I stood looking at this angel, for even in a dream where all things are possible, this angel took my breath away.

The angel spoke: "Callie, I've come to talk to you about your brothers. There has been a mistake. Which one do you want to send back?"

With a start I woke up. The dream flew away and I found myself touching my lips and realizing that the sensation of cold was coming from the tangerine that Ben T. was pushing against my lips. He was standing over me saying, "Callie, wake up! Santy's already come."

I thought as I rubbed my eyes, Of course it wasn't the milkman on Christmas morning.

"Look Callie, Come on in here!", the boys called out.

I got up, but still felt uneasy from my dream. As I pushed back the covers to get out of the quilt-warmed bed, the note I had written the night before floated off the side of the bed. The boys folded the paper and made it into an airplane.

Delighted with the joke he'd made out of my note which lay at our feet, Raider said sarcastically, "Come on, P.C., we've already opened ours." I cut my eyes at him and let the two littlest boys lead me into the front room.

My stocking was now a big knotty thing, the bulges mysterious and grotesque. I eyed it as the boys hopped around in their footed pajamas. Daddy was sitting in the big chair putting the tracks of an electric train set together. Toys and torn wrapping paper were scattered over the rug. I took my Christmas stocking down and they watched me pour the contents out: fruit, nuts, candy. And in the toe, under a tangerine, a little box containing a birthstone ring. As I looked into the shine of the peridot I could see the lights from the tree reflected in its greenness.

The boys weren't paying much attention to me gazing at my ring. I could hear Ben T. whispering to Raider, "A girl at school told me that Santy Claus and the stork were the same thing." The boys were standing under the tree.

"Hey, there're still some presents under here!" Raider called out.

I had to laugh. There were five little red cellophane packages. It was the fudge Mother had helped me make as presents for the boys. The fudge hadn't gotten hard but she helped me spoon it into the cellophane anyway and tie it with a ribbon at the top. I thought they were pretty sorry-looking gifts, but the boys smacked their lips and looked pleased. The baby was chosen as the one to give me a little box from under the tree. The tag read: "From the boys." I opened it and found a small brown diary. Written in my mother's fine Palmer Method handwriting were the words:

"Callie's secret thoughts." I ran my finger over the smooth unlined pages and thought of the days when I would write private words and lock them in with my little gold key.

Stuck inside the back page was a picture. It was a snapshot of the boys lined up on the back door steps, each bright face just a little bit taller than the other. They had their hair slicked down for the picture.

I stood there holding the picture and I started feeling so funny around the heart that I thought I was going to cry. They were looking out of the picture at me with such a trusting look, I could see just how different each one was from the other. Raider's thin wrists stuck out of his sweater sleeves the way they did when he played the piano; Marion's sock had fallen down and didn't meet the bottom of his knicker; Ben T. was biting his lip like he always did when he was self-conscious; Rob cupped his chin in his hand to hide the scar where he had fallen the summer before, playing ball; and the baby was looking at me with big blue eyes.

I thought about how the picture would look with even one of them gone. They were as different from each other as I felt I was from anyone else.

I guess mother saw me standing there, blinking, because she set the five-layer coconut cake down on the dining room table. I glanced at it uneasily. She pulled her long pink robe closer around her and came and put her arm across my shoulders just as though she could read my thoughts.

"Let's sing our Christmas song now," she said, and we all went over to the piano. Raider slid in on the stool and started playing the song we had all made up over the years. Everybody sang out, our different-pitched voices all blending together:

"Soft are the words we're singing,
Warm are the smiles we send
Hushed is the music playing
As peacefulness begins.
Close as a loved one's memory
Held in a candle's light
Warmth, love and peace we send you
From our silent night."

The notes left our mouths and curled around the room like silver strips of tinsel. They rose past the turkey smells, up the chimney, higher than the flames, up, up and out into the cold sky.

JULIA ALVAREZ

An American Surprise

Back home on the island from his latest trip, Father walked in the door, and his three girls raced to him with happy cries, "Papi!" He picked each one up and gave her a twirl. The chauffeur followed, carrying the bags. "In the study, Mario," Dr. Bermudez directed and then he rubbed his hands together and said, "Oh, do I have a wonderful surprise for my girls!"

"What is it?" the children cried, and Ana, the youngest, took a guess because last night at prayers Mother had promised that one day soon she would see such a thing. "Snow?" she asked.

"Now, girls, remember," Mother said, just in case they needed reminding, "let Father relax first." Then Mother whispered something to Father in English, and Father agreed, "After dinner then. We'll see who leaves her plate clean." Then, added, "Oh, what a surprise!"

Lydia and Marie, the two older girls, exchanged triumphant looks and skipped off, hand in hand, to tell their cousins next door that Father was back with a wonderful surprise from New York City where it was winter and the snow fell from heaven to earth like the Bible's pieces of manna bread.

But Ana was not about to wander off, for supposing, just supposing Father finished his drink and decided to open his bags right then. As the only one there, she would get first pick of whatever the surprise was. If only Father would give her a small clue!

But Father was no good for clues. He was sprawled beside Mother, his arms spread out across the back of the couch as if he were about to embrace everything that was his. They were talking in those worried voices that grownups use when something had gone wrong.

"Prices have skyrocketed," Father was saying. Mother ran her hand through his hair and said, "My poor dear," and off they went to their bedroom for a nap before dinner.

Then the house grew quiet and lonesome. Ana lingered by the coffee table, taking sips from what was left in the glasses until the ice cubes rattled down to her mouth, tattletales, and her eyes squeezed shut with the burn of Father's drink. From down the hall came the sound of tinkling silverware and the scrape of a chair being settled in its place. Then Gladys, the new pantry maid, began to sing:

Yo tiro la cuchara,
Yo tiro el tenedor,
Yo tiro todos los platos,
Y me voy para Nueva York.

Ana loved to hear Gladys' high sweet voice imitating famous singers on the radio, but Mother said Gladys was only a teenager and didn't know any better than to sing popular tunes in the house and wear her kinky hair in rollers all week long and then comb it out for Sunday mass in elaborate hairdos copied from American magazines.

Gladys' singing stopped abruptly when Ana entered the dining room. "Girl, you gave me a scare!" she laughed. She was setting the table for dinner, taking spoons from a bouquet of silverware in her left hand, executing fancy dance steps before stopping at each placement and reminding herself, "Spoon on the right, wife to the knife." In the absence of sisters, Gladys was fun to be around.

The maid stood back from the table and cocked her head critically, then tucked a chair in, gave a knife a little nudge like someone straightening a picture on the wall. "Come," she nodded towards the back of the house. Anita followed her through the pantry where everything was in readiness for dinner: the empty platters were out, waiting to be filled; the serving spoons were lined up like a family, tall ones first, then littler and littler ones.

In the passageway that connected the maids' room with the rest of the house, Gladys stopped and held open the door. "So! Your Father is back from New York City!"

Ana blushed. She bowed her head with pleasure and entered past Gladys. The room was dark and hot. Most of the windows were shut against the strong Caribbean sun. A hazy, muted light fell from a high, half-opened window. On a cane stool, a humming fan turned this way and that.

Slowly, as her eyes adjusted to the dimmer light of the room, Ana made out the plastic statuettes and holy pictures of saints which cluttered the bureau top. An old mayonnaise jar with a slit in the bottle cap glinted with the coppery dregs of a few pennies. As the fan blew upon it, the flame of the votary candle swayed and flickered. Two of the three cots were occupied. On one, the old cook, Zoila, laid, fast asleep, her fat black face looking pleased at the occasional cool breeze. On another, sat Pila in her slip, head bowed, murmuring over a rosary that dangled between her knees.

As the door clicked shut, Zoila opened one eye, then closed it. Ana hoped she had fallen back to sleep since the old cook liked to scold. "You know your mother doesn't like you back here," Zoila started in. Ana looked to Gladys for defense.

"No harm, Cook," Gladys said cheerfully. She led Ana to her cot and patted a spot beside her. "The Doña won't mind today seeing as Don Eduardo just got in."

"Tell me the hen doesn't peck when the rooster crows," said Zoila with heavy sarcasm. She let out a grumpy sigh and turned herself over to face the wall. Softly the fan tickled the pink bottoms of her feet. "I was changing Doña Laura's diapers before you were born!" she quarreled. "I should know how the dog bites, how the bee stings!"

Gladys rolled her eyes at Ana as if to say, "Don't mind Cook." Then she said in an appeasing voice, "You certainly have put your time in!"

"Thirty-two years," Cook said. She let out a dry laugh.

"I wonder where I'll be in thirty-two years," Gladys mused. A glazed look came across her face; she smiled. "New York," she said dreamily and began to sing the refrain from the popular New York Merengue that was on the radio night and day.

"Dream on," Zoila laughed. And now she was laughing. The fat under her uniform jiggled. Her body rocked back and forth. "Your head is in the clouds. Watch out for the thunderbolt, Girl!"

"Oh, Cook," Gladys reached over and gently patted the old woman's feet. She seemed as unfazed by Zoila's merriment as her bad humor. "Every night I pray," she said, nodding towards her makeshift altar. Gladys had once explained to Ana how each saint on her bureau had a specialty. Santa Clara was good for eyesight. San Martiń was a jackpot, good for money. Our Blessed Mother was good for anything. Now she picked out a postcard Ana's mother had thrown out a few days before. It was a photo of a robed woman with a sharp star for a halo and torch in her raised hand. Behind her was a fairytale city twinkling with Christmas lights. "This one is a powerful American Virgin," Gladys handed the card to Ana. "She'll get me to New York, you'll see."

"Speaking of New York," Pila began. She hurried her sign of the cross and kissed the crucifix on her rosary. Pila, the laundry maid, was a curious looking woman: she had splotches of white on her black arms and legs and one blind eye and one good eye, but no one ever knew which was which. Now either the blind eye or the good eye was trained on Ana. "Show us what your father brought you."

"Lucky, lucky," Pila continued before Ana could explain. "These girls are so lucky. What a father. He doesn't go on a trip that he doesn't bring back a treasure for them!" She enumerated for Gladys, who had been in the Bermudez household only a month, all the treasures El Doctor had brought his girls. "You know those dancing dolls from the last time?"

Ana nodded. It would not do to correct Pila, who was known for her sharp tongue, and risk being called a young miss-know-it-all, but the dancing dolls were from two trips ago. From the very last trip, the gift had been tied shoes that were good for their feet, a very bad choice, but that's what came of Mother's being in charge of what the surprise would be. Before he left on a trip, Father always asked, "Mother, what do the girls need?" Sometimes, as with this trip, Mother replied, "Not a thing. They're all set for school." And then, oh then, the surprises were bound to be wonderful, because, as Father explained to Mother, "I didn't have the faintest idea what to get them. So I went to Schwarz and the salesgirl suggested . . ." And off would come the wrappers from three suggested dancing dolls or three suggested pair of roller skates or this very night, three wonderful surprises!

Gladys took the postcard back and smiled at it. "What did he bring you?" she asked.

"Not yet," Ana sighed, disappointed that she could not oblige their curiosity, for even Zoila had given half a roll over to hear what the surprise had been. "We have to eat supper first," she explained.

"Speaking of supper," Pila reminded the two maids. "Our work is never done," she added pointedly. "Night and day, and what surprise do we get!" She grumbled on as she braided her kinky, black hair into dozens of tiny braids. Her complaints were different from Zoila's. They were bitter and came capriciously upon you even during the nicest conversations. Zoila's were a daily litany, sometimes cried out at the dog, sometimes scolded at the rice kettle she had to scrub, sometimes mumbled under her breath at Doña Laura whose diapers she had changed and whose actions, therefore, she thought she had a right to criticize.

Ana drifted away and, in no time, supper was ready. It was spaghetti and meatballs, thank goodness, so it wasn't going to be difficult to clean her plate. Ana spooled the strands on her fork and rolled her two meatballs around until she was tired of her game, and ate them both. Mother was nice about vegetables tonight, allowing Ana to serve herself, which she did, peas, but not enough to go around her neck in a necklace had they been strung together. The three girls ate quietly, open-eyed, while Father told stories about taxis and bad snowstorms (how could a snowstorm be bad!) and the Christmas decorations on the streets. They felt the blessedness of the weeks ahead: this very night, a wonderful surprise, and in less than twenty days, according to the little calendar whose doors they opened with Mother every night at prayers, Christmas! And more surprises then! They were lucky girls; Pila was right, oh so lucky.

Finally, Father turned to Gladys, who was pushing the rollaway cart around the table, clearing off the plates, "Eh ——"

"Gladys," Mother reminded him; after all, she was the new girl and Father had not had much occasion to use her name.

"Gladys," Father said, "would you bring me my briefcase?"

"In the study," Mother directed, "On the desk next to the smoking table."

Away Gladys hurried, her slippers frantically clacking, delighted to be sent on such an errand; then she was back, his leather briefcase held like a child in her arms.

"Good girl!" Father gave Gladys a bright, approving smile and snapped open the locks. The lid flew up like a jack-in-the-box. Inside were three packages, wrapped up in white tissue paper and clustered together in a tender, intimate way like eggs in a nest. Father handed one to each girl and then lifted a tiny box of perfume from the side pocket of the case and smiled at Mother.

"Oh you dear," Mother said, patting his hand, "I've been out for weeks."

There was the sound of ripping paper and Father cheering them on, "Oh, oh, oh!" Gladys lingered by her cart, organizing the dirty dishes into neat stacks before rolling them away to the kitchen where Pila and Zoila would wash them. Then, the boxes were torn open . . . and a baffled look appeared on each child's face. Mother leaned towards Lydia and lifted a small cast iron statue from her box: an old man sat in a boat looking down at a menacing whale, its jaws hinged open. Marie set hers on the table and tried to look pleased: it also was an iron statue — a little girl with her jump rope frozen in midair. Ana did not even bother to unpack hers. She stared down at a girl in a blue and white gown who stared up at a puffy canopy of clouds. What could the Schwarz salesgirl have been thinking of?

"What on earth are they, Eddie?" Mother asked, picking up Marie's little jump roper and looking into the dotted eyes.

"Guess. . . ." Father smiled coyly, then added, "They're all the craze now. The girl at Schwarz said she had sold half a dozen already that day."

Mother turned the statue over. On the underside of the platform she felt something with her finger. "Made in U.S.A.," she murmured, and then she noticed a keyhole for a tiny key. "Why!" Mother looked up at Father, "it's a bank, isn't it?"

Father beamed. He took the jump rope girl and set her down on the table before him. She stood poised on her stand, an arc of wire rose over her head and looped through two needleholes in her fists. The polka dots on her dress and the yellow in her hair had been painted on the iron. "Watch this," he said, picking a penny from the pile of change he had rattled on the table. The coin fit in a groove on a fencepost beside the girl. Father pulled a lever at the base of the stand, the lever popped back in, the coin dropped with a tinkle and tap, and then — the three girls and Mother and Gladys blinked — for the girl took a skip and the jump rope turned a turn.

"Oh," a sigh of wonder passed around the room.

"Mechanical banks." Father grinned and picked another penny from the pile. "So that my girls start saving their money to take care of us, Mother —" he gave her a wink — "when we're old and grey."

"Do mine," Lydia begged, and Father placed a penny in the old man's slotted hands so that the coin looked like the wheel of a boat. When he pulled the lever, the sailor turned and the coin rolled into the whale's mouth.

The girls laughed. "Jonah's Bank," Mother read the name on the side of the boat, and then with a look of mischief in her eye, she said, "Oh Eddie, I wonder what the nuns would say!"

Father's eyebrows rose up. "But wait till you see this one!" He laughed, lifting Ana's bank out of its box. "Actually, these Jonah and Mary banks are supposed to encourage children to save for their offerings at church. Surely the nuns can't object to that!" He stood a penny in a slot on the canopy of cloud and pulled the lever at the base. The coin disappeared; the young woman, her halo painted on her hair, rose up towards the clouds, her arms lifted at the joints of the shoulders. As the lever popped back, she descended to the ground.

"Blessed Mother!" Gladys whispered. Then everyone, including Mother, laughed because they had forgotten Gladys was still in the room, and there she was, neck craned forward, her eyes as round and coppery as those very pennies that had worked such wonders.

Father held up a coin to her. "Here, Gladys, give her a spin." But Gladys backed off and looked shyly at her slippers. "Go on," Mother encouraged her, and this time she came forward, wiping her hands in her apron, and took the coin from Father, who directed her to stand it on the cloud. Again the coin rattled down, and Mary ascended for a moment, then fell back to earth until the next penny saved. Gladys' face was radiant. She made a slow, dazed sign of the cross.

"They're like children," Father said tenderly when Gladys left the room. "Did you see her face? It's as if she had seen the real thing."

After dinner as Mother and Father gossiped over their expressos and cigarettes, the three girls shared a disappointed look. Ana tried giving her Mary a shake to see if she couldn't get the pennies out and buy herself a box of Chicklets.

"Oh no! They stay in there saved." Father patted his pocket. "Papi keeps the keys."

The banks turned out not to be such a disappointment after all. They were far better than tie shoes, that was certain. At school they created a stir among the other children. Girls elbowed each other in line to stand next to Ana. She was invited to help herself to her favorite red lifesaver when it was the next one unwound from its wrapper in the roll, and even when it wasn't the next one, several were collapsed to get to it. Sister read Doña Laura's note explaining that this was an offertory bank, and everyone got to work a penny in the cloud and watch the little figure rise. Then Sister, whose job it was to make a lesson out of everything fun, told the class how Our Blessed Virgin did not die but got to take her body to heaven, she was so good. The class gazed dreamily at the bank, half-expecting it to shoot up to the ceiling in a puff of smoke.

Ana's bank went back home heavy with coins. Father unlocked the bottom and out came a few less than a hundred pennies, and he kindly made up the difference and gave Anita a big silver dollar that looked more like jewelry than money. Then business slowed. Once in a while Mother's friends, who declared they hated pennies in their purses, disposed of them gladly in the whale's mouth or the canopy of cloud. Of course, the jump rope girl was the favorite, lucky Marie. But Gladys protested that the best one of all was the Mary bank, and she used up all the pennies in her mayonnaise jar to work the miracle. The pity was it didn't take quarters.

Finally, the banks found their way to the shelf with other neglected toys. Soon Christmas was upon the Bermudez household. Mother complained that she would die of exhaustion — there was so much to be done. The girls' pageant costumes had to be sewn. Next door Aunt Estelle needed help getting the garden and house ready for the big Christmas night bash to be held there this year. Then the grape tree had to be cut down at the beach, painted white, and hung with silver and gold balls and showered with tinsel. What a sight! Especially at night when Mother turned off all the lamps and the tree blazed with lights, blinking on, off: little vials like the stoppers of nose drops filled with colored water and drained out.

As the day approached with less and less windows to open on the Advent calendar, the children were unruly with excitement, but the grownups seemed too busy to care. The house was fixed up as if there were going to be a party. The giant poinsettias in the courtyard looked like flaming torches. Nuts and fruits filled the silver platters at the centerpieces of tables and sideboard. An elegant soldier took a walnut in his mouth and cracked it open for you, and every time he did so, Mother sighed and said, "It's a pity there's no national ballet for the girls." Gladys was busier than ever, polishing silver, preparing canapes, following Mother through the house with vases of calla lillies and bougainvillea. Instead of the radio merengues Gladys now sang an endless repertoire of Christmas carols:

Glo-oh-oh-oh-oh-ohh-
Oh-oh-oh-oh-ohh-
Riah!

Best of all, Mother seemed not to mind the singing anymore and once or twice broke out into song herself in a delicate, quavery soprano:

> A Santa Claus le gusta el vino,
> A Santa Claus le gusta el ron . . .

And of course, at the Christmas eve pageant, all the children sang:

> Adeste fideles
> Laeti triumphantes . . .

Ana, costumed in a nightgown with a tinsel crown on her head, was to announce to the poor shepherds tending their flocks by night:

> Do not be afraid
> For behold I bring you
> Tidings of great joy:
> The baby Jesus is born!

But she was so flustered by the lights in her eyes and the sea of faces in the packed auditorium that she stumbled over her lines and said, "The baby doll is born!" instead of "the baby Jesus." Mother said no one but she, who knew Ana wanted a baby doll from the baby Jesus, had caught the slip.

The next morning the baby doll was under the tree, a ribbon in her gold hair, and a bottle tied to her wrist. She cried out "Mama" when Ana lay her down and wet her diaper after she drank a bottle through a little hole in her mouth. And that was not all! The room was piled with gift-wrapped boxes. "Something for everyone!" Father laughed, and a lot for his darlings. Each one sat at the center of a wake of ripped paper and empty boxes, surrounded by gaily colored toys. Zoila and Pila and Gladys opened their gifts carefully so as not to tear the bright tissue paper. Their faces lit up: a wallet with a pretty lip of green in the billfold!

That night, although she had got to bed much later than usual, Ana could not sleep. Even when she shut her eyes tightly in an honest effort, she saw now her new doll, now her holster or coloring book loom larger than life in her vision, and she had to turn on her light and look at her gifts to make sure they were real. Mother came by briefly from the noisy party next door in a long, silvery gown, her pale arms bare, one arm linked to Uncle Arturo's arm. She wagged her finger at Ana for having her light on, but she didn't seem to mind really, and she laughed a lot when Uncle shot himself dead several times with Ana's new revolver. Much later, Gladys stopped in on her way back from helping out next door. "It's past midnight, young lady!" But instead of turning out the light, she sat herself down on Ana's bed, took off her slipper, and began massaging her tired foot. They could hear the uncles and aunts and Mother and Father singing carols in the distance. "It is a gay old time next door," Gladys said. Doña Laura had danced a bolero with El Doctor that was as good as in the movies. Uncle Arturo had taken off his shirt and done a workman's jig on top of the dining room table. Crazy Aunt Estelle had been thrown or threw herself into the swimming pool, you couldn't be sure.

Gladys' gaze wandered around the room, taking in the clutter of new toys before alighting fondly on the shelf. A timid look spread over her face. From her pocket she brought out her new wallet, opened it, and took the ten dollar bill from the fold. "I'll buy the bank from you," she said in a hesitant voice.

The bank! Why that old thing was certainly not worth ten brand new dollars. Not since the gadget had gotten rusty from its being left out in the patio overnight. Half the time the spring didn't work at all. "Why Gladys," Ana advised her.

Gladys' glance faltered. She put the bill back in the fold and held the wallet out. "I'll throw in the wallet too."

For the first time she could remember, Ana did not know how being good worked. One was not supposed to give away gifts once received. Gladys should keep her wallet. But that meant Ana should keep her old bank — which to give away would be a generous deed. Muddled, she looked up at the shelf.

"You can have it," Ana said. Gladys' mouth dropped open. The surprised look in the young maid's eyes confirmed Ana's suspicion that she had done something she would get punished for if caught, so she added, "Don't tell, Gladys, okay?" The maid nodded solemnly as she left the room, the bank bundled in her apron and tucked under her arm.

Mother was one to notice the stain on one's place setting at the table or the bruise accidentally punched on little cousin's arm or the empty space on the bedroom toy shelf. "That reminds me," Mother said a few weeks after New Year's when the whole household had been mobilized to look for her reading glasses on top of her head. "Where's your Mary bank, Ana?" Just then, as Gladys and Ana exchanged a guilty look, Mother found her glasses on her head and slipped them down on her nose. She looked curiously from Ana to Gladys.

"My bank?" Ana asked as if she had never heard of such a thing.

"Come, come," Mother said, and again she looked at Ana and again she looked at Gladys.

"Oh *that* bank," Ana answered and explained that it was "around."

Mother was very patient and said quietly, "Well, let's find it, shall we?" And when they didn't, of course, find it anywhere in Ana's room — Ana gave a very credible, thoroughgoing search, looking even inside her tie shoes — Mother did not persist but let the matter drop.

That Sunday after the maids went off to early mass, Mother inspected their quarters while Father kept watch by a window. Later, Ana heard her parents' concerned voices behind the closed door of the study. Then the door flew open, and Father came down the hall followed by a scowling Mother, and just in time, Ana ducked behind the wicker chair as they went by. Then they were back again in a sombre single file, Father, a grumbling Zoila, and Mother bringing up the rear. The same procession went back and forth with Pila, and, last of all, with Gladys, her eyes small and round. The door shut. Voices were raised in the study. Ana watched a powderpuff of dust turn cartwheels in a cross-breeze. In the corner, a shred of tinsel glimmered with leftover holiday cheer. Finally, the door opened, and Gladys, sobbing into her apron, scurried down the hall.

Ana's heart sank. Trouble was brewing in the big house. It had already landed on Gladys, and it was no use hiding, for sooner or later, it would fall on her too. She rose and lay the doll on the cushion of the chair, ignoring its cry of "Mama."

At the door of the study she paused, overcome as always by the high shelves of books and the dark wood of the walls and lattice windows. Mother was pacing up and down the room as if neither direction would do and smoking steadily. Father sat at the edge of his recliner, his hands drooped over the armrests, his head bowed. On the small smoking table beside the stand of pipes, Ana caught sight of the mechanical bank, swaddled in an apron. She took a step into the room. But no one noticed her. "It was a present," she blurted out. Mother stopped and looked at her absently. "I'm sorry," Ana wailed.

Father glanced up at her, then exchanged a glance with Mother.

"We're sorry too," Mother said quietly. "Next time your father brings you a gift —" she began to scold, but Father cut her off.

"We're just going to have to get better presents, Mother," he said, winking at Ana. "I don't see the dancing dolls being left out in the rain or being given away to the maid!"

Ana's heart soared at the thought of a better surprise than any that had come before. What could it be? She looked about the room expansively for ideas, anything, anything. Her gaze fell on the bank.

Mother put out her cigarette with nervous, little jabs. "I guess I better go explain to the others." She sighed and brushed past Ana. The door slammed behind her. A rack of pipes jiggled and rattled. A whole wall of lattice windows collapsed open.

Out in the driveway the car pulled up to the entrance, and Mario was putting a cardboard suitcase and a burlap sack in the backseat. Suddenly, Gladys appeared, her head lumpy with rollers, dabbing at her eyes with a kerchief. She climbed in beside her bags, and with a flash of chrome, the car disappeared down the driveway, past the guard at the gate, to the world.

"Papi!" Ana cried, turning around. "Don't make Gladys go away, please!"

Her father reached out and pulled her towards his lap. His eyes were dull as if they'd been colored in brown and smudged. "We trusted her," he began. Then he added, "Gladys asked to leave, you know . . . she'll get a job in no time. Maybe even end up in New York." But the glum look on his face did not convince her. He gazed past her, out the window. The distant sound of a car engine died to a hum, then was gone.

His glance fell on the little bank. He smiled and reached in his pocket, withdrawing pennies. "Give her a spin," he said.

Ana was not in the mood for play. But he was as sad as she so it was up to her to cheer him up. Bravely, she picked up a penny from his hand, stood it in its slot and pulled the knob as far as it would go. The coin dropped with a clink to the bank below. But the lever jammed and would not fall back in its groove. The little figure rose, her arms swiveled. Then she stopped, stuck, halfway up.

CHARLIE DANIELS

A Carolina Christmas Carol

I might as well go ahead and tell you right up front: I believe in Santa Claus. Now, you can believe or not believe, but I'm here to tell you for a fact that there is a Santa Claus, and he does bring toys and stuff like that on Christmas Eve night.

I know, I know. It sounds like I've had too much eggnog, don't it? All I ask is that you wait till I get through telling my story before you make up your mind.

When I was a kid, Christmas time had a magic to it that no other season of the year had. There was just something in the air, something that you couldn't put your finger on, but it was there, and it affected everybody.

It seemed like everybody smiled and laughed more at that time of the year, even the people who didn't hardly smile and laugh the rest of the year.

"You reckon it's gonna snow? Boy, I sure do wish it'd snow this year. Do you reckon it's gonna?"

Heck no, it won't gonna snow. As far as I know, it ain't never snowed in Wilmington, North Carolina, at Christmas time in the whole history of man. It seemed like everybody in the world had snow at Christmas except us.

In the funny papers, Nancy and Sluggo and Little Orphan Annie had snow to frolic around in at Christmas time. The Christmas cards had snow. Bing Crosby even had snow to sing about. But not one flake fell on Wilmington, North Carolina.

But that didn't dampen our spirits one little bit. Our family celebrated Christmas to the hilt. We were a big, close-knit family, and we'd gather up at Grandma's house every year. My grandparents lived on a farm in Bladen County, about fifty miles from Wilmington, and I just couldn't wait to get up there.

They lived in a great big old farmhouse, and every Christmas they'd fill it up with their children and grandchildren. We'd always stay from the night of the twenty-third through the morning of the twenty-sixth.

There'd be Uncle Clyde and Aunt Martha, Uncle Lacy and Aunt Selma, Uncle Leroy and Aunt Mollie, Uncle Stewart and Aunt Opal, and my mama and daddy, Ernest and Nadine. I won't even go into how many children were there, but take my word for it, there was a bunch.

There'd be people sleeping all over that big old house. We kids would sleep on pallets on the floor, and we'd giggle and play till some of the grown-ups would come and make us be quiet.

All the usual ground rules about eating were off for those days at Grandma's house. You could eat as much pie and cake and candy as you could hold, and your mama wouldn't say a word to you.

My Grandma would cook from sunup to sundown and love every minute of it. She'd have cakes, pies, candy, fruit and nuts setting out all the time, and on top of that, she'd cook three big meals a day. I mean, we eat like pigs.

Christmas was also the only time that my Granddaddy would take a drink. It was a Southern custom of the time not to drink in front of small children, so Granddaddy kept his drinking whiskey hid in the barn. When he'd want to go out there and get him a snort, he'd say that he had to go see if the mare had had her foal yet.

It was a good, good time. A little old-fashioned by some people's standards, but it suited us just fine.

If I'm not mistaken, it was the year I was five years old that my cousin Buford told me that there wasn't any Santa Claus. Buford was about nine at the time. He always was a mean-natured cuss. Still is.

Well, I just refused to believe him. I said, "You're telling a great big fib, Buford Ray, cause Santa Claus comes to see me every Christmas, right here at Grandma and Granddaddy's house."

"That ain't Santa Claus. That's your mama and daddy."

One thing led to another and I got so upset about the prospect of no Santa Claus that I went running in the house crying.

"Grandma, Grandma! Buford says there ain't no Santa Claus! There is a Santa Claus, ain't they, Grandma?"

"Of course there is, Curtis. Buford was just joking with you."

Aunt Selma heard me talking to Grandma and walked to the door. "Buford Ray, get yourself in this house right this minute!"

When he came in, Aunt Selma grabbed him by the ear, led him into the front room and swatted him.

Granddaddy was also a big defender of Santa Claus. He would talk about Santa Claus like he was a personal friend of his. And the more he went to check on the mare, the more he talked about Santa Claus, or "Sandy Claws," as he called him.

"Yes, children, old Sandy Claws will be hitching up them reindeers and heading on down this a-way before long. Wonder what he's gonna bring this year?"

He'd have us so excited by the time we went to bed that I reckon if visions of sugarplums ever danced in anybody's heads, it was ours.

Christmas Eve night, after we had eat about as much supper as we could hold, we'd go in the front room. There'd always be a big log fire crackling in the fireplace, and Granddaddy would always say the same thing.

"Children, do y'all know why we have Christmas every year?"

"Cause that's when the Baby Jesus was born."

"That's right. We're celebrating the Lord's birthday. Do y'all know where He was born at?"

"In Bethlehem," we would all chime in.

"That's right. He was born in a stable in Bethlehem almost two thousand years ago."

Then Granddaddy would put on his spectacles and read Saint Luke's version of the Christmas story. Then, after we'd had family prayer, Granddaddy would always get a twinkle in his eye. "I reckon I'd better step out to the barn and see if that old mare has had her baby yet."

There was always a chorus of, "Can I go with you, Granddaddy?"

"Y'all had better stay in here by the fire. It's mighty cold outside. I'll be right back."

When Granddaddy came back in the house, he'd always say, "I was on my way back from the barn while ago, and I heard something that sounded like bells a-tinkling, way back off yonder in the woods. I just can't figure why bells would be ringing back in the woods this time of the night."

"It's Santa Claus! It's Santa Claus!"

"Well, now, I never thought of that. I wonder if it was old Sandy Claws. You children had better get to bed. You know he won't come to see you as long as you're awake."

Then it was time to say good night. All the grandchildren would go around hugging all the grown-ups. "Good night Grandma, good night Granddaddy, good night Uncle Clyde, good night Aunt Mollie," and so forth.

We would always try to stay awake, lying on our pallets until Santa Claus got there, but we always lost the battle.

It sounded like the Third World War at Grandma's house on Christmas morning. There was cap pistols going off and baby dolls crying, and all the children hollering at the top of their lungs.

By the time the next school year started, I was six years old and in the first grade. I kept thinking about what Buford had said. I didn't want to believe it, but it kept slipping into the back door of my mind.

At school, Buford was three grades ahead of me, but I'd still see him sometimes. Every time he'd see me that whole year, he'd make it a point to rub it in about Santa Claus.

He'd do something like get me around a bunch of his older buddies and say, "Hey, you fellers, Curtis still believes in Santa Claus." And they'd all laugh and point.

Away from any adult persuasion, I guess Buford finally wore me out. I returned to Grandma's house the next year not believing that there was a Santa Claus. Christmas lost a little of its mystique. Oh, I still enjoyed it. I even pretended that I believed in "Sandy Claws" for Granddaddy's benefit, but it wasn't the same.

Well, as you know, time marches on, children grow up and leave home, including me.

I was living in Denver, Colorado, married, with a child, and I hadn't been home for Christmas since our little daughter had been born. Dawn was three that year, and this would be the first time that she really knew about Santa Claus, and she was some kind of excited.

We had the best time shopping for her, buying all the little toys that she wanted.

Daddy called me about three weeks before Christmas and said, "Son, you know that your grandparents are getting old. They've requested that all the children, grandchildren and great-grandchildren come home and spend Christmas with them at their house, the way we used to. Can you make it, son?"

"We'll be there, Daddy."

I couldn't think of a better place in the whole world for little Dawn to spend her first real Christmas, so we packed up and headed for North Carolina.

Grandma was eighty-two years old, but she still cooked all day long, and she still enjoyed every minute of it. Granddaddy was eighty-four, but he still had a twinkle in his eye and a mare in the barn.

The old house was fuller than ever, with a whole new generation of children in it. Everybody was there. Even Buford. He had married, but he didn't have any children. He didn't want any. One of my cousins said he figured Buford was too stingy to have children.

Buford was still the same, except that he had changed from a boy with a mean nature to a full-grown man with a cynical nature and a know-it-all attitude.

Just before we went into the front room for family prayer and the reading of the Christmas story, I overheard him say to somebody, "I don't know why Granddaddy keeps filling the children's heads full of that Santa Claus nonsense. I think it's ridiculous. If I had children, I wouldn't let him tell them all that junk."

I looked hard at Buford. I had never liked him, and I liked him even less now.

Our little daughter was so excited when Granddaddy started talking about "Sandy Claws" that she jumped up and down and clapped her hands.

When I took her up to bed, there was pure excitement in those big brown eyes. "Santa Claus coming, Daddy! Santa Claus coming, Daddy!"

I got a warm feeling all over, and I sure was glad to be back at Grandma's house at Christmas time.

After all the children had gone to sleep, the grown-ups started going out to their cars to get the toys they had brought for Santa Claus to leave under the Christmas tree.

I decided to wait until everybody else had finished before I put Dawn's presents out. This was a special time for me and I wanted to enjoy it.

After everybody had gone up to bed, I went out to the car to get Dawn's toys. To my shock, I couldn't find them. I ran back into the house to my wife. "Sylvia, where did you pack Dawn's Christmas presents?"

"I thought you packed them."

I was close to panic, but I didn't want Sylvia to know it. I said, "Oh well, you just go on to bed, honey, and I'll look again. I probably just overlooked them."

I kissed my wife good night and went back downstairs.

I knew I hadn't overlooked them. We had somehow forgot to pack them, and they were two thousand miles away in Denver, Colorado.

I was a miserable man. I just didn't feel like I could face little Dawn the next morning. She'd be so disappointed. All the other children would have the toys that Santa Claus had brought them, and my beloved little daughter wouldn't have anything.

How could I have been so dumb? Here it was, twelve o'clock Christmas Eve night, all the stores closed, everybody in bed, and me without a single present for little Dawn. I was heartbroken. I went into the front room and sat by the dying fire, dejected and hopeless.

I don't know how long I sat there staring at the embers, but sometime later on I heard a rustle behind me and somebody said, "You got a match, son?"

I turned around and almost fell on the floor. Standing not ten feet from me was a short, fat little man in a red suit, with a long white beard and a pipe sticking out of his mouth.

I couldn't move, I couldn't speak. He looked at me and chuckled.

"Have you got a match, son? I ran out and I want to get this pipe going."

When I finally got my voice back, all I could say was, "Who are you?"

"Well, people call me by different names in different parts of the world, but around here they call me Santa Claus."

"No, I mean who are you really?"

"I just told you, son. How about that match?"

I stumbled to the mantelpiece, got a kitchen match and gave it to him.

"Much obliged." He stood there lighting his pipe, with me looking at him like he was a ghost or something.

"How did you get in here?"

"Oh, I've got my ways."

"I thought you were supposed to slide down the chimney."

"That's a common misconception. Would you slide down a chimney with a fire at the bottom?"

"Well, no. I mean, no, sir."

"Well, neither would I."

"How did you get here?"

"I've got a sturdy sleigh and the finest team of reindeer a man could have."

"But we ain't got no snow."

Santa Claus laughed so hard that his considerable belly shook. "I don't need snow. Half the places I go in the world don't have snow. Besides, I like to get out of the snow once in a while. We have it year-round at the North Pole, you know."

"You mean you really live at the North Pole?"

"Of course, I've always lived at the North Pole. Don't you know anything about Santa Claus, son?"

"Well, yeah, but I thought it was all a big put-on for the children."

"That's the trouble with you grown-ups. You think that everything you can't see is a put-on. It's a shame grown people can't be more like children. They don't have any trouble believing in me."

"You mean you've really got a sleigh, with reindeer named Donner and Blitzen and stuff like that?"

"That's right, son. There's Comet and Cupid and Donner and Blitzen and Dasher and Dancer and Prancer and Vixen. Of course, there's no Rudolph with the red nose. I don't know who came up with that one. Rudolph really is a put-on."

"But what are you doing here? Why did you come?"

"Because there's a little girl in this house who believes in me very much. Now, she'd be mighty disappointed to wake up Christmas morning and have nothing under the tree."

"You mean you came all the way here just because one little girl believes in you?"

"That's right, son. There's magic in believing. Besides, she's not the only one in this house who believes in me."

"Who else?"

"Why, your grandfather, of course."

"You mean Granddaddy wasn't putting us on all those years? He really believed in you?"

"Of course he believed in me."

"Well, why do you do this?"

"It's my way of celebrating the most important birthday in the history of man. Our Lord has given us so much. How can we do less?"

Santa Claus consulted a piece of paper he pulled out of

his pocket and started taking a doll and other toys out of a big bag he had brought with him.

"Well, I've got to go, son. I've got a lot of stops to make before sunup. It's been real nice talking to you. Thanks for the match."

"Can I help you with your bag, Santa Claus?"

"No, that's all right, son. I'm used to carrying it."

I walked outside with him. "Where's your sleigh, Santa Claus?"

"It's parked right over there in the edge of the woods. You can come over and see it if you like."

I started walking over to his sleigh with him, but then I had a thought.

"I'm gonna have to miss seeing your sleigh and reindeer. Thank you so very much. You saved my life. God bless you, Santa Claus. I'll see you next year."

"God bless you, too, son, and a Merry Christmas to you and yours."

Santa Claus started across the yard toward his sleigh, and I went running back in the house like a wild man. I raced up the stairs. "Buford, Buford, get up!"

"What's the matter, is the house on fire?"

"No, but hurry. Come out on the upstairs porch."

Buford grumbled as he got up and followed me out on the upstairs porch.

"What in the heck do you want? It's cold out here."

"Just hush up and listen."

Well, we listened for a full minute and nothing happened.

"You're crazy. I'm going back to bed."

"Buford, if you go back in the house, you're gonna miss something that I want you, above all people, to see."

We waited for a little while longer and I had almost given up hope when I heard it. It was just a little tinkle at first, hanging on the frosty air and getting louder by the second. It was sleigh bells!

Buford looked at me and said, "Curtis, is this some kind of a joke or something?"

"No, Buford, I swear it ain't. Just wait a minute now!"

The sound of sleigh bells was getting louder and Buford's face was getting whiter. "You got somebody out there doing that, ain't you? Admit it! You got somebody out there, ain't you?"

I didn't say a word. All of a sudden it sounded like somebody had flushed a covey of quail. That sleigh came up out of the woods and headed west, hovering just above the treetops.

Buford was speechless. I thought he was gonna pass out. He held on to the banister and took deep breaths.

Even if you believe so far, I know you ain't gonna believe this next part, but it really happened. Santa Claus made a big circle and turned and flew right around the house. I bet he won't over twenty feet from the upstairs porch when he passed by me and Buford. Old Santa Claus could really handle them reindeer. Then he headed west again, moving at a pretty good clip this time.

I hate to even tell you this next part, cause you'll think I took it right out of the book, but I didn't. Anyway, just about the time he was getting out of our hearing, he hollered, "Merry Christmas, everybody!"

And then he was gone.

"Curtis, do you know where Granddaddy keeps that bottle hid in the barn? I need me a drink."

I don't believe that Buford ever told anybody about seeing Santa Claus. I know I didn't, not until now. But I just had to tell somebody about it. It's been hard keeping it to myself all these years.

I'm a granddaddy myself now. That little girl that caused all this to happen with her faith in Santa Claus is grown and married and has a three-year-old girl and five-year-old boy.

Me and Sylvia moved back to North Carolina many years ago and bought a big old farmhouse. Now my grandchildren come and spend Christmas with me and their grandmother. There's not as many of us as there was at Grandma's house, but we have just as big a time and celebrate Christmas just as hard.

In fact, Christmas is about the only time of the year I'll take a drink. I always get me a pint of Old Granddad at Christmas time. Since the grandchildren are so small, I don't like to drink in front of them, so I keep my drinking whiskey hid out in the barn. When I want to go out there and get me a snort, I always tell the grandchildren that I've got to see if the cows got corn.

Of course, all the grown-ups know why I'm going out to the barn, or at least they think they do.

I always make my last trip to the barn after I've read the Christmas story and had family prayer. Everybody thinks I'm going out to get me a snort, but they're wrong.

I'm just going out to hear the sleigh bells ring.

TOM TURNER

Blue Bethlehem

al had swallowed bubblegum before, and even a baby tooth, but this was the first time he had ever swallowed a dime. From the way it had slid and slipped and rolled down his throat, he knew it was too late to try to cough up the dime. It was probably all the way down in his left hind foot by now.

Maybe if I was to stand on my head, Cal thought, *I can shake the dime loose and let it fall out my mouth*. He tried this, but each time he got ready to unbend his knees, the rest of him collapsed and his head swam so he couldn't keep his mouth open even if the dime had wanted to roll out. It was just too many things to try to do at the same time.

In his hand, the dime had seemed small, but on the tip of his tongue it had felt so heavy Cal never dreamed of swallowing it.

Folks that swallows catfish bones eats bread, Cal remembered. *If I had the dime, I could buy me some bread, but if I had the dime back, lightbread the LAST thing I'd get with it.*

Cal had been headed for Mr. Godown's Store when he swallowed the dime. Mr. Godown was a deaf old grouchy white man who didn't like to crouch down behind his candy case too long at a time. This was why Cal had put the piece of money in his mouth to start with: so he could concentrate on what he was going to buy with it before he got there. When he left the house, he had intended to buy a yard of yellow satin hair ribbon for his sisters, Doris and Amber. But the nearer Cal drew to Mr. Godown's store, the more he came to realize what a sorry Christmas present hair ribbon would be. And besides, his brother, Roosevelt, had sent him the dime from the Army and it was the only case dime he had ever owned before.

Something good to eat would make more sense than old hair ribbon, Cal was thinking. *A Mound or something.* He could almost taste the rich chocolate and coconut. This was when he had swallowed the dime.

Suddenly, Cal remembered that Mr. Godown could get blood out of a turnip. He had heard his mother say this many times. It stood to reason that if Mr. Godown could get blood out of a turnip, he ought to be able to get the dime out, too.

Mr. Godown was sitting by the stove behind his newspaper when Cal got there. He knew it was Mr. Godown behind the newspaper because he could smell his old cigar and see the smoke coming up.

"Mr. Godown!" Cal yelled.

The newspaper made a terrible racket between Mr. Godown's hands. "Jesus, boy!" Mr. Godown said. "You nearly give me a heart attack!"

Cal bowed his head. He was too shy to ask Mr. Godown to get the dime out now. He tried to grin, but his lips wouldn't budge.

"Well, what can I do for you?" Mr. Godown frowned.

Cal shrugged and blinked and shook his head side-to-side.

Mr. Godown creased the newspaper and took the cigar out of his mouth.

"Mr. Godown," Cal said, and stopped.

"What is it?" Mr. Godown said.

"Mr. Godown," Cal said and stopped again.

"I haven't got all day," Mr. Godown said.

"Mr. Godown," Cal tried again, "what happen if a boy worse to swallow a dime?"

"How's that?" Mr. Godown said.

I finally got it out, Cal thought, *and Mr. Godown can't hear thunder.* "Mr. Godown," he said again, very carefully, "this boy I know swallowed a case dime."

It took a long time for it to reach Mr. Godown, but Cal knew he had heard. He could tell by the way the old man finally squinted and jabbed the cigar back in his mouth.

"Is this boy a close friend of yours?" Mr. Godown puffed.

"Nosir," Cal said. "He just a boy."

"Because swallowing money is a serious thing," Mr. Godown said. "If you swallow money, you'll die."

This was the last thing Cal expected Mr. Godown to say. *Die, die, die, dime!* The word rolled down and down until Cal had to clamp his hands over his ears.

"Hold on," Mr. Godown said. "Wait a minute."

But Cal was the deaf one now. He brushed past Mr. Godown's candy case without even looking through the glass. *Deaf and dumb and swallowed a dime.*

Cal knew next to nothing about dying, and what he did know was confusing. His grandfather had died and gone to heaven, but not from swallowing a dime. His grandfather had swallowed a clock. The doctor said it was a blood clock, and when it reached his heart he died. Cal wanted to get home before the dime could reach his heart. If he kept his legs stiff, the dime could not move around much and he would be able to do what he had to do. He would march like Roosevelt in the Army.

He decided he would not tell his sisters that he was going to die. He had already ruined their Christmas by finding their Santy Claus on top of the chifforobe. He and Amber and Doris had eaten every tangerine, banana, orange and most of the apples that their poor old mama thought she had hidden. It was bad enough that Santy Claus couldn't come, without telling them he was going to die, too.

By the time Cal got home, he had stopped marching and was pulling himself along. When he came through the door, Doris and Amber were just taking a bite out of some apples. They were big red noisy apples, but Cal barely noticed.

"Where Mama?"

The two girls did not answer, but took their apples from their mouths and looked at one another like something was up.

"Howcome you dragging your feet thataway?" Doris asked.

"She here?"

"You think we be in these apples if she was?" Amber asked.

"She taking back washing," Doris said.

"Get the Bible down."

"What you done done now, Cal?" Amber wanted to know.

"Get the Bible and get a pencil, too."

Ordinarily, they only took the Bible down to hide bad report cards in, but Doris and Amber did as they were told.

"Hurry up," Cal said. He knew how to put what he meant to say, but Amber would have to write it. "Put down: I THE ONE EAT ALL THE SANTY CLAUS."

"I ain't writing that," Amber said. "You and Doris eat just as much as me."

"Put it down," Cal said, "and let me sign it."

"You can't sign for what we eat," Doris said.

"I might not can write," Cal said, "but I can sign."

"Howcome you want to sign for us?" Doris asked.

"Cause I the one found it," he said.

"We all three found it," Amber said.

"No," Cal said. "Y'all say it smell like Christmas coming, but I the one smell where it coming *from*."

Doris, who was not much older than Cal, began to cry. "We should not have did it," she sobbed. "Now Christmas done ruined."

"We ought to all three sign it," Amber sniffed.

When Cal saw that Amber was crying he decided to join in, too. He could outcry Amber and Doris put together. Cal cried for the fruit, and he cried for Roosevelt's dime and he cried all around what he was really crying about; but he never let on that he was going to die.

It was dark when their mother got back home. The whole time she was cooking supper, Cal was so good and quiet that finally she had to stop and feel his forehead.

"I don't know what's come over you, Cal," she said, "unless it a bad case of Santy Claus coming."

Cal could feel his heart begin to pull in two. It was sad as any blood clock, ticking, but still he never let on. *Roosevelt wouldn't let on,* he told himself. He was going to be brave to the last, just like Roosevelt.

Christmas morning, Cal woke up in the strong arms of his brother Roosevelt. At first he thought Christmas had come, but then he remembered the dime and knew he must have died in his sleep. The trip to heaven had been so smooth, it hadn't even waked him up. *It must be heaven,* he thought, *'cause Christmas can't come, and folks in dreams don't give you fuzzy kisses and squeeze you till your eyes pop out.*

The Roosevelt angel toted him to the table where there were Pepsi Colas, baloney, lightbread, a soldier hat and a brand new basketball. And not only this, but every piece of the fruit that he and Amber and Doris had already eaten and signed for in the Bible. His mother was standing beside the table. She had on a red dress God must have given her. It caught the light from the fireplace like new money. And Amber and Doris were there, too. Doris had a yellow ribbon in her hair and Amber was dabbing perfume on herself from a pretty bottle blue as Bethlehem.

The angel Roosevelt grinned down at Cal. "Old Timer," he said, "you sure don't act surprised much."

"Nosir," Cal rubbed his eyes. "I ain't surprised. I always figured it would be something like this."

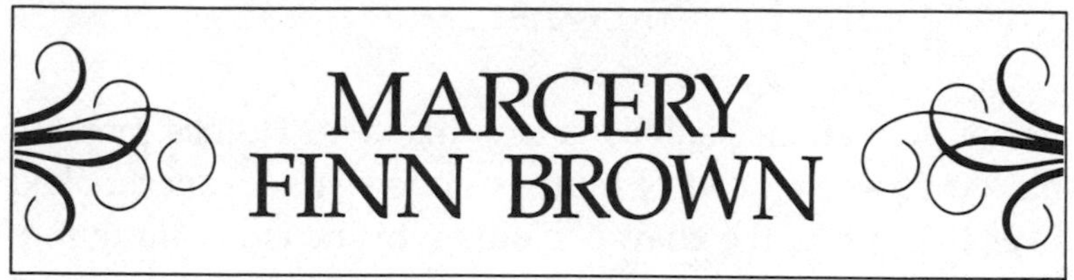

MARGERY FINN BROWN

New Acquaintances

It's ten-thirty on Christmas Eve, and Astrid and John Donovan's party is beginning to wind down. Their house in Berkeley — brown shingles hennaed by the sun — sits high and aloof on Grizzly Peak. Outside the tall windows, a grid of amber streetlights shimmies through the darkness, and stretching to the horizon is the inky-black bay. After paying homage to the view, guests circulate and chatter while white-coated waiters pass canapés and cups of holiday cheer.

There's a fieldstone mantel at one end of the room, under which a hysterical fire hisses and spits. At the opposite end of the room, next to a picture-perfect Christmas tree, sits a handsome, severe-looking gentleman. He's wearing an impeccable gray cheviot suit with a softer gray silk tie. A heavy gold chain scallops across his vest. He has piercing blue eyes and a head of tempestuous hair. A cane hooked over the arm of the chair explains why he is not mingling. He's the host's father, Judge Thomas Donovan, who arrived yesterday.

When his son John called him in Boston with an invitation for Christmas, he said they were all anxious to see him. Just the other night, Pauli had asked why her grandfather never came to visit. Didn't he like them? Weren't they family? John also said the weather would be balmy. Balmy? Since Thomas arrived it has been raining steadily, a penetrating rain that makes a beeline for the space between his shoulder blades. He's taken his daily allotment of pills, but when his arthritis is this bad, there's nothing to do but bite the bullet.

The pain makes him irritable. He's detached from the party faces that swim in and out of focus. Is it possible to be lonely without wondering how much of it is your own doing? Ann had been his link with the world, he thinks to himself. You shouldn't have left me, Ann. We made a deal. Without you I've grown stiff in my ways. The old enthusiasms are gone.

When he turns, he sees his granddaughter, Pauli, at the top of the stairs, looking down at the party. Is she ten or eleven? He's ashamed to ask. He raises his hand in a mock salute. She whisks off like a scalded cat.

Pauli is the magnet that's drawn him across the continent, but she hasn't said fifty words to him since he arrived. Pauli's not rude — quite the opposite. She's too polite. There appears to be no friction with her parents — not much warmth, either. She was a lively endearing baby, but now that carefree air has chipped away. Unlike her twin brothers, Eric and Lars, a pair of brawny Viking jocks at Yale, Pauli is difficult to classify. Is she starting that Golden Age of Adolescence? Why not? he thinks. Kittens turn into cats.

Pauli's indifference shouldn't hurt him, but it does. When Ann was alive, he passed his feelings to her. Now that he is alone, he is embarrassed, sometimes swamped by feelings he never knew he possessed, feelings that Christmas always intensifies. When you're happy, Christmas adds width and an extra sheen. When you're hopeful, Christmas sends your hopes through the air like a gaudy meteor. But when you're lonely, Christmas encourages you to think you're the most godforsaken soul in the universe.

Not wishing to be a specter at the feast, he gives a semi-smile.

"What's this?" he asks the waiter proffering a tray of canapés and cups.

"The brass cups contain glögg."

"Grog?"

"No, sir, glögg, with an umlaut. It is an alcoholic punch of Scandinavian origin. The recipe has been handed down in Mrs. Donovan's family."

"Fancy that," says Thomas. He takes what appears to be a cheesy square from the tray. It's so sweet he coughs violently, causing Astrid, his daughter-in-law, to stride across the room.

"Father," she says, in an unchummy whisper. "Are you all right?"

John and Astrid are stockbrokers. They're tall, thin, and tanned from skiing. Standing together they look like a pair of matching golf clubs.

Astrid says she and John will drive to the airport to meet the boys when the guests have gone. Would he care to come? He would not. Pauli, she says, is upstairs washing her hair. If he wants anything, he should just ask Pauli.

"I'll do that," he says, lying.

How he wishes he were home. Calvin would have his bed turned down, by the bed a bottle of Remy Martin and a brandy snifter. Every night he pours himself a snort — one, never two — and raises his glass. *"Zusammen im Himmel,"* he says. Together in heaven. It's the toast he and Ann always used.

All the old Christmases are still so fresh in his mind. When his family moved from Dublin, Thomas was a sturdy sixteen. His first Christmas in Massachusetts, his presents consisted of six oranges and a hockey stick. That afternoon he tooled around Sargent's Pond. Out of nowhere comes this kid with a tam over his eyes and skids into Thomas. The stick breaks. The kid lands on the ice and scrambles for his tam. Long black curls, furious black eyes. He's a *girl*.

"Why don't you pick on someone your own size?" she yells. Thomas skates off red-faced and furious. Back on her feet, the girl twirls off across the ice. He had to admit she was a crackerjack skater.

He forgot about her, or so he thought. His last year at Harvard Law, he was driving an SS Pierce delivery truck when he saw a blue Rolls pulled off the road, hood up, steaming. There she stood in a white dress, a look on her face that said, "Which one of you lucky guys is going to help me?"

Fourteen months later they eloped. Both families were furious. Money was scarce. But after his first few big wins in court, they started a family: John, Vincent and Paul. They moved to a sprawling gray-shingled house in South Hamilton where they drank better wine and gave Sunday-night buffets. Thomas helped in the kitchen because she was such an appalling cook. The years went so swiftly and with such flourish, they took for granted their good fortune until it ceased to be. Ann noticed a lump on her neck. Chemotherapy helped. Two operations helped. Then nothing helped.

Has he nodded off? The inevitable party debris has been whisked away. Soft red ashes glow in the fireplace, and the lights on the Christmas tree blink off-on, off-on. The stairway creaks. With his eyes partially closed, he can see Pauli coming down in a long white robe. Around her shoulders is a blue towel, and over the towel her damp hair falls like a fountain. He doesn't see the blanket in her arms until she approaches his chair and gently folds it over him, tucking the fringe away from his face. The gesture almost undoes him. He watches her cross the room to the fireplace. Her face in profile is finely etched, fragile. Beneath her robe he can see her feet, long, glossy and bare.

"Put something on your feet!" What made him roar like that when all he really wanted to say was thank you?

She whirls around. The gaze she directs at him is intensely cool. All she says is "Oh, Grandfather" and sits on a stool, idly hitting the carpet with a bare foot.

"It occurs to me," he says, to take his mind off the apology he should but would not make. "You're the only one who calls me Grandfather."

No comment.

"The truth is I hate 'Grandpa.' It makes me feel older than God's dog."

No comment.

"I didn't see you at the party, Pauli," he says, trying to fill the silence.

"*Yes*, you did. I was sitting on the top step."

"Ah, I did see you there."

"Is arthritis what you call a fatal disease?"

"No. Actually, I'm in pretty good shape for the shape I'm in."

"Grandfather, did you have a good time at the party?"

"Yes and no. Christmas is a big family time. I was thinking of the people I love who aren't around anymore. I'm not much for parties these days."

"Me neither. I never feel comfortable. Everyone's yukking it up. Sometimes I think they're laughing at me."

It was as if she had rehearsed the questions in her mind, blurting them out with a combination of shyness and hauteur. Without any proof whatsoever, he senses in her a tremendous vulnerability. Her cool exterior doesn't entirely mask a depth of feeling the more frightening because she doesn't express it. He's glad to see she's comfortable enough to leave the fireplace and walk toward him. Her eyes are crisp — the color of a blue poker chip. In the middle of her mouth she has two Bugs Bunny teeth, with gaps on both sides. She'd grow into those teeth, he thought. She'd be tall . . . a silvery blond Ice Maiden, enigmatic.

"Grandfather, did you have a lot of friends at my age?"

Thinking back he says, "All the years I went to school I never belonged to a gang."

"Are you sorry you didn't?"

"No, I was lucky enough to meet your grandmother. There's an old saying: You can't choose your relatives; thank God for friends. When there's a person in your family who's also your friend —"

"You mean you and Grandmother hit the jackpot?"

"Exactly."

"I wish I knew how to talk to people," Pauli says. "On my birthday — my birthday was September fourteenth. I guess you forgot."

"I did. My birthday was September sixth. Everybody forgot."

"I didn't know you were a Virgo, too. Our horoscope in the paper today said: 'Avoid stagnation. New acquaintances prove rewarding.'"

Thomas really felt like smiling, but he didn't think it was the right time.

"For my birthday I got my own telephone. But when I dial the number of one of the kids in my class, soon as I hear hello, I hang up."

"All you need is a couple of opening lines. If you felt like a little practice, you could call me in Boston."

"Who'll pay for the calls?"

He resists the impulse to say reverse the charges. "You pay for yours; I pay for mine."

"Okay. I'll call on weekends when rates are cheaper."

He allows himself a smile.

"Do I have to tell jokes?" she asks. "I never make people laugh."

"I've heard enough jokes in my day."

Perched opposite him like a bird, she looks happy with his answer.

"Enough of this serious talk," says Thomas. "Would you care for a bit of song, as they say in Ireland?"

He hasn't sung for years. The sound that emerges isn't shameful; he starts with "McNamara's Band" and "Galway Bay," then launches into "I'll Take You Home Again, Kathleen," ending on a tricky bit of falsetto.

She applauds, and after a moment says, "I was just wondering. The day after Christmas, would you —" she hesitates, unsure of herself.

"I won't be able to do it, Pauli, unless you tell me."

"All right then. Day after Christmas, do you think you might like to come to the rink and watch me skate?"

"Skate?" Surprise crackles in his voice. "I didn't know you could skate."

"Mr. Osgood's my coach, and I practice almost every day after school. I'm not going to make the Olympic team; but Mr. Osgood says, 'You're a winner, Pauli, I think you're one in a million.'"

Sitting there on the ottoman with her legs tucked under her, she looks at him with those astounding eyes, wondering if he thinks she's bragging, waiting for his response. What he would like to do most of all is put his arms around her and shield her from all harm and heartache. But she doesn't need to be protected. He feels a world of tenderness for her, but what he doesn't know is how to express it. He closes his eyes for a moment, the better to contain the unexpected spark of anticipation. He'd known it often as a young man when he thought ahead of life to be lived, goals to be reached. He'd thought it was gone forever with Ann, but here it was again, the same little sprig of joy snatched out of time.

"Remind me sometime to tell you how I met your grandmother, Pauli. As for Mr. Osgood, he's absolutely right. You *are* one in a million."

He watches her gap-toothed smile. It melts and sparkles and dazzles its way to his heart.

When John and Astrid and the boys return from the airport — the plane had been delayed — Thomas is facing the fire, with Pauli on the floor beside him. There is an empty brandy snifter and a glass of milk on the table in a sahara of cookie crumbs. They are talking about the day after Christmas, and the days after that, and when spring comes, perhaps she would like to come and visit him in Boston. Autumn in New England *is* beautiful. Everything considered, however, they prefer not to wait till autumn. Although the words are never said, they both feel the need to make up for lost time.

STEPHEN DIXON

A Christmas Story

t's Christmas Eve and I'm on the street. That's okay. That's what I want. I look at the apartment windows with the wreaths and lit trees and people around them, some still decorating the trees, and I think that's for them, not for me. I haven't got the spirit, plain as that. I can't afford the spirit, even plainer. I almost never had the spirit, though did as a kid, sure, but that was because I was taken care of then and all my friends had it and my folks and they gave it to me and I took it and Christmas became fun. But not as an adult. Takes too much. I can't even pay for a dingy room of my own, I can a lit tree? Sure and where my going to stick it: on some street corner or in a basement I might find to flop out in tonight? Look, the spirit's gone and it's not coming back. And I'm not going to get upset about it tonight and let it sink me as it does most other bums.

But it's the best night for handouts, I can tell you that. People see me and they get especially generous. They feel sorry for me. Well I kind of feel sorry for them. Look at what they got to do to keep it all going. Work most every day so they can have Christmas off? Also fixing the house, getting the car started when it's way below freezing, getting Johnny off to school when school begins again and now seeing he has something to do during his vacation. So neither of us are better off. We're equals you might say and equals in what we got coming in too. They got their Christmas joys to look forward to and me my Christmas handouts. So we all gain. Hey: three cheers for Christmas, I say.

There's a couple. "Howdy, sir, evening, ma'am, spare some change for Christmas?"

"You can't work for a living like the rest of us?" he says.

"Come on," she says, "it's Christmas Eve, leave the guy alone. Here," and she gives me a quarter from her purse. Then he says "All right" and sticks his hand in his pocket and comes up with a half dollar.

"Well thanks," I say. "And Merry Christmas to you both."

"Merry Christmas to you," she says.

So I got about three times as much as I would have if he didn't put up a stink. And Merry Christmas? Merry Christmas my eye. That's what I'd like to tell them, but a man's got to live and I don't want that guy running back and taking what he gave me as some other people have done when I said something that wasn't nice.

Another couple. Look like two cheery people and stuffed to the gills with cash.

"Spare some change for a Christmas dinner?" I say.

"Get lost," he says.

"Up yours," she says.

"Same to you," I say, "and many many more."

Now those two got the spirit. They'd make good bums.

I keep on walking, mostly to keep warm. Coat's old and the rest of the clothes aren't that heavy and I still got to find a place to sleep tonight. Which hallway shall have this prince? Getting tougher though. Either the cops poke you back to the sidewalk or the landlords or supers just throw you out there themselves. Christmas Eve and all day Christmas is usually better. Once, about ten years ago, a family invited me into their house. Saw me on their doorway. Suddenly that old Christmas kindness came over them and they said, "Come in and have dinner with us and stay the night in our son's bed — he's away at war." Okay by me. I went in, ate a couple bellyfulls. Slept in luxury. Next day they gave me breakfast and even a present — couple of handkerchiefs with somebody else's initials. Then they sat me in their best easy chair and turned up the steam for me and handed me that skimpy Christmas day newspaper to read and asked me to join in a little carol singing around the piano and fed me a Christmas dinner that made me sick for two days it was so much and the food so rich. Then the old guy stuck a ten spot in my pocket and gave me one of his hats which I still wear and his wife held out my coat for me so I could stick my arms in and I left and rang their doorbell the next Christmas Eve and the man answered and I said, "Remember me?" and he said, "Oh yeah, from last year, well have a heart, pal, once isn't enough?" "Sure it is," I said and I left and can truthfully say now that I haven't had a more successful and pleasurable night and day anywhere since.

Hey, there's a nice looking young lady. Fine face. Good coat. Fur. Fancy boots. Walking with a fancy dog. If she doesn't jump out of her skin at the sight of me, she should be good for a quarter or more.

"Good evening, ma'am, spare some change for a holiday dinner? I'm a little down on my luck these days and haven't had a bite for two days."

"You should go to Salvation Army then. They always have a turkey dinner Christmas day, though this year I understand it's chicken."

"I do go, ma'am. Almost every year when I'm in town. But I'm talking about for tonight — Christmas Eve."

"Tonight's Christmas Eve? Completely skipped my mind. What day is today . . . in fact, what month? I never look at the calendar anymore. In fact, I don't even have a calendar anymore. Come along, Josh," and they go.

"What about a dime then?" I say. "I can get a half cup of coffee with it. And a third of a doughnut if you also throw in a nickel." But she was gone. That's what lots of money sometimes does to you. Or she was putting on an act. That's okay. Any way people want to get out of giving me and even on this night, I don't mind. I don't say anything's owed me. All I want now is to make as much money possible in the time available to me before the city closes up for the night and I can't find a place to sleep.

So I walk around the most populated areas — the main avenues, getting a dime here, nickel there, pennies, lots of pennies, times are supposed to be tougher than usual these days, so not many quarters and no more half dollars for the night. Though one well-dressed lush does give me a dollar bill and say "Buy yourself a Christmas stocking with it."

I tell him, "I got two feet so I'll need two stockings," and he says, "I might be drunk but I'm not sober," which I still think I get the meaning of, even if I feel he mixed up the words in his joke.

Anyway, in a few hours I count my take and find I have more than five dollars, not my biggest haul for the year but my best in months. Now to start looking for a place to sleep. I try all the basement doors I'm familiar with around here. All locked. I try some of the lobbies of the shabbier buildings. But the two warm ones where I've found sleeping places before, the cops are called and I'm ushered out.

"Give me a break," I tell the last two cops and one of them says, "And you give us a break too. You think we like working late this night or putting you on the street or even just getting out of our car in this cold to do it? You know where to go. Find some less conspicuous place. And if you can't and you made some scratch tonight like you should've been doing on Christmas Eve, then treat yourself to one of your fleabag hotels."

Finally some good advice from a cop. I hate paying for my sleeping space, but I do have more cash on me than usual and it's as cold as they say. So I go to one of the bum hotels and they tell me they're all filled up.

"What are you talking about?" I say. "Because you never turned me away before when I had real cash."

"Tonight's the big E, buddy," the clerk says. "Plenty of you guys made some money tonight and got a sack long before you came."

I try all the other dives but it's always the same. Filled up.

"What about the floor?" I say to the last one.

"All our floor mattresses are taken also," he says.

"Then just the floor, cold and hard as it is. I'll lay out my coat."

"Can't do. They've been cracking down on us lately and too many residents over the maximum and we can lose our license. You should've been here hours ago. You know bums like to be with people on holidays too."

So I'm on the limb again. But I've gotten off every other limb without falling off. What about the churches? But they're all locked by the time I get there when if I came an hour sooner during the last Mass I might have found a nook to hide out in when the place closed. I try the bus and train stations but the private cops there kick me out. I try a hundred parked cars, a thousand. Every single one of them is locked. People start getting afraid their cars will get stolen and who suffers most: the bums. I try everything. The few lobbies where nobody bothers me for a half hour are so cold that I know I'd freeze to death there by morning.

Then I think: what about the couple who took me in ten years ago? I've given them nine years to recuperate from that good turn. Maybe tonight, when they hear my story and see my teeth chattering, they'll give in and let me have a couch to sleep on or just their basement. I don't have to have the Christmas Eve dinner and easy chair and hankies and the rest.

So I walk across town. By now I just about have frostbite. And ring their first floor bell of the three story building they own. A lady comes to the door and says through the door crack over the chain "Yes?"

"Hey," I say, "remember me?"

"No, who are you?"

"I was your Christmas Eve and day guest here ten years ago. Kenneth Fisk."

"Sorry, Kenneth, but I only moved in here four years ago."

"That's why you don't remember me, of course. Well listen. That last couple who lived here — where'd they move to?"

"They're both dead."

"Oh, that's too bad. They were real nice folks. You see, I was a blood relative of theirs. And whenever I was down on my luck they'd put me up for a while. And when things were going well with me, I did the same for them if they happened to be hard up. But now, as you can see —"

"Excuse me, Kenneth, but I'm tired. You sort of woke me up, so if you don't mind?" and she starts closing the door.

"Sure, sure, but listen. Don't rush away. I'm down in my luck again, that's what I want to say. Haven't any place to sleep. All I'm asking for is an evening in a warm place. Not in your house, but the basement. Near the oil burner if you got. Anything, because I'm freezing to death out here. Been on the streets all night collecting enough money to live on for the next few days. And all the cheap hotels are booked solid with bums like myself for the night and the more expensive ones are either too expensive for me or just wouldn't let a guy looking and dressed like me in."

"I'm sorry," she says, "but I'm especially afraid of people like you. As much as my heart tells me to let you in, my head can't."

"Lock your basement against me once I'm down there and only let me out when it gets to be morning. I swear I won't be any harm. I never touched a person to injure them intentionally since I was a little kid. You don't want to see me get very sick and die?"

"Of course I don't. But I don't want to die myself. And people like you would terrify me even if I had you locked in five cages inside a sixth in my basement, so what more can I say?" and she shuts and bolts the door.

"You can say Merry Christmas," I yell at the door.

"Of course. I forgot. Merry Christmas."

"I was getting bitter."

"And I wasn't — I swear," and I hear her clunk upstairs.

So I've about run out of ideas. All it needs now is to snow. And sure enough, when I'm trying to jimmy open the window of a parked car, here comes the flakes. Little ones at first. I break a couple of them in the air with my hands. Then they get bigger and more in number till I can hardly see in front of me. In fifteen minutes the city's covered with the stuff and looks like some dumb fairy tale while I'm still trying to find a basement door to open or break into if it's loose enough. But there are none and my feet are getting frozen I can tell you. Also my hands in their holey gloves which can't even turn another doorknob. And my nose is frozen, my face caked with snow and ice. My whole body feels frozen. I feel sick. I look for a cafe to go have coffee and warm up and rest in, but all the all-nighters are closed too. Sure: it's that night when everyone wants to be with their family and friends. I push my way into a few vestibules and lean my forehead on the bells of all the tenants. The buildings I do get into to sleep on one of the hallway landings above — always a last resort for me because for this I can be thrown in the clink — the tenants show up in their pajamas and tell me to get lost.

Well okay, I say. I understand. And I'm not complaining either. I lead my life and they lead theirs and that's the way it goes I guess, isn't that right? And I like my life, though I don't like it tonight. I'll probably freeze to death if I don't find a place to stay quick, but can't I still say I like my life? It's what I choose. Not the snow. Not the cold. Not a station-house cell where some creep inmate might try to knock me around or steal my pants or get in them or worse. And not standing here in the middle of the street freezing to death, you can be sure. But being free is what I like about my life most of all. That's right. I don't mind having no place to go. Not anymore. Let it snow. Hey, come on — let's have some more snow. What do I care anymore? At least I've lived the way I wanted to and now I'm not afraid to die.

I go down the subway, the last place I like to stay because the conductors and cops never let me get much sleep and all the chances of muggings. I'm kicked from car to car and train to train all night and the bunch of punks who steal my money and try to set me on fire on the platform I'm eventually able to run away from, but I don't freeze to death and do manage to get in a few winks. In the morning I have a free snack and go back to the streets asking for handouts, since as days go, people are more quick to give today than any other.

"Merry Christmas," lots of people say, giving me coins.

"Sure . . . Thanks very much . . . Same to you . . . Hey, you bet."

JOAN WILLIAMS

Going Ahead

In the middle of the city was a park, on Main Street, a square; there, inside a hut, Santa Claus sat, with a heater to warm him. Tad stood in line with the other children thinking what he would do; go in one door, speak to Santa, receive candy, come out on the side where the grown-ups waited. He could tell his grandfather was cold waiting, and he was cold too. Children around him wore rubber boots, though it was not raining; his grandfather said later it was because of the cold and the frost slowly melting, leaving the grass wet. He had on the everyday, heavy work boots he wore even to the barn. Usually, to Delton, he wore Sunday-school shoes, but his mother had said she did not care if they called him "country," if he looked country; he had to be warm. He had not admitted that his shoes made no difference; he always felt country arriving, bouncing along in the cab of the dusty or muddy pickup, looking down on everyone. City people in ordinary cars sped by below or, worse, crawled impatiently behind, waiting to pass. Once he had asked his grandfather, "Can we ever get a car?"

And Grandpa had said, "A pickup's always served us. Why change?"

Another time Grandpa had said, "Boy, damn if you ain't got big enough for me to carry to Delton by yourself. I been waiting a long time. In the springtime, we'll go up yonder to a ball game and the zoo. Now, I reckon I'll have to carry you to see Santa."

He had planned the trip with Grandpa ever since he could remember, but his father had said, "Poppa, you and the boy don't have any business going up there to Delton. There's too many things happening on the highway with the Negroes bothering folks in Mississippi cars."

His grandfather had said, "I'm not going to bother none of them, why are they going to bother me?"

"Because you're white," his mother had said, turning from the stove; then his father had said, "That's exactly right." But Tad had said nothing.

He had watched his father and Grandpa get ready to go to the barn to milk. His father had stomped into a boot and said, "I don't know what you want to go for anyway. I hear the Negroes have taken over downtown Delton. Everything's integrated. Things have changed, Poppa. You're going to have to realize it."

Grandpa had said, "I've never had any trouble with Negroes. I don't expect to start now. Ain't any of them going to bother an old man and a little boy on the highway."

He had known his mother would tell the story again. She had said, "Ellie Watkins was driving back and saw a pickup on her tail. She slowed to let it pass, but it wouldn't. So, she went faster, but it did. Went on down the highway that way, until finally it did go by, flying. She wanted to get home then and went faster too. Suddenly the truck came almost to a stop, in the middle of the road. No reason in the world, except to make her bump it. She skidded so, she said sparks came out of her tires. As soon as she got stopped, the truck went on. It turned off onto a side road and when she passed, she saw three Negro boys looking back at her, dying laughing."

"If you're bound and determined, Poppa, you, number one, put that pistol in the glove compartment and, two, be back here before dark, and I mean plum before," his father had said before going out with Grandpa. He had thought they looked like giants the way they were huddled into their outdoor clothes. They had opened the door, and cold had come in and traveled the room like a whisper before the fire warmed it again after they went out. He had hugged his knees. "Mother," he had said, "can I tell Grandpa I don't believe in Santa Claus anymore?"

"Goodness, no," she had said. "You'll spoil his fun. You can pretend, can't you?"

"Sure," he had said.

This morning he had had no chores. He and Grandpa ate leftover corn bread with sorghum, and then they started. His wool gloves were worn at the ends, and his fingers had felt frozen when he came into the morning. It was twenty miles over a winding gravel road to the main highway, then fifty more over blacktop to Delton, into Tennessee. He and Grandpa had lost time looking for the pistol; then his mother had remembered it was already in the truck. She went nowhere without it, though in north Mississippi there had been no serious trouble since things had been settled at the university. But his mother had said there was a differentness: beneath their ordinary lives there was a feeling of waiting, of always wondering if something would happen.

For the first time in his life — Grandpa said for the first time in *his* — people locked their doors. If his mother went for a loaf of bread, she shut up the house. His grandfather said folks had went crazy; they ought to remember what FDR had said about being afraid. His mother had said locking doors made strangers; it was as if they all hid something from each other; she was afraid to express her views anymore; you didn't know how the other fellow would react to what you thought. He thought that all grown-ups thought about was change. His father had said they had to go along with it, the best they could.

This morning nothing had happened on the highway. Cars with Negroes had passed, and no one paid any attention to him and Grandpa. Once, a car ahead of them had slowed and a farmer turned into a field, a Negro helper sitting beside him. "You see any trouble there?" Grandpa had said.

"No," he had said, and looking into Grandpa's eyes had been like looking into the cistern: he had seen himself reflected. His grandfather's eyes, his hair, his mustache were all the same silver-gray color as the flat, still water. They had gone on, looking at a sun so pale it was hardly distinguishable from the white winter sky.

Now, waiting to see Santa Claus, he stood warming his hands, squeezing them and pulling the ends of his gloves longer, the way Grandpa had taught him. Behind him a girl spoke, her breath jumping in spurts like steam, telling another child the lake at the zoo was expected to freeze; people could skate there. He tried to imagine ice-skating, wondering if the pond behind his house would freeze; he had no skates if it did. Long ago winters in Mississippi had been very cold. Grandpa had skated every year on the pond behind the house, and Tad tried now to imagine him as a little boy.

Santa Claus called him, and he stepped over the doorsill into the hut. Immediately, warming, his fingers were full of pain. He wondered how the man stood it so hot with all that stuff on his face, and why he painted his nose red. Was that what little children expected? If he had to pretend for Grandpa's sake, he would have to pretend for the man's too, he had decided. He shook hands, looking the man in the eye, as Grandpa always said to, and said, "How do, Santa Claus."

"Have you been a good boy this year?" the man said.

"Yes, sir. I guess so," he said.

"What can I bring you?"

"A twenty-two," he said. "Single-shot."

"I'll have to ask your mother and daddy about that, son. Maybe when you're older."

"I've used my dad's a year," he said. "I killed a moccasin on the back steps, and there's always something after the chickens."

"Keep on being a good boy then," the man said. "Here's a little gift. Come in, little girl. Come and see old Santa." Tad turned toward the exit and stepped out, holding the candy cane, glad he was small for his age, and hoping no one else would know he was nine.

As soon as he was out, Grandpa said, "How was old Santa?"

He said, "Fine."

"He don't keep you in there long," Grandpa said.

"I reckon he's trying to hurry folks out of the cold," he said.

"I reckon so," Grandpa said, feeling better. "What'd you want?"

He said, "A twenty-two," and knew he was getting the gun from the way Grandpa gave a little bounce. "Uh-huh," Grandpa said. "What else?"

"Shells," he said.

"For shore. You need a gun, you need some shells," Grandpa said. "You asking for anything else?" Tad knew the shells were bought too. He had nothing else in mind, but suddenly he said, "Grandpa, if the pond freezes over, can I get ice skates?"

They walked on, Grandpa pulling his scarf tighter. "Well," Grandpa said. "We'll have to see."

He knew there would be nothing to see. His father would say: "Son, if we had the money, just to throw away, I'd get you the skates in a minute. But that pond might stay frozen one, two, at the most three days and never freeze again." He knew that made sense, but anything he mentioned, Grandpa would bear in mind. Once he had overheard his grandfather say, "The closest I'll ever come to heaven is watching that boy grow up." Tad had felt a sudden huge swelling in his chest. He had that feeling now, walking beside Grandpa, knowing he was worrying over how to get him something. "Grandpa," he said, "we better forget about the skates. That pond might stay froze a day or two and never freeze again."

"That's so," Grandpa said. But a tag end of thought seemed, still, to remain in his mind.

They chose first to pass the peanut man who stood outside the Planters shop wearing a plastic peanut head, carrying a cane, and passing out a spoonful of nuts to anyone who held out a hand. He and Grandpa could not understand those who did not. "Nothing like goobers," Grandpa said, tossing peanuts into his mouth.

"Nothing like goobers," he said, tasting fuzz from his wool glove with them.

Grandpa could not understand parking meters but would not spend money on a lot. Now, as they were passing their truck, Grandpa gave him the dimes and he punched in two for two hours and tried to explain. Still Grandpa said he could not understand those machines and walked away shaking his head and said, "We got to get your momma's and daddy's presents. Eat some dinner, look at toys, then get on home early like we promised. What you got in mind for your daddy?"

"I don't know," he said. "What does he need?"

Grandpa said, as always, "He could use something to hep him if he gets snake-bit."

Every year they bought his father a bottle of rye together. His father opened the present as if in surprise and said how glad he was to have his supply of snake-bite medicine replenished. Then Grandpa would say he had thought he was about to run out; even if they didn't use whiskey much, when you needed a drink, you needed it. Last Christmas, Grandpa had said, "You never know. This boy's liable to be coming in here any day now telling us he's got married. We'd have to drink to that."

"Shoot!" Tad had said, "I'm never going to get married."

"Why, what about the little redheaded girl I saw you walking along the road with?" Grandpa had said.

"Her!" he had said, and this past year had gotten off the school bus early never to have to get off with the little redheaded girl again.

Where he lived, whiskey was sold only by bootleggers — Baptists had voted the county dry — and he followed Grandpa into the liquor store with a sense of guilt. But Grandpa stepped straight up to the counter and said, "We'd like to take us a fifth of Four Roses, please, sir."

On the counter Tad put a dollar of the two he had in change. The storekeeper brought the bottle and swiftly, with one finger, separated the coins spread on the counter and counted them again. "Dollar even, son," he said. "Thank you." Grandpa gave the rest of the money, and the man said, "Merry Christmas."

Grandpa stepped back, onto the foot of a Negro customer, and turning said quickly, "I'm sorry."

"That's all right," the Negro man said. "I wasn't watching myself."

"Merry Christmas," Grandpa said.

"Merry Christmas," the Negro said.

"Merry Christmas, son," the storekeeper said.

He said, "Merry Christmas," and opened the door, and bells jingled.

When they were on the street, Grandpa said, "Well, we got that over with," as if he had not known what to buy.

Tad said, "Now we have to get Mother's presents; that's harder," and he followed Grandpa into another store. They went up and down aisles looking at things they knew ladies liked, and Tad spent his dollar on a small straw basket with a bottle of perfume inside.

Grandpa said, "I think you know more about ladies than I do. You hep me decide." Though the present was not for Tad, his heart beat faster at the idea of spending five dollars. His grandfather always said the money had to be spent on foolishness, meaning something his mother would not buy for herself. He and Grandpa finally decided on pearls that could be worn many ways; the saleslady showed them, hung them in one long strand down her neck, wound them once, then twice around it. "Now that's sho nuff some foolishness," Grandpa said, handing over the money. "We ready to eat dinner now?"

"Can't we see the toys first?" he said.

"Can't you wait?" Grandpa said.

"No," he said; then, in the elevator, Grandpa said, "Boy, I bet your stomach's going to be waiting when you get there."

His mother had said to remember his grandfather was an old man. "You want to rest?" he said, but Grandpa said he could go on a while longer. He led Grandpa to the counter where there were toys having to do with space and science. One by one, he picked up models of the latest planes and explained them to Grandpa, who could hardly believe how fast the real ones flew. In one corner of the store was a toy spaceship large enough to walk inside. He and Grandpa went in, and he picked up the helmet of a space suit and put it on. "Just think, Grandpa," he said, "when I'm grown, I'll probably be flying to the moon."

"Well, when you learn how to fly this thing, son, take me to the moon with you," Grandpa said.

"Grandpa, you wouldn't go," he said. "You've always said you never wanted your feet that high off the ground."

"I'd take them off for you," Grandpa said. Then he put a helmet on Grandpa's head, and they laughed at each other a long time through the transparent flaps. They decided on the dime store for lunch. It was past the usual eating time when they arrived, and no one else was there. Only one counter was open. Grandpa, sitting down, said he guessed he would have to have some fried clams. His mother had said Grandpa was not supposed to eat fried food. "But if I'm not there, he does," she had said. "I'll bet he comes home sick."

Now Tad said, "You're not supposed to eat fried things," and Grandpa said, "That's just some foolish notion on the doctor's part. What are you going to have?"

"I think I'll have a foot-long hot dog," he said.

When they were eating, Grandpa said the clams were good, even if they had come out of a box, frozen. Tad said the hot dog was good too, but when he bit into one end, mustard squirted out the other. He put his head as far back as possible and licked the bun, hearing other people sit down. When he sat up straight, he saw the other people were Negroes. Grandpa was not eating, and he said, "Are you already sick?"

"No," Grandpa said. "Come on, we've got to go."

"We haven't finished our dinner," he said.

"Come on, we've got to go," Grandpa said and stood up, taking the packages.

He followed Grandpa to the cashier and up the steps and out onto the street. Then he said, "Was it the Negroes, Grandpa?" But Grandpa would not say anything; he just kept walking.

In a little while they were in the truck again, moving

higher than anyone else, and he said, "You've sat next to Negroes before, Grandpa."

"They've never set to the table with me," Grandpa said.

"They've sat in the truck, close as this," he said.

"They've never set to the table with me," Grandpa said.

"You broke open watermelons and ate them in the field."

Grandpa said in a flat voice, as if something had been taken from him, "They just set right down there, with me."

It was nearly evening when they got back, after driving without speaking between frozen fields over the same road that no longer seemed the same. Lights coming on in houses and barns were like scattered pieces of the fallen pale sun. Doors were shut against the cold; no one was on the road; and it was suppertime. The only store open was where the old men stayed as long as possible to play checkers. Tad looked in, going by, and saw them. Grandpa's friends, he thought. Maybe his father had been right: Grandpa should have stayed at home. When they were at home, Tad told what had happened, and his father said, "We warned you, Poppa."

Grandpa said that he was never going to Delton again; traffic had been so heavy it gave him a nervous stomach; he was going to bed. "Would you bring me some soda?" he asked.

When his grandfather was gone, Tad said, "Grandpa ate fried clams." But when his mother took up the soda she said, "This'll help that old nervous stomach."

"Why does Grandpa eat what he knows will hurt him?" Tad said.

His father said, "He doesn't want to admit he can't do everything he did when he was young."

There were a lot of things Grandpa couldn't admit, Tad thought: what he had eaten, that he was old, that times had changed. And Tad could not tell him he no longer believed in Santa Claus.

His mother said that Tad had had a long day; he had to go to bed.

He went, but he was not sleepy. He lay awake a long time, looking out, studying patterns of the stars against the early night sky, and planning. If Grandpa couldn't change himself enough to go seventy miles to Delton, Tad thought, Grandpa couldn't change himself enough to go to the moon. He would have to go on ahead without him. He guessed he could not tell Grandpa that either.

JOHN UPDIKE

The Carol Sing

urely one of the natural wonders of Tarbox was Mr. Burley at the Town Hall carol sing. How he would jubilate, how he would God-rest those merry gentlemen, how he would boom out when the male voices became Good King Wenceslas:

"Mark my footsteps, good my page;
  Tread thou in them boldly:
Thou shalt find the winter's rage
  Freeze thy blood less co-*oh*-ldly."

When he hit a good "oh," standing beside him was like being inside a great transparent Christmas ball. He had what you'd have to call a God-given bass. This year, we other male voices just peck at the tunes: Wendell Huddlestone, whose hardware store has become the pizza place where the dropouts collect after dark; Squire Wentworth, who is still getting up petitions to protect the marsh birds from the atomic power plant; Lionel Merson, lighter this year by about three pounds of gallstones; and that selectman whose freckled bald head looks like the belly of a trout; and that fireman whose face is bright brown all the year round from clamming; and the widow Covode's bearded son, who went into divinity school to avoid the draft; and the Bisbee boy, who no sooner was back from Vietnam than he grew a beard and painted his car every color of the rainbow; and the husband of the new couple that moved this September into the Whitman place on the beach road. He wears thick glasses above a little mumble of a mouth tight as a keyhole, but his wife appears perky enough.

> The-ey lo-okèd up and sa-haw a star,
> Shining in the east, beyond them far;
> And to the earth it ga-ave great light,
> And so it continued both da-hay and night.

She is wearing a flouncy little Christmassy number, red with white polka dots, one of those dresses so short that when she sits down on the old plush deacon's bench she has to help it with her hand to tuck under her bottom, otherwise it wouldn't. A lively bit of a girl with long thighs glossy as pond ice. She smiles nervously up over her cup of cinnamon-stick punch, wondering why she is here, in this dusty drafty public place. We must look monstrous to her, we Tarbox old-timers. And she has never heard Mr. Burley sing, but she knows something is missing this year; there is something failed, something hollow. Hester Hartner sweeps wrong notes into every chord: arthritis — arthritis and indifference.

> The first good joy that Mary had,
> It was the joy of one;
> To see the blessèd Jesus Christ
> When he was first her son.

The old upright, a Pickering, for most of the year has its keyboard turned to the wall, beneath the town zoning map, its top piled high with rolled-up plot plans filing for variances. The Town Hall was built, strange to say, as a Unitarian church, around 1830, but it didn't take around here, Unitarianism; the sea air killed it. You need big trees for a shady mystic mood, or at least a lake to see yourself in like they have over to Concord. So the town bought up the shell and ran a second floor through the air of the sanctuary, between the balconies: offices and the courtroom below, more offices and this hall above. You can still see the Doric pilasters along the walls, the top halves. They used to use it more; there were the Tarbox Theatricals twice a year, and political rallies with placards and straw hats and tambourines, and get-togethers under this or that local auspice, and town meetings until we went representative. But now not even the holly the ladies of the Grange have hung around can cheer it up, can chase away the smell of dust and must, of cobwebs too high to reach and rats' nests in the hot-air ducts and, if you stand close to the piano, that faint sour tang of blueprints. And Hester lately has taken to chewing eucalyptus drops.

And him to serve God give us grace,
O lux beata Trinitas.

The little wife in polka dots is laughing now: maybe the punch is getting to her, maybe she's getting used to the look of us. Strange people look ugly only for a while, until you begin to fill in those tufty monkey features with a little history and stop seeing their faces and start seeing their lives. Regardless, it does us good, to see her here, to see young people at the carol sing. We need new blood.

This time of the year is spent in good cheer,
  And neighbors together do meet,
To sit by the fire, with friendly desire,
  Each other in love to greet.
Old grudges forgot are put in the pot,
  All sorrows aside they lay;
The old and the young doth carol this song,
  To drive the cold winter away.

At bottom it's a woman's affair, a chance in the darkest of months to iron some man-fetching clothes and get out of the house. Those old holidays weren't scattered around the calendar by chance. Harvest and seedtime, seedtime and harvest, the elbows of the year. The women do enjoy it; they enjoy jostle of most any kind, in my limited experience. The widow Covode as full of rouge and purple as an old-time Scollay Square tart, when her best hope is burial on a sunny day, with no frost in the ground. Mrs. Hortense broad as a barn door, yet her hands putting on a duchess's airs. Mamie Nevins sporting a sprig of mistletoe in her neck brace. They miss Mr. Burley. He never married and was everybody's gallant for this occasion. He was the one to spike the punch and this year they let young Covode do it, maybe that's why Little Polka Dots can't keep a straight face and giggles across the music like a pruning saw.

Adeste, fideles,
Laeti triumphantes;
Venite, venite
In Bethlehem.

Still that old tussle, "v" versus "wenite," the "th" as hard or soft. Education is what divides us. People used to actually resent it, the way Burley, with his education, didn't go to some city, didn't get out. Exeter, Dartmouth, a year at the Sorbonne, then thirty years of Tarbox. By the time he hit fifty he was fat and fussy. Arrogant, too. Last sing, he two or three times told Hester to pick up her tempo. "Presto, Hester, not andante!" Never married, and never really worked. Burley Hosiery, that his grandfather had founded, was shut down and the machines sold South before Burley got his manhood. He built himself a laboratory instead and was always about to come up with something perfect: the perfect synthetic substitute for leather, the harmless insecticide, the beer can that turned itself into mulch. Some said at the end he was looking for a way to turn lead into gold. That was just malice. Anything high attracts lightning, anybody with a name attracts malice. When it happened, the papers in Boston gave him six inches and a photograph ten years old. "After a long illness." It wasn't a long illness, it was cyanide, the Friday after Thanksgiving.

The holly bears a prickle,
As sharp as any thorn,
And Mary bore sweet Jesus Christ
On Christmas day in the morn.

They said the cyanide ate out his throat worse than a blowtorch. Such a detail is satisfying but doesn't clear up the mystery. Why? Health, money, hobbies, that voice. Not having that voice makes a big hole here. Without his lead, no man dares take the lower parts; we just wheeze away at the melody with the women. It's as if the floor they put in has been taken away and we're standing in air, halfway up that old sanctuary. We peek around guiltily, missing Burley's voice. The absent seem to outnumber the present. We feel insulted, slighted. The dead turn their backs. The older you get, the more of them snub you. He was rude enough last year, Burley, correcting Hester's tempo. At one point, he even reached over, his face black with impatience, and slapped her hands that were still trying to make sense of the keys.

Rise, and bake your Christmas bread:
  Christians, rise! The world is bare,
  And blank, and dark with want and care.
Yet Christmas comes in the morning.

Well, why anything? Why do *we?* Come every year sure as the solstice to carol these antiquities that if you listened to the words would break your heart. Silence, darkness, Jesus, angels. Better, I suppose, to sing than to listen.

I Am Dreaming of a White Christmas: The Natural History of a Vision

[1] 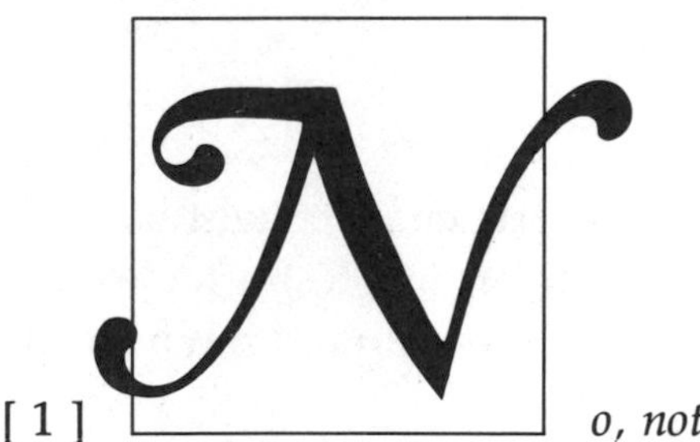 *o, not that door —*
never! But,
Entering, saw. Through
Air brown as an old daguerreotype fading. Through
Air that, though dust to the tongue, yet —
Like the inward, brown-glimmering twilight of water —
Swayed. Through brown air, dust-dry, saw. Saw
It.

The bed.

Where it had
Been. Now was. Of all
Covering stripped, the mattress

Bare but for old newspapers spread.
Curled edges. Yellow. On yellow paper dust,
The dust yellow. No! Do not.

Do not lean to
Look at that date. Do not touch
That silken and yellow perfection of Time that
Dust is, for
There is no Time, I
Entering, see.

I,
Standing here, breathe the dry air.

[2]

See
Yonder the old Morris chair bought soon
After marriage, for him to rest after work in, the leather,
Once black, now browning, brown at the dry cracks, streaked
With a fungoid green. Approaching,
See.

See it.

The big head. Propped,
Erect on the chair's leather pillow, bald skin
Tight on skull, not white now, brown
Like old leather lacquered, the big nose
Brown-lacquered, bold-jutting yet but with
Nostril-flanges gone tattered in Time. I have not

Yet looked at the eyes. Not
Yet.

    The eyes
Are not there. But,
Not there, they stare at what
Is not there.

[3]
    Not there, but
In each of the appropriate twin apertures, which are
Deep and dark as a thumb-gouge,
Something that might be taken for
A mulberry, large and black-ripe when, long back, crushed,
But now, with years, dust-dried. The mulberries,
Crushed and desiccated, each out of
Its dark lurking-place, stare out at
Nothing.

    His eyes
Had been blue.

[4]
    Hers brown. But
Are not now. Now staring,
She sits in the accustomed rocker, but with
No motion. I cannot
Be sure what color the dress once was, but
Am sure that the fabric now falls decisively away
From the Time-sharpened angle of knees. The fabric

Over one knee, the left, has given way. And
I see what protrudes.

See it.

Above,
The dry fabric droops over breastlessness.

Over the shrouded femurs that now are the lap, the hands,
Palm-down, lie. The nail of one forefinger
Is missing.

On the ring-finger of the left hand
There are two diamond rings. On that of the right,
One. On Sundays, and some evenings
When she sat with him, the diamonds would be on the fingers.

The rings. They shone.

Shine now.

In the brown air.

On the brown-lacquered face
There are now no
Lips to kiss with.

[5]
The eyes had been brown. But
Now are not where eyes had been. What things

Now are where eyes had been but
Now are not, stare. At the place where now
Is not what once they
Had stared at.

There is no fire on the cold hearth now,
To stare at.

[6]

On
The ashes, gray, a piece of torn orange peel.
Foil wrappings of chocolates, silver and crimson and gold,
Yet gleaming from grayness. Torn Christmas paper,
Stamped green and red, holly and berries, not
Yet entirely consumed, but warped
And black-gnawed at edges. I feel
Nothing. A red
Ribbon, ripped long ago from some package of joy,
Winds over the gray hearth like
A fuse that failed. I feel
Nothing.

Not even
When I see the tree.

Why had I not seen the tree before?
Why, on entering, had I not seen it?
It must have been there, and for
A long time, for
The boughs are, of all green, long since denuded.

That much is clear. For the floor
Is there carpeted thick with the brown detritus of cedar.

Christmas trees in our section always were cedar.

[7]
Beneath the un-greened and brown-spiked tree,
On the dead-fall of brown frond-needles, are,
I see, three packages. Identical in size and shape.
In bright Christmas paper. Each with red bow, and under
The ribbon, a sprig of holly.

But look!

The holly

Is, clearly, fresh.

I say to myself:

The holly is fresh.

And

My breath comes short. For I am wondering
Which package is mine.

Oh, which?

I have stepped across the hearth and my hand stretches out.

But the voice:

No presents, son, till the little ones come.

[8]
What shadow of tongue, years back unfleshed, in what
Darkness locked in a rigid jaw, can lift and flex?

The man and the woman sit rigid. What had been
Eyes stare at the cold hearth, but I
Stare at the three chairs. Why —
Tell me why — had I not observed them before? For
They are here.

The little red chair,
For the baby. The next biggest chair
For my little sister, the little red rocker. Then,
The biggest, my own, me the eldest.

The chairs are all empty.

But
I am thinking a thought that is louder than words.
Thinking:

They're empty, they're empty, but me — oh, I'm here!

And that thought is not words, but a roar like wind, or
The roar of the night-freight beating the rails of the trestle,
And you under the trestle, and the roar
Is nothing but darkness alive. Suddenly,
Silence.

And no
Breath comes.

[9]

Where I was,
Am not. Now am
Where the blunt crowd thrusts, nudges, jerks, jostles,
And the eye is inimical. Then,
Of a sudden, know:

Times Square, the season
Late summer and the hour sunset, with fumes
In throat and smog-glitter at sky-height, where
A jet, silver and ectoplasmic, spooks through
The sustaining light, which
Is yellow as acid. Sweat,
Cold in arm-pit, slides down flesh.

The flesh is mine.

What year it is, I can't, for the life of me,
Guess, but know that,
Far off, south-eastward, in Bellevue,
In a bare room with windows barred, a woman,
Supine on an iron cot, legs spread, each ankle
Shackled to the cot-frame,
Screams.

She keeps on screaming because it is sunset.

Her hair has been hacked short.

[10]
Clerks now go home, night watchmen wake up, and the heart
Of the taxi-driver, just coming on shift,
Leaps with hope.

All is not in vain.

Old men come out from the hard-core movies.
They wish they had waited till later.

They stand on the pavement and stare up at the sky.
Their drawers are drying stiff at the crotch, and
The sky dies wide. The sky
Is far above the first hysteria of neon.

Soon they will want to go and get something to eat.

Meanwhile, down the big sluice of Broadway,
The steel logs jerk and plunge
Until caught in the rip, snarl, and eddy here before my face.

A mounted policaman sits a bay gelding. The rump
Of the animal gleams expensively. The policeman
Is some sort of dago. His jowls are swart.
His eyes are bright with seeing.

He is as beautiful as a law of chemistry.

[11]
In any case,
I stand here and think of snow falling. But am

Not here. Am
Otherwhere, for already,
This early and summer not over, in West Montana —
Or is it Idaho? — in
The Nez Percé Pass, tonight
It will be snowing.

The Nez Percé is more than 7,000 feet, and I
Have been there. The first flakes,
Large, soft, sparse, come straight down
And with enormous deliberation, white
Out of unbreathing blackness. Snow
Does not yet cling, but the tall stalk of bear-grass
Is pale in the darkness. I have seen, long ago,
The paleness of bear-grass in darkness.

But tell me, tell me,
Will I never know
What present there was in that package for me,
Under the Christmas tree?

[12]
All items listed above belong in the world
In which all things are continuous,
And are parts of the original dream which
I am now trying to discover the logic of. This
Is the process whereby pain of the past in its pastness
May be converted into the future tense

Of joy.

EVE SHELNUTT

Partridges, 1950

oon it was the hunting season, the woods behind our house opening paths of sunlight, the ground, padded with decaying leaves, invitational. Even the weather, after the humid days of September, seemed soft, to be calling.

I had planned to go among the hunters; I had a vest, a cap, my eyes, trained. Then, suddenly, I ceased going to the fort of twigs I had built there. I felt too old or, more likely, my body, wanting to be touched, for I was twelve, grew cautious, as if Johnny from the trenches of experience was teaching me its need for substantial cover.

From the porch, I watched Ralph go alone. Daily he grew thinner and his jowls drooped, like a dog allowed to stalk only what flew, its training strained by the residual thrumming of wild blood never carried by wing. His face said, *I am chastened.* His body, shuffling, asked why.

Johnny, if he knew what was good for him, packed himself in behind boscage. The newspapers called the event in Korea a conflict. Would his body understand it was a war?

Even though he turned his eyes upward, the gun also slanting upward in the crook of his right arm, Ralph listened to thickets move almost imperceptibly around him, a harvest of noise — scraping fur, muscle-weight shifting, dense bone growing more dense, preternatural sleep beginning in burrows, which he could sense, a ruffle of leaves, he imagined, around small animals' necks — amulets. He wanted one for himself, for Johnny. And then, I imagined, he wanted a cover of snow until all cold had passed. When not dreaming, he asked, *Will* Johnny's eyesight hold?

When Ralph came back from an outing, we wanted to pat his head, ruffle its fur, rub the red-veined eyes. We did not remind him it was truly winter in Korea, every bush frozen into light. After all, we weren't sure, never having been there, knowing from habit what we could feel. Momma knitted wool socks for Johnny, for any friends he had still living. I felt the balls of wool.

And Momma played Mahler on the phonograph. Sukie said it should be Bach, *pure* majesty, and I argued, from habit, I thought.

But remember, Sukie, how Momma once told us — it was a Sunday, we were riding over the rail road tracks beyond Church — how Mahler went to Freud once to complain that, in the midst of soaring notes, his mind distracted him with pleasant ditties? So I imagined girls in tiered skirts dancing on packed ground outside a cottage in sunlight, before all the leaves had fallen, stray fans of red leaf sticking to their braids. Mahler conducted from a tree stump.

Fear was a bird in Ralph's mouth, held there carelessly, as if from birth his mouth had shaped itself for retrieving. When he held perfectly still, as he did especially on Sundays, standing before the mantle, he seemed sleek in his thinness, as if having lost fur in the thickets. One hand raised, the head stilled — he was listening, over continents and water.

Lying on our beds Sunday afternoons, we considered Ralph's gift to us. It was as if he had taught us Johnny's true condition. And, if Johnny died, it would be accidental. Quick, a turn of the head at the wrong sound; he would be lifted into death's jaws like a wilted bird. During naps, we panted. And I know all of this, Sukie, because self-sympathy ran in our veins, we were so young then. And compassion came out panting.

On a wall in the kitchen were stuck picture post cards Poppa had sent from Santa Barbara — the Santa Ynez mountains, the adobes of Canon Perdido Street — and a Chamber of Commerce map with Poppa's radio station circled, a brown dot ringed with red. Some Sundays Momma had spread the map across the empty platters, our useless dog barking by her side at the sound of rattling paper, as if Momma were filling a bag with bones.

Now Ralph spread his map, black on white, not cream-colored with California light, as ours. He had drawn a line across it, like a fence running through pasture, and circled Seoul, saying mail probably went by truck from there. We left Poppa's map on the kitchen wall and, finally, using the same tacks, Ralph thumbed his over it. "Gotta see it day-to-day, Kiddos," he said.

"*Me?* A 'Kiddo'?" Momma asked, turning from the stove and smiling, as at Poppa when he visited. Sukie kicked me as water flowed over our hands — *see?* For Ralph wasn't one of us by birth but inherited through Lela, and Sukie had her eye on Ralph and Momma. Sukie said Poppa didn't come often enough to "fix her." How often, Sukie, I want to ask now, does a woman have to be fixed? Does a body sleep while waiting or prowl in its darkness?

When Johnny was drafted, Lela, *sick unto death,* said Momma, *sick unto death,* meaning body first, the mind agreeing, took a bus with one suitcase filled with flannel nightgowns out to Los Angeles, to live with Estelle in Estelle's four rooms near the canning factory.

Calling Momma from the farm during the summer, Ralph had reported that Lela had slept all the way, forgetting even to eat her baby food, and Estelle had said she had to lift Lela off at the station, people staring. Then, as an afterthought, Estelle had sent Ralph a post card, asking, "Are all of you crazy?"

Lela wanted to be nearer the side of the world she imagined Johnny would return from. It may have seemed to her a race over water — Lela's body held to its slip by the thinnest rope and Johnny's tacking toward her.

"What could I *do*?" asked Ralph.

For a time, he went on, mostly outside, on the land, seeing to the cows and the team of black boys who navigated the cows from the fields at milking time.

I think Ralph spent time moving the salt licks closer to the house. Suddenly, it seemed, I discovered them when we went to check on him. They were dull yellow from the cows' tongues, the color *they* were, Ralph said. "Johnny, shooting at someone yellow. . . ."

When Momma brought Ralph to live in the back room of our house, off the kitchen, Sukie said, "Oh God," sighing the words, as if she were already tired. For days after he unpacked, she only trailed her fingers over the piano keys, listless, sweat beading on the back of her neck, the rest of her dry as August grass.

Later, when school began and Momma brought the junior grades together for the weekly music lesson, I looked across the aisle to see that Sukie wouldn't open her mouth. She kept her eyes closed, her head tilted back on the wooden seat, strands of her yellow hair trailing over it. Her long fingers laced in her lap.

I thought, then, how quiet it must be in our house, Ralph in his room with the door open, the piano in the dining room with its lid shut, and Ralph listening to the faucet drip in the kitchen.

When Momma gave her Saturday violin lessons, Ralph listened at first from the front stoop. He sat smoking, the Camel cupped in his right hand as if to hide it, and I asked him, "Won't you burn your hand that way?" He said it was how Johnny smoked over there. "Can't let them see even a bit of light, Kiddo." Then he shut his eyes as the twins murdered Mendelssohn inside.

Then Ralph moved to the low, upholstered chair without arms by the windows in the dining room. He watched Momma with sun coming over his left shoulder, and he didn't smoke. Blood flowed to his hands, the fingers swelling, reddening, he sat that still. In his overalls, he looked like an uncle who had brought his brother's girls for their lesson because something tragic had happened at home which no one would tell them. I almost liked the twins when Ralph sat watching.

"He's thinking of Lela," Momma said. "I can feel it in my back."

Johnny's letter came by way of Rufus, the oldest of Ralph's black boys, the one permitted to drive the truck and, Momma said when she took the damp letter from between the quart milk bottle, the dumbest. Johnny's handwriting would be seeping across the envelope even as she carried it to Ralph before we went to school. Seeing the letters unopened, we thought they would tell us all we wanted to know. Momma drove better on a day of one of Johnny's letters.

But, those evenings, at the supper table, Johnny's words were like pebbles dropped down a bottomless well. Ralph said, "He acts like I'm Lela and can't hear the truth."

Momma said, "Well . . . ," beginning, herself, to sigh.

I thought, each time I heard Momma sigh, of how Poppa ran his station in climate which was always warm, where girls wore Bermudas any time, even down his street. I imagined, looking sideways at Sukie, she saw what I saw: Poppa's Oriental weather girl calling the national weather bureau each morning and reporting, "Sunny and mild." From her smile would come a flare of teeth.

The days grew colder. Ralph had Rufus come over one Saturday and assemble the oil heater Momma stored during summer under the porch. When Ralph stood by the mantle, he had now to stand to one side, where the mirror couldn't reflect the back of his head; the patch of light which previously shone from the bald circle disappeared from the mirror.

Sometimes he put both hands, palms flat, across the top slats of the heater, forgetting as he daydreamed, until his palms were ribbed with heat. Then — he had long given up wearing his overalls and wore now his shiny, black Sunday pants — he hooked his fingers inside his belt, the lattice of welts, I imagined, heating his stomach through his white shirt.

While Sukie practiced after the twins had left, their dollars curled on top of the piano, Ralph drove Momma's car to the farm, Momma beside him, me in the back. They leaned on a fence, Momma with the collar of her camel's hair jacket turned up, Ralph in his navy blue sweater that buttoned down the front.

Looking out at the cows, he talked to her, almost a whisper. From the seat of the tractor I watched their heads become circled with red as the sun lowered.

After they finished talking, Ralph stood still, looking across the wavering fields to the horizon. Momma stomped her feet to keep warm. I was sure that when Ralph turned, he couldn't see Momma, saw, instead, two red circles separated by the width of her nose. Maybe I was the only one, then, to remember Poppa's circle on the map, the sunlit streets of Santa Barbara.

When we got back, Momma's dollars would be sticking from the notebook in which she kept stamps and the record of lessons. The piano lid would be down. "It's freezing," Momma would say, wrapping her coat more closely to herself. "Put it there," Ralph would say, slapping Momma's padded backside and turning her toward the heater. Sukie, from the sofa with her piano score and pencil, would roll her eyes. I want now to write to Sukie, asking: How old *was* Ralph then? *Old enough,* she would say, words spitting. But, Sukie, I would answer, he grew younger than Johnny and younger, we *all* know, than Lela.

Estelle sent a telegram, short, to save money — Estelle's way: *Lela died*. Momma's breath sucked in, one hand found her stomach, the other, holding the telegram, raised across her eyes, as if shading them from glare. "Get him," she said to me and, for the first time, I knocked on Ralph's door.

"It's Lela," I said, and he trotted through the kitchen, past Johnny's map, past the piano and his armless chair, his arms held close to his sides as if he would run for miles.

When he read the telegram, he said, softly, "Poor Lela, poor Lela," and I noticed his feet were bare.

Sukie jumped from the sofa. She screamed, "Is that all you got to say, 'Poor Lela'? Is that *it*?," and she ran from the house, sweaterless, the door slamming behind her.

Ralph took the telegram to his room and I heard his door close quietly. Momma looked into my eyes, hers a searing vacancy, then she followed Sukie outside.

From a window I watched her standing over Sukie, who sat on the Hudson bumper, her legs stiff before her on the gravel. I saw Momma's right hand lift, as if to encompass L.A., Korea, Santa Barbara, all the world. And finally Sukie lifted the hem of her dress to her eyes.

After that, Sukie grew quiet. If she played the piano, she trailed her fingers over the keys, beginning always at the high notes, one arm resting on the left side of the piano, her head resting on the crooked arm, yellow hair draped. We mourned by no song, many notes.

Estelle had Lela cremated; it was the way they did things there. This news came by letter, which asked, too, why Ralph couldn't have flown out.

Momma answered Estelle. Did you ever see that letter, Sukie? As if writing to a child, she told Estelle that decency is not always obvious; some water, Momma said, can be vile with disease while looking clear as glass. She wrote, "Ralph loved her purely. He fears for Johnny. Johnny came from her."

On the 15th day of November, Momma began baking the fruitcakes she would send to Poppa, to Estelle, to Johnny if he lasted. The kitchen filled with the odor of cinnamon, nutmeg; cartons of green and red candied cherries, green and red citron sat like jewels on the counter. Ralph sat on his bed with the door open, a bowl of nuts in his lap, which now and then he would remember, lifting a pecan, turning it in his fingers, then crushing the shell with pliers he had found in the Hudson trunk.

Momma baked to the sound of his radio tuned to news and gospel songs. She believed all news was too old to be worthy and she hated the songs. She called to him once, "You should get your boys to take you to church sometime. See what those songs are *supposed* to sound like. Not watered down, you know?"

"I know," said Ralph. "I *do know*." Meaning what, his voice flat?

Later, she soaked the heavy, rectangular cakes in rum. I remember: Ralph came out of his room, sniffing. He laughed. The sound startled us.

Was it his laughter, rising from desire so buried none of us could have named it, that made me, later, hearing the sound again, smell the odor of rum? It was years, Sukie (we were closed off too long), before the first man I loved entered me. Holding over him as if I were a hummingbird frozen mid-air, I heard him laugh as Ralph had laughed. Catching me, a piercing, it was rum I smelled.

Do men love you to the strains of Bach? Bless them, it would be better to straddle them on a stump.

It became the spent breath of love, a ritual, to unwrap Momma's cakes, dribble on the rum. Ralph smiled each time, that weak reminder. I breathed the original of my heart. Yes, I loved him.

Johnny's letters came, irregularly. We drank less milk. We spread Ralph's map more often across the emptied plates. Before Thanksgiving, because he had given up his walks with his gun, Ralph said, one morning, he would try his hand at getting us a turkey at the Tryon annual shoot. "Can't let myself get rusty," he said, to which I added the words *with dread:* How I saw things then, some feathery with light filtering through leaves, some flat, no beating heart, no quivering in quasi-sleep.

Do the fingers always remember, as the body in water remembers lungs pushing the head above water? The turkeys flew and his polished rifle swept from the crook of his arm, and the turkeys fell. Heavy bodies without wingspan gathering air. "He's on a *roll,*" a man called from the bleachers, and, for a second, I saw Ralph curled into a ball, his black suit coat grown to him, rolling him down a hill, gunfire grazing his fur as he rolled. A breath of air rolled from my mouth. I almost cried out in warning.

On the way home, Rufus and I brought turkeys from the truck bed for some of Rufus's kin living between Tryon and Greer. The turkeys' feet were tied; we slung them over our shoulders, Rufus whistling at their doors. Ralph waited in the car, engine humming.

We plucked ours by the old pump, Ralph using the hacksaw to sever the head and feet from the naked body, burying them beneath the first tree of the woods. He shivered, burying the head, its eyes open. How could we eat now, Ralph and I?

But we ate. Does Sukie remember: the table clothed in white, Momma's swans of salt, all four of them sitting by the water goblets? We said a blessing, I remember, but no one mentioned Lela or Johnny or Estelle or Poppa. No need; they seemed to assemble behind our chairs, changing places behind us as if looking over our shoulders at cards we held, placing bets in whispers, Johnny, was it?, laughing softly. I imagined his lips.

That dinner was the first piece of felt on a picture such as we made in Sunday School. A mauve wedge, the color of roses. The days turned even colder — medium blue, a rectangle, like the cakes. Frost closed light from the windows until, when we looked through them, it seemed the sun was moonlight.

Sukie took a job at Kresses (green and white) for Christmas money, and Poppa's huge box came, filled with oranges, grapefruit, lemons, limes. Our mouths ached, puckering inside. And for me, he sent a doll of straw, tiny and intricately woven, as if Momma had sent pictures and he could see I was old, now, for a doll to hold in my arms. Yet we took no actual pictures then.

For Momma he sent a basket woven in Mexico, and for Sukie bottles of nail polish, a different color for each nail. She let them grow long; they made a tapping sound on the piano keys when she trailed her rainbow nails over them in passing.

Momma called a florist to ask, in early December, what it would cost to send Estelle a dozen yellow roses and, later, Ralph and I drove in Momma's car to the florist shop where he signed a card, to be mailed inside a larger envelope to a shop in L.A. We sent the cakes, the postman saying, "Rum!" and laughing.

During our holiday from school, Momma sent the twins away so even Saturday seemed ours, as if, as in a frame, we were closed off, assembling colored from four corners. We were quiet, as if pressed behind glass, secretive, not with excitement of gifts hidden from each other in the house. It was habit imbued by occasion, like the sudden odor of rum.

Ralph had Rufus come for him in the truck one Wednesday night when Momma was at choir practice, and I thought he went to hear gospel songs and shouting. I imagined Ralph sitting on a bench in the back, his thin legs crossed, hands fingering the cloth of his trousers. He would look up now and then as words and music swayed like trees around him.

For days Momma sat by the oil stove with her feet up on the blue hassock, reading Robert Browning, then letting the book fall to her lap as she slept, little puffs of air seeping through her half-opened lips. Sometimes Ralph stood on the other side of the stove, watching her as she slept. How old, Sukie, would he have been then?

It is odd that I cannot remember what gifts she gave me on Christmas morning, taken by Ralph one by one from beneath the tree in the dining room where his armless chair had sat. Johnny sent a handkerchief with a half-moon embroidered in blue in one corner. On Ralph's tie was the same half-moon, in red on a background of blue. Momma wore a pink nightshirt which tied across the front. "I think he meant it for Lela," she said. "Originally," and she looked off into nothing. Sukie got from him a miniature music box in the shape of a piano. From her room we heard what sounded like tiny bells coming in snatches — seconds of bells at first, and then minutes. What was the whole song?

Much of that morning has receded. Of course!, I say, memory a filter — so much silt on the bottom we could drown in silt.

Before church on Christmas Eve, Momma gave the dog her package of bones to chew on while we were gone. Ralph put on the suit coat which almost matched his pants, a duller black. Momma pulled from the table arrangement a red carnation to put into his jacket lapel. He kissed her once, on the cheek. Maybe I saw her shiver.

As she conducted the choir, Ralph sat between us on the padded bench. He jiggled his right knee until Sukie put out one hand, gloved, to stop it. He looked up startled, as if he had been sleeping and was suddenly awakened. I expect we all prayed for Johnny, don't you?

When it was over, Momma rushing to gather us together toward the car, her maroon choir robe flung over one arm, Ralph began smiling, and they whispered together by the driver's side of the car before Momma got in to drive. She let Ralph off at Palmetto Street where there were no street lights. "What for?" I asked, and Momma said, "Hush. Don't spoil it for him."

Inside our house, Momma plugged in the tree, lit candles, turned on the oven for reheating the carmel rolls she had made before taking Ralph to look at his cows in the afternoon. Momma poured herself sherry from the cabinet over the stove and sat with it by the heater. Sukie brought a blanket to the couch. I got the broom with which to pull the dog's bones from under the couch, throwing them to her across the rose-patterned rug.

We listened to the clock's humming, then to the chime on the half-hour. I remember turning once to ask Momma about Ralph. She shook her head as my mouth opened and, seeing Sukie's head burrow into the pillows, raised one finger to her lips.

I think, now, that Rufus must have pushed Ralph up from the yard and over the sill of his window. I think I remember the sound of their whispering. I think I remember looking up to where Momma sat with her feet against the stove. She must have smiled.

I heard his pillowcase of small boxes thumping behind him through the kitchen. At the doorway to the dining room, he cleared his throat, as if trying out his voice, and Sukie slept on.

I heard him slowly raise the piano lid. With two fingers he began to play a melody from Sukie's favorite piece by Bach, a thread of the whole, looping to her on the couch, all he had taught himself while we were at school.

I saw her head move once, then sink again into the pillows. Momma got up and tiptoed to sit beside him at the piano. I imagine it: she leans into his left shoulder and gently taps his hands away. He slides off the bench, he quietly stoops to lift the pillowcase. Not a note is missing.

Sukie, no matter, later, how he dissembles, *this* is how we will remember him, even you: Candlelight shines on the red velvet jacket belted over Momma's choir robe. His face is almost covered in a field of cotton.

You rise from the couch as Momma plays louder with all fingers, both hands. We see his red-tinged lips break into a smile. A flock of tiny partridges fly from the field of white. They lift, circling your head. Oh! you cry.

And he bows to the flapping of wings and Bach.

from *The Broken Door: An Autobiographical Fiction*

Until I was nine we always went home to Coatesburg, South Carolina, for Christmas. Coatesburg was my father's home. We went back to the house he was born in.

My father's people were South Carolina Methodists, and my grandfather was a businessman of some kind. He ran a dry goods store, or sold hardware, or something like that. I never understood exactly what he did. He failed at whatever it was, and the family didn't like to talk about it.

In *Loftin* terms most of my father's brothers and sisters also failed in life — all of the men did, except my father — but they never got over the idea that failure was shameful. Also they didn't like to talk about my grandfather's business, because *being* in business in the first place was below the traditional expectations of the family, and a little shameful in itself. You could say that it doubled my grandfather's failure according to the terms of their family pride — except that he had made so much money doing it for awhile.

"He trusted everybody." Uncle Polk didn't talk about it much either, but he was the only one who talked about it at all. *"Everybody,"* he repeated. "Even niggers. Make his mark, and promise to pay, and any coon in Edgefield County could go driving off in a brand new Coleman buggy. Gene Loftin held paper from everybody in Edgefield County — black *and* white." He stopped and fiddled with his pipe. "It wasn't worth five cents on the dollar when the bank called it in. After he went to the wall."

The Loftins had mostly been professional men, with a sort of inborn disdain for commerce and the people who engaged in it, though a good many of them had been farmers. One of my grandfather's brothers, Wilbanks Loftin, was a Methodist minister. Before he died, he was presiding elder for the State of South Carolina. His other brother, Bonneau, was a lawyer. Those were successes in Loftin terms.

I never met Grand Uncle Bonneau. He was still living when I was born, but he had moved to the southern part of the state — somewhere across the river from Louisville, Georgia — and we had lost touch with that branch of the family. He was the oldest of the three brothers, and there were more stories about him than about my grandfather, who was dead before I was born, or of Grand Uncle Wilbanks, whom I did meet.

"Uncle Bonneau killed fifty-two men." Uncle Polk lowered his voice when he talked about Uncle Bonneau. He also forgot to gesture with his pipe. Telling stories about the killing uncle flattened out his voice. I must have been six or seven the first time he talked about Uncle Bonneau when I heard him.

"Four Yankee soldiers." He held up four fingers. "Four bluebellies — those were the first ones. He wasn't but ten or twelve at the time." I remember being particularly impressed because that was only three or four years older than I was myself the first time I heard the story.

"They came into Lawton. Four of them outriding when Sherman went up to burn Columbia." The old family place was at Lawton, which is still there — at least it is on the maps — out in the sandhills about fifteen miles south of Coatesburg. There isn't anything left now but the family graveyard and a Missionary Baptist Church. The house was burned down just after the war. We found what looked like the hearthstone in the weeds, and near it were several overgrown rose bushes.

"Bonneau shot them through the parlor window. Them standing on the veranda talking to the niggers in the yard. Shot them with a Colt cap and ball." The wicker chair hissed gently. "They buried them out in the woods." He stopped, tamping his pipe absentmindedly. The chair was quiet. "Gene showed me the place once. It was grown over with pines." He thought a minute. "Gene wasn't but six or seven when they did it, but he said he remembered the spot very distinctly." He nodded to himself. "Very distinctly." He fiddled with his pipe. "Gene's the one told me he used a Colt cap and ball. He may have confused it with the one he used later."

Uncle Polk leaned back in the chair and it groaned under the hissing. "Shot the mounts and buried them too. So nobody wouldn't find out." He thought a minute. "Must have been a hell of a hole they had to dig. *Four* mounts."

"As low as the food was, they should have cooked the horses and eaten them," said my mother. My mother's Uncle Toby Walsh told stories about the war that were always concerned with how short the food supply was — them having to eat boiled grass and stewed fence lizards — things like that.

"Wouldn't nobody eat horsemeat in those days," said Uncle Polk. He thought a minute. "I'd sooner eat a spring lizard myself," he said.

"They ate those too," said my mother.

"Well," said Uncle Polk.

The family always claimed that Uncle Bonneau killed the Negroes one at the time — in personal grudges, man to man. "Bonneau never did ride with the Klan. He was a lonesome and solitary man. He didn't hold with mobs. I guess he liked to settle his own scores."

According to Uncle Polk, Uncle Bonneau didn't go armed. So when he took offense, he would have to go home to get his weapon. And he always let the black man know what he was doing, so he would have a head start.

" 'You got an hour's start, boy,' he'd tell him." Uncle Polk would point his finger, imitating Uncle Bonneau giving the boy the warning. "It didn't make any difference if the colored boy ran or not. Bonneau never was in a hurry. He'd go home and load his Colt, and have the stable boy saddle his mount. Sometimes he'd shave himself." Uncle Polk made scraping motions along his cheek. "Just to fill up the time he'd give the boy." He thought a minute.

"Couldn't any of them run fast enough. The longest one he chased went up into North Carolina. Bonneau caught him and shot him dead on top of Grandfather Mountain. Sometimes he'd be gone two or three weeks." Uncle Polk shook his head. "Forty-eight," he said. "Georgia. Tennessee. All over South Carolina. He always brought the body home and buried it in Coatesburg."

I couldn't tell about the expression on my father's face when Uncle Polk would tell the story. The way the stories were told, I think everyone was ashamed of Uncle Bonneau for *what* he did, but they were proud of him for doing it so well.

There was a picture of Uncle Bonneau that I saw once. He was a benign looking, small man, with long white hair and a moustache. He looked serious, as did all the people in the nineteenth century photographs I ever saw, but the photographer had missed the implacable quality that was the main point of Uncle Polk's stories about him. I wasn't very impressed with the sepia colored photograph.

"Edgefield County niggers stepped light around Uncle Bonneau," Uncle Polk said. He lit his pipe. "Forty-eight of them didn't step light enough." He opened the box with his finger and slid in the spent match, facing away from the good ones. "Even after he moved down to Louisville, they worried about 'Mr. Bonny'."

There were nine children in my father's family. Half of them were raised rich, and half of them were raised poor. It depended which side of my grandfather's failure they were born on. The older children had their own horses and took piano and painting lessons, and lessons from an elocution teacher.

My father was the fifth child — the third boy — so he was right in the middle and had some of it both ways. I remember hearing my father's younger brother Waddell talk about it in 1958, and he was still resenting it at the time.

"They had their own *horses*!" he said. He had stopped by to visit my mother in Savannah. None of the other Loftins were there when he said it.

The Coatesburg house was paid for at the time of my grandfather's death in 1912 — my Grandmother Loftin had seen to that. Aunt Sarah, my father's younger sister, lived in it with her husband Sam Leech and their three children. They were the ones we visited. Though, to a large extent, we visited the house.

It was a wooden house. Not elegant, and too small for nine children and a hired hand. Or it seemed so to me, according to my suburban standards. It was built on high brick piers, and until I was twelve years old I could walk right under it without bending over. The dirt was dry and powdery, and we would go there to twirl doodle bugs out of their craters.

It was a cold house. Just physically it was cold. Probably it was cool and pleasant in the summer time, but my memories of it were of the visits we made there at Christmas. I'm sure we went in the summer too, because I remember Uncle Sam showing us how to make a whistle out of a willow twig. But I don't remember the house as ever being warm.

The way the house was laid out was peculiar. At least I was never in another one that had quite the same arrangement of rooms. It was almost like two houses under one roof, with the living room and parlor and the three bedrooms in one section, separated from the kitchen and bathroom by an "L" shaped gallery that was open at both ends of the ell.

I would have to say that, morally, it was superior to any house I ever lived in, particularly in the winter time, because of those open halls with the wind whistling down them. Going to breakfast was especially brisk and character building. But once you had made the dash across the gallery — the floorboards rang like steel plates on those cold mornings — you felt you had really earned the warmth of the kitchen.

Aunt Sarah did her cooking on a wood stove, so the room was always pulsing with heat. And she cooked hot breads for every meal — biscuits and yeast rolls in the mornings, and cornbread, loaf bread, and biscuits for the other two meals. It clouded the room with the smell of yeast bread baking and lightwood kindling from the stove. But the kitchen wasn't big enough to hold the crowd on our visits, so we had to eat in shifts. Between the warmth of the stove and the pinesmoke smell of the bread baking, I could have spent the whole visit right there in that room. But I was always having to make way for someone else to take his turn.

The bathroom wasn't nearly so pleasant as the kitchen. It was big and drafty, with a clawfoot tub, and an electric heater with a round reflector. The floor sagged so precariously that the tub seemed on the point of launching itself through the window onto the back porch. I don't remember what color the walls were painted. The light was so dim it may be that I couldn't tell. There was one bare forty-watt bulb that hung by its cord from the ceiling, and was turned on and off by a surface mounted rotary switch on the wall. The way it was placed, the only way to read in there was to sit sideways on the toilet. None of the light got onto the page, but at least sitting sideways kept it from shining in your eyes. The red glow of the element in the heater provided more light than the bulb did.

The fact that my father had been raised in that spartan house was something that I used to ponder a good deal after our visits. Living in it must have been a rigorous kind of training, full of the need for exertion, and pleasure after pain. It seemed to go along with the stories about the snake and the railroad trestle and the time he was shot in the leg. Later I realized that the bathroom and the running water in the kitchen were relatively recent improvements, and hadn't even been there when my father was a child.

Aunt Sarah worked in a ten-cent store in Coatesburg, and Uncle Sam kept the house. I am sure that everybody in the family noticed that arrangement, but I never heard anyone comment on it. Uncle Sam was a wonderfully gentle man, but not in the least effeminate. He was stocky and firmly built, with thick forearms and wrists. His hair was dark brown and coarse, like an Indian's, and hung down over his forehead in a fan. He had a natural feel for the soil, and we always came home from our visits with Mason jars full of butterbeans and peas and tomatoes put up out of his kitchen garden. His voice was deep and hoarse, with a phlegmy resonance in it, and he loved to tell stories for children, which he illustrated with small, delicate gestures of his hands. Aunt Sarah was absolutely devoted to him.

There were three children — James Fletcher, Billy Wynne, and Leigh, the youngest, who was a girl. She loved silver bells — the Hershey chocolate drops that came wrapped in tin foil — and my father always used to take her a bag of them as part of her Christmas present.

James Fletcher was the oldest. He was a waterhead, and from the time he was two or three years old he had been bedridden. They kept him in the first bedroom, the one behind the living room and off the kitchen gallery, on a small iron bed under a window that always had the shade drawn. For as long as I could remember, he had been paralyzed from the neck down, and when he tried to talk he sounded like he was choking. I can remember standing across the room and watching my father in the dim light trying to talk to him where he lay in the bed, rolling his head from side to side and making noises like there was something stuck in his throat.

I was afraid of James Fletcher, and would never approach his bed very closely. The top of his head was as big as a watermelon, but his face seemed smaller than average. He looked like a bottle-nosed dolphin, or a sperm whale, or the kind of creature that was always helping Ming take over Mongo in the Flash Gordon comic strips.

At first my father tried to force me to come up to the bed and talk to him. "Come on, son. I want you to meet Buddy." My father called James Fletcher "Buddy."

I guess I must have felt like Isaac did when Abraham called him to come in the Bible story. I ran out of the room and hid myself under the house. My father tried to insist, but I ended up making such a scene that my mother stepped in and put a stop to it.

The family always told each other that James Fletcher could hear my father, and that he looked forward to our visits in Coatesburg. Aunt Sarah and my father would discuss the signs that their belief rested on.

"Did you see his *eyes*?" she would say. "Old Buddy understands more than we would think. A lot more than we would think."

"He understands good as you or me," Aunt Sarah would nod her head. "You can see it in his eyes."

"There's a lot of life in Old Buddy," my father would say, agreeing with her. I believe I heard him talk more, discussing James Fletcher with Aunt Sarah on those Christmas visits, than I would hear from him the rest of the year taken altogether.

At odd times of the day I would look in on James Fletcher. For me he was some kind of lesson in the potential for treachery that life might have in store for me, and I always hoped that my father and Aunt Sarah were mistaken about how much he was able to understand. He had *always* been that way. That was what I couldn't get over. Every time I looked he would be lying there on his back, in the same position he had been in the last time I'd seen him — rolling his head on the pillow and moving his lips. Once I was brave enough to creep up close to him and try to look at his eyes. But I couldn't see anything. The bulge of his forehead put them into shadows that were too deep to penetrate.

To me it was a terrible thing. A terrible thing that he was alive at all. I never saw him out of the low iron bed under the shaded window, though I am sure Aunt Sarah or Uncle Sam must have moved him around the house sometimes — when no one was there. If I had had the courage, I would have pulled down the covers to see what the rest of his body looked like.

Even then I knew that the grown-up members of the family recognized that James Fletcher was living a terrible life. But they didn't seem to be outraged about it to the degree that I thought they should. There were times when I felt we should all be beating a drum. The dark room was unspeakably awful to me, with that swollen head rolling on the pillow. It was like looking at what death itself was going to be.

Billy Wynne was four years older than I was, and Leigh was four years older than my sister, who was two years younger than myself.

Billy Wynne was a paragon to my father in a way that I never was. I don't remember resenting that — though it was the kind of thing I feel that I would have resented. Partly I didn't resent Billy Wynne because my father only saw him once or twice a year, while he saw me all of the time, and naturally would have less patience with me. But the rest of the reason I didn't resent him was that *I* thought Billy Wynne was a paragon too. My father never talked about him except in general terms. He never explicitly put him up to me as a model.

Billy Wynne deserved better of the world than he ever got as a child. He was always working to bring money into the house, which he never got to spend on himself, but gave to Aunt Sarah to use for household expenses. Sometimes he would keep out a dime or fifteen cents to buy a barrette or a comb for Leigh.

He also did interesting things, which he was willing to share with me, in spite of the difference in our ages. The first time I shot a shotgun, it was Billy Wynne's. He was hunting squirrels for meat before I was even allowed to have a B.B. gun for plinking at tin cans. He also built model airplanes. Great red and yellow ones that he hung by wires from the ceiling of his room. Sometimes he would take them out into a field behind the house, and he would let me help him fly them. He kept the boxes that the kits came in, and every box was accounted for by a finished airplane hanging from the ceiling. Building model airplanes got to be a sore point between my father and me later on.

"Couldn't you *finish* one? Just once? I'd like to see what one *looks* like when it's finished."

That was my father, talking about model airplanes — the kind you made by cutting out little pieces of balsa wood and glueing them together. It got to be an obsession with him, and I believe more words passed between us over model airplanes than anything else we ever talked about.

Between 1941 and 1944 I must have started a hundred ten-cent *Comet* and *Whitman* airplane models. I would always get the balsa wood frame glued together, but when it came to putting on the tissue paper covering, something happened to my momentum. The only one I remember finishing was a Beechcraft biplane. The tissue was green and black, and it looked really good. But my father never got to see it. I sailed it out the window of my upstairs bedroom to see if it would fly, and a stray dog picked it up in his mouth and ran away with it. I never finished another one, and my father never would believe me when I told him about the dog.

"Wouldn't *you* like to see what one looks like?"

"Of course," I'd say.

"All right," said my father.

I worried about it a good deal myself, reading a gloomy omen of my life to come when I would remember those beautiful red and yellow models that Billy Wynne had hanging in his bedroom. But worrying didn't help me to finish them.

For Christmas of 1938 my father bought a bicycle for Billy Wynne, and a big doll for Leigh, which my mother wrapped up in a package with a two-pound bag of silver bells.

We took the bicycle up to Coatesburg tied to the radiator of our car, and my father worried the whole way that something would happen to it before we got there. Fitzgerald, Georgia, is where we were living at the time, which is down in the southern part of the state, and the trip to Coatesburg was an all-day affair. Usually we spent Christmas Day at home, and would go up to South Carolina the day after Christmas, but because of the bicycle my father wanted to be there on Christmas Day to see Billy Wynne's face when he got it. We left Fitzgerald about the middle of the morning on Christmas Eve.

It was a gray, overcast day, as Christmas often seems to be in Georgia and South Carolina — but cold, which it usually isn't. My father was driving, with mother beside him in the front seat, and my sister and I in the back, with Grandmother Hoskins between us to keep us from fighting. Grandmother Hoskins was the most benign presence imaginable, and just about perfect for a boundary marker on our long trips. She would get into the car, cross her ankles, and fold her hands in her lap, and, except for her eyes, she wouldn't move for the rest of the trip. Only my father had to stop every fifty miles or so to let her go to the bathroom.

Across the river from Augusta, Georgia, on the South Carolina side of the river, there was a long, steep hill. It must have been a mile up from the bridge to the crest — maybe a mile and a half. In those days the Highway Department hadn't gotten around to paving it yet.

When we got to Augusta, the light was beginning to fail. I remember the lights on the Christmas trees had been lit, and we could see them through the windows of the houses as we passed. It must have been raining the whole day all over Georgia, and by the time we got onto the South Carolina side of the bridge, the road up that hill looked like a swath cut by an avalanche, with red water boiling in the ditches and overrunning the culverts, and mud in the roadbed that seemed to be moving down toward the river like a lava flow. There weren't any cars on the road, but there were several in the ditches — one with its hood buried up to the windshield in the red water.

As we came off the bridge, my father stopped the car and looked up the hill. He didn't say anything, but we all thought when he stopped that he had decided not to risk the climb, and we would have to take the long way around. My mother gave a sigh of relief. The long pull after Augusta was always the worst part of the trip for her. It made her nervous, even when the road was dry. Two hours would be added to our trip by avoiding it, but she was clearly happy when my father turned the car around and pointed it in the opposite direction. Only, instead of going ahead, back over the bridge, he shifted into reverse and started backing up the hill. *Backing.*

My mother couldn't believe it. "What are you going to do, Loft?" Her voice cracked when she said it. She sounded like she was going to cry. I almost never heard that tone in my mother's voice.

My father didn't answer directly. "Billy Wynne's bicycle." That's all he said. I guess he thought he would be less likely to damage it if he took the hill in reverse.

My father was always a mild and reasonable man, and almost never committed himself to a course of action irrevocably. As mother said, he had a temper. But in 1938 he was forty years old, and the only time the temper came out was over small, exasperating things — a wood joint he'd made in his shop which fitted badly, or the car not starting when the battery had run down. The worst I ever saw him lose himself over anything big was that Christmas Eve on the North Augusta hill.

Maybe he took offense at my mother telling him how to drive. He might have thought his judgment was being called in question. Or it could have been that the eight hour drive in the rain had just worn him out. Whatever it was, there just wasn't any talking to him about backing the car up that hill — notwithstanding it was like trying to paddle a canoe up Niagara Falls.

There were houses on both sides along the road, and until the car windows caked over with the mud flung up by the back wheels, we could see the Christmas trees and wreaths in the windows, and people standing in them watching as we crept by with the engine screaming like a diesel on a greased track.

"Look at the pretty wreaths," said my grandmother, pointing to a house that had wreaths with red electric candles in all four of its front windows.

My Grandmother Hoskins was absolutely one of the loveliest people I have ever known. In the thirty-seven years I knew her, I never saw her angry or confounded by life. I do not think it ever occurred to her that the world could have a demonic side to it. My grandfather had presided over their house, cooked the meals, given orders to the servants. And there were two grandmothers living there to take care of the children. The only times grandmother ever went into the kitchen were to make cole slaw and egg custard. You could call them her specialties, but they weren't exactly that, because she didn't know how to prepare anything else. She played the piano — usually "The Glowworm," always slowly, and with a little pause after the first four bars while she rearranged her fingers for the change in chords. To sum up her life, as far as the overt facts were concerned, you could say that she had seven babies (the last of which weighed fourteen pounds and was born dead) and she was taken care of. She was a lovely, lovely person, but the trust she put in others almost amounted to stupidity. Everyone who ever met her came away feeling he had learned a lesson in goodness. But there were times when it just wasn't a lesson you could bear.

"Mother," said my mother. "Shut up."

We crept up the hill, the back tires sending roostertails of mud over the top of the car, with people coming out in the rain to stand on their front porches silhouetted by the Christmas trees and wreaths to watch as we went creeping by. The sounds the car was making were more like some big animal in pain than a piece of machinery.

It took us half an hour to slither to the top. The rate of progress we made, relative to our expenditure of energy was absurd and nerve-wracking — like a centipede trying to climb out of a soapy bathtub. The way the back wheels were spinning, if we had been on firm ground we would have been doing a hundred and twenty-five miles an hour — but our actual rate of progress was about two.

The whole way my mother sat braced sideways in the front seat, one hand on the dash and the other twisted in the doorpost strap, looking at my father. His head and shoulders and arms were all caked with mud, since he had to hang his head out the window to see where we were going. And mud was spattered over the inside of the windshield and the dash.

At the top of the hill he cut off the engine and got out of the car. There were popping and cracking noises coming out from under the hood, and the sound of steam hissing.

My father took off his coat, folded it carefully, and laid it over the back of the front seat. Then he went around to the front of the car to see about the bicycle.

"It's all right," he said when he came back. "The bicycle's all right." He made an "o" with his thumb and index finger.

Down the hill we could see the lights of the houses, and the city lights of Augusta across the river. Some of the people were still on their porches looking up at us.

My father leaned down and put his head into the car. All I could see were his teeth and the whites of his eyes, and the white sleeves of his shirt, with a dark "V" stenciled in mud where his coat had been. There was a little smile on his lips that was not a smile.

"The bicycle is okay," he said.

"We could have been killed," said my mother.

My father was standing with his foot on the running board, his head ducked down below the roof of the car. "We could have gone in the ditch," he said. "Nobody was going to be killed."

"Get back in the car," said my mother. "It's raining."

The feeling in our house was always one of calmness. I believe that was mostly my mother's doing. The Hoskins were all low-keyed people, but my mother was the kindest and the steadiest of the six children. There was never a harsh word between my mother and my father that I remember. And there weren't any harsh words that night on the hill outside Augusta either. Except for mother telling grandmother to shut up — which, because of its tone, would have amounted to an obscenity in our house.

But the way that my father looked, talking to my mother, stooped over with his foot on the runningboard of the car — the way he looked brought to my mind the stories about the water moccasin and the railroad trestle and the time he was shot in the leg. Then I thought about him knocking down the man who had insulted my mother, and I imagined how it might have been if he had missed the man and had hit her instead. My father had a hard hand, and I knew it would hurt terribly to be hit by him, even if it happened by accident.

I had been excited by the climb up the hill, but after it was over, watching my father and my mother, I became frightened. Something had happened between them, and it was having an effect on all of us. They were no longer an entity to me — something that I am sure the poet E. E. Cummings must have somewhere called "momndad." They had become two separate people.

My father had a little trick that he liked to perform. It was a very simple trick, and he even taught me how to do it. You would take five toothpicks and break each one in the middle to form a "V." Then you would put them together on a smooth surface, like linoleum, with the bottoms of the breaks touching so they formed a skinny five-pointed star. To perform the trick, you placed a drop of water in the middle where the arms of the star came together — and right before your eyes it would blossom into a fat, fully drawn star like the ones on the American flag. It was one of my favorite tricks, because even though it was simple, and you knew what was happening, you couldn't *see* the water flowing into the arms of the star.

Something like that slow and inexorable motion took place in the car among the members of my family on top of that hill. Each of us seemed to retreat into a compartment of his own. It was the first time I remember feeling that I was not the main concern of my father and mother. The first time I actually saw that they had lives of their own to live and that a time might come when I would be alone.

My father's face was covered with mud from hanging out the window, but the whiteness of the shirt where his coat had covered him was shining in the rainy darkness. I thought that if he washed off the mud, right there at the top of that North Augusta hill, then I would be able to see for myself what he had looked like that night the boys fell out of the roof at D. Ford Crowther's tobacco warehouse in Brattleboro, Georgia, the night they had the fight.

The mud from the North Augusta hill was still thumping under the fenders of the car when we came into the back yard of the Coatesburg house. It streaked and caked the windshield, except for the fans made by the wipers. My mother was no longer braced in the seat, but she and my father had not spoken for a long time. In the back seat my sister and I rolled down the windows so we could see. Uncle Sam and Billy Wynne were standing on the porch waiting for us, and Leigh came out of the kitchen door as we pulled up. When he saw them, my father tooted the horn.

"Merry Christmas!" Uncle Sam said. He had his hands in his pockets, and after he said it he took out his right hand and made a small gesture with it. Then he peered at us in the darkness. "Loft?" he said. Billy Wynne was standing beside him with his hands behind his back.

My mother had wiped some of the mud off my father with her handkerchief, but he still looked like the end man in a minstrel show. The car was solidly caked with mud, and must have resembled the kind of vehicle in which some life or death message might have been delivered to the commander of a winter army.

"Merry Christmas!" said my father, waving out the window of the car. He drew out the "merry" — "mehhhh—ry."

Aunt Sarah came out of the kitchen door, wiping her hands in her apron. "Sweet Jesus, Louis. What happened?"

"That North Augusta hill," said my father, getting out of the car. "It looked like Verdun." He went around and opened the door for my mother while my sister and I piled out of the back. Uncle Sam helped my mother up the steps to the porch while my father held the door for my grandmother.

"You hit a bicycle?" asked Uncle Sam, looking at the front of the car in the light from the kitchen door.

"That what that is?" said my father. "I thought it was a shoat." Both of the men laughed. "Help me get it off, will you, Sam?"

They untied the bicycle and brought it up onto the porch. Billy Wynne knew it was for him, but he made no move to claim it. He was very dignified and reserved. While they brought the bicycle up onto the porch, he stood with his hands behind his back, looking out into the dark of the back yard, his mouth tight and his chin pulled back.

My father took out his handkerchief and wiped some of the mud off. "You reckon that's a bicycle, Billy Wynne?" he said.

Billy Wynne looked at the bicycle, then he looked back into the yard, "Yes, sir," he said.

When I saw the shiny red paint where the mud had been wiped away, I suddenly began to feel a mountainous resentment at my father. There was a little voice inside my head that kept saying, "Unfair! Unfair!" Unfair that my father would give the bicycle to Billy Wynne instead of me — though I knew that it was not unfair at all. I had been seeing the bicycle for a week on the back porch in Fitzgerald, and my mother had told me that it was Billy Wynne's Christmas present. I had been pleased for him in Fitzgerald, but now we were in Coatesburg and the bicycle and Billy Wynne had actually come together.

I *already* had a bicycle. My father had gotten it for me the previous summer. And, anyway, I hadn't learned to ride it yet. So Billy Wynne's wouldn't have been any use to me. And, most of all, I knew that Billy Wynne had *earned* it. Because he worked and gave the money to his mother to buy groceries with.

With Billy Wynne standing there in the light from the open kitchen door, his hand behind his back but getting ready to claim the bicycle, I went over all the reasons why it should go to him instead of me. I was a fair-minded child, and I could see that the arguments were all on his side. When I had summed them up and was sure that justice demanded Billy Wynne get the bicycle — that there was nothing in my father's decision that I could complain about — I stepped up and pointed my finger at it.

"Daddy," I said.

He looked at me.

"I want that goddamn bicycle," I said.

He looked at me for a minute. "What did you say?" he said. He was too surprised to be angry at me right away.

"You heard me," I said.

I was eight years old at the time, and profanity wasn't tolerated in our house in any case, except for Uncle Polk. I remember once making a list of all the dirty words I knew, writing them down on a piece of paper. It went something like: "pee pee, doo doo, vomit . . . ," things like that. I got the worst spanking of my life when my mother found it and reported it to my father. Nobody in our house said "damn" out loud, much less "*god* damn."

"Mary . . . ," said my father, looking at my mother.

She looked at him, and I felt them coalescing into an entity for the first time since we had started up the hill in North Augusta.

My father took me by the arm, gripping me so hard his fingernails almost made the blood come. He marched me to the bathroom that way, holding me at arm's length. When we went inside, he locked the door and turned to me. The expression on his face was one of puzzlement more than anger, and I could see that he didn't know exactly what to do. He was nonplussed. Of course he didn't want to spoil Christmas for everybody, and maybe he also felt a little guilty about the bicycle. I don't think I had ever defied him so openly before.

He looked at me for a long time. "It's Christmas Eve, Nate," he said. His voice was much softer than I had expected it to be.

"I want the bicycle," I said. It wasn't exactly what I wanted to say, but I couldn't think of anything else.

"You have a bicycle," he said. "You won't learn to ride it." He looked around the bathroom for a minute. There was a sad expression on his face.

It was a sore point with both of us. He had threatened to give my bicycle away if I didn't learn to ride it, but I was afraid that I was going to fall and hurt myself. I can remember whole afternoons we would spend in the street in front of our house, with my father pushing me on the bicycle, running along with his hand on the seat until his face was red and swollen and he was gasping for breath.

"Now, Nate! Now!" he'd say, and would give me a final push to send me off on my own. As soon as he let go I would become rigid with fright. The bicycle would coast for a little way, but as soon as I felt myself losing my balance I would jump off and let it crash. "Pedal, Nate! PEDAL!" He would be shouting at me as I coasted away. I enjoyed the feeling of coasting when he would be pushing me down the street and I could feel his hand on the seat under me. It was glorious. But I was afraid the moment he let go. In the bathroom of the Coatesburg house I tried to put that out of my mind.

"I want a *new* bicycle," I said.

I suddenly remembered something that had happened to me when I was three or four years old. We were living in Macon, Georgia, at the time, and a boy my age invited me to come to his house to play. Maybe the boy was younger than I was. He lived on the edge of our neighborhood, and I didn't see much of him. My mother let me go and we played with lead soldiers in his back yard. There was a fish pond, and I remember that we threw some of the soldiers into the pond. Then we started fishing them out with a piece of string that had a hook on the end of it. As I was fishing out one of the soldiers I decided to run away with it. Just — click — and I turned into a thief. I ran off dragging the soldier at the end of the string. He chased me down the street, but not all the way back to my house. I told my mother that he had given the soldier to me. Later, when I was playing with it, I tripped and cut myself on a piece of broken glass. It was a bad cut at the heel of my hand, and my mother told me that if it had been a little nearer my wrist I might have cut an artery and would have bled to death. I thought about bleeding to death. But I never did tell her that I had stolen the soldier.

I still had the scar on my hand, and I looked at it in the light from the forty watt bulb.

"I want a *new* bicycle," I said.

"Billy Wynne *needs* a bicycle to deliver his papers," said my father.

"I know," I said.

"I couldn't get two bicycles," he said.

"I know," I said. "I know you couldn't get two bicycles." Then I started to cry, rubbing the heel of my scarred hand on my pants leg. I had the feeling that I had done something that was irrevocable, and I knew that Billy Wynne needed the bicycle more than I did.

My father was sitting on the toilet looking at me, with his hands on his knees and his elbows turned out. I was standing in front of him. I tried not to cry too loud, because I didn't want the others to hear me. I was embarrassed enough already.

For a minute I stood there sobbing as quietly as I could. My father watched me without saying anything, and then he leaned forward and put his arms around me and pulled me to him. As soon as he did, I could feel him sobbing too.

He did it without making any noise. I think that he was crying because he really did love me, and also because of what had happened on the North Augusta hill.

"I know he deserves it," I said.

For a minute my father didn't say anything. I felt him stop sobbing, slowly, like an engine running down. When he spoke, his voice was almost a whisper. "You wouldn't want a *red* bicycle anyway, would you?"

"No," I said. I didn't know why I shouldn't want a red bicycle.

"*Everybody* has a red bicycle," he said. I could feel him moving his hands to his face, wiping his eyes. "We'll get you a blue one."

"How about a black one?" I said. A red one was what I wanted.

"Yes," he said. "We'll get you a black one." He held me at arm's length. "When you learn to ride the one you've got, I'll get you a black one."

"Okay," I said. I didn't know whether I would learn to ride my bicycle or not. But there really wasn't anything else to say.

He turned on the water in the tub and wet the washcloth. Then he wiped my face. Afterwards he wiped his own which was streaked with the mud from the crying.

He put the washcloth back on the rack. "Listen," he said. "Let's not spoil Christmas."

I nodded. "I'm sorry," I said. "Billy Wynne deserves the bicycle more than I do."

He looked at me for a minute. "Billy Wynne *needs* it." he said.

"Yes sir," I said.

He got up and looked at himself in the mirror over the sink. "I'm a mess," he said.

I didn't say anything, even though I agreed with him.

He got the washcloth and wiped his face again. After he put it back on the rack he looked at me. "Do you think you could apologize?" he said.

I thought about it for a minute. "I could write them a note," I said.

He seemed to think about that for awhile. "No," he said. "You couldn't do that."

I thought about it again. "I suppose I could do it," I said.

He nodded. Then he looked at himself in the mirror again. "Do you think you're ready to go out now?" he asked.

I felt like I might start crying again, but I nodded, "Yes, sir," I said.

Before he opened the door, he put his hand on my shoulder. "Merry Christmas, son," he said.

"Yes, sir," I said. "Merry Christmas to you."

The bicycle my father had given to me was part of something that was another sore point with me through most of my childhood. Like all of the big toys I received as a child, it was secondhand. Of course I was happy to have them, those toys. But there was always something missing — something that didn't work the way it was supposed to. There were two or three pieces that had been lost from my Erector Set before I got it, so I couldn't build the ferris wheel. And the transformer of my electric train stuck when I tried to run it too fast. I didn't feel that I could complain about little things like that, but I couldn't help being aware of them either.

As with most of the other toys, there was no particular occasion on which the bicycle had been given to me — only that my father had found a good trade just then.

My father was a great trader, and the only big item that we always got new was the automobile. My father had to use that in his job, and the Highway Department paid a part of the cost. But even so, I don't think he would have taken a chance on a used one. That was the way he felt about automobiles.

But nearly everything else that came into the house had the marks of wear on it. And for everything that came in, something went out. I don't know how my father's mind worked when he was trading — it moved along lines that I could never make out. He wouldn't trade a stove for a stove, for instance — nor even for another piece of kitchen equipment. I remember once he traded a Shetland pony for a Delco home generating plant. A *Delco* home generating plant. I didn't even know what that was at the time. Once he traded two hunting dogs for five thousand board feet of cypress lumber. There was never any connection that I could make out. It was always a puzzle to me.

I finally decided that the way he traded was a sign that my father was thinking about the world in wide and general terms. Years later, going back over it, the thought came to me that there was a sort of inspiration in the lack of connectedness in his trades. And I became proud of him because of it.

My father was a good trader. He enjoyed the action involved, and was, in fact, a bit vain about how good he was. He didn't talk any more during a trade than he did in general, perhaps he talked less. But that worked to his advantage it seemed. The times I saw him engaged in it, the men he was swapping with seemed to feel that they had to argue on both sides of the trade, because my father almost wouldn't talk at all. It was strange to see the man doing the talking for both of them, while my father just stood there and listened to him — nodding his head now and then and smiling right along. Finally the man would get smiled and nodded into something like a frenzy so that he always developed the best arguments on my father's side of the swap, and would wind up cheating himself. It was always terribly one-sided.

Uncle Polk said that in one series of swaps, my father started out with a Barlow knife and traded it all the way up to a Ford automobile.

"He wouldn't *say* anything. It was nerve-wracking. You wouldn't believe how nerve-wracking it was to watch him." He stopped and thought about it. "I love Loft," he said. "But I wouldn't swap with him for all the tea in China." He raised his eyebrows and nodded his head. *All* the tea in China," he said.

Christmas Eve night turned off bitter cold, and the wind got up after the rain had stopped. Billy Wynne and I shared a bed in the back bedroom, which had been a storeroom of some kind, and wasn't finished on the inside. The cold came in through the cracks in the clapboards, and when the wind subsided, between gusts I could hear the house creaking and moaning like a glacier as it tightened itself in the cold. The only way to keep warm was to pile on the blankets, and there must have been a dozen of them on the bed. After mother pulled them over me and kissed me good night I couldn't move. It was like sleeping under a sandbag. I felt like I had been buried alive.

I was ashamed of myself for the way I had acted, and although I had apologized in front of the family, I felt that I needed to do it in private as well. Just to make it something between myself and Billy Wynne.

"Billy Wynne," I said, when we were alone in the bedroom.

He didn't answer me.

"I'm sorry for what I said about the bicycle," I said. "Can you hear me?"

It took him a minute to answer. "I *need* it, Nate," he said.

"I know you do," I said. He sounded like a grown man.

"Uncle Louis will buy you a new one."

He said it matter-of-factly. The calmness and resignation in his voice made me want to cry again.

Before I fell asleep I listened to Billy Wynne's regular breathing for a long time, and to the house creaking in the cold. Finally, just before I went to sleep, I moved my foot over into his warm place.

Christmas morning I had to wait for Mother to come and get the covers off before I could get out of bed.

"A bag of switches for me, I guess," I said. I meant it as something of a joke, but after I said it I wasn't quite sure that it was.

"Santa Claus knows that you apologized," she said.

When I put my bare feet on the floor it was so cold it felt hot. I danced around like a spider on a stove top until I got my stockings on.

In the kitchen no one said anything about the way I had acted the night before. Uncle Sam told a Christmas story at the breakfast table, and he seemed to be directing it at me just so I wouldn't feel so badly. Only Aunt Sarah looked at me in a way that made me feel uncomfortable, but she didn't say anything.

After breakfast we went into the living room and opened our presents.

The living room had bright yellow walls, but it always struck me as a gloomy room — and never more gloomy than on that Christmas morning. It wasn't as naturally depressing as the parlor across the entrance hall, which was all maroon and white and dark mahogany. I had never actually been in the parlor, but once I had opened the sliding doors enough to be able to see what it looked like.

There was a fire in the living room fireplace, but Aunt Sarah would only burn four lumps of coal in the grate at one time — even for company — and the floorboards leaked air freely. All of the rooms had fireplaces in them — except Billy Wynne's back bedroom — but the living room was the only one that ever had a fire in it that I remember — and that never did any good. I suppose it was a gesture of hospitality on Aunt Sarah's part, but as far as the heat was concerned, you would have had to sit on an andiron to feel it. The draft sure worked without a stint though. It sucked like a Kansas tornado. All the women's dresses, and the skirts on the upholstered furniture, billowed out from the air coming up through the cracks in the floor.

The Christmas tree was a big personal disappointment to me. It was a pine that Billy Wynne had cut down in the woods — just a plain pine tree, scraggly and bare. It looked like the framework that you might start with if you were going to build a real Christmas tree. And it didn't have any lights on it. There was a long popcorn chain that wound around and around. And little stars and bells cut out of cardboard and covered with tinfoil from old pipe tobacco packages that Billy Wynne had collected. And chains with links made out of colored construction paper. At the top was an angel that had been cut out of the Sears Roebuck catalog, with a dress and wings made from tinfoil. But there weren't any lights at all.

It would take more than twenty-five years for me to see how beautiful Billy Wynne's scraggly pine tree was, with its tinfoil ornaments made one by one. I should have been a quicker study, though that is a lot to ask of anyone as middle class as I have been. All the valuable lessons I ever learned had to be written into my hide. That is a tedious but emphatic way of bringing home a point, though it has the advantage finally of being indelible — if only it doesn't come too late.

Still, in 1938 I loved colored Christmas lights. Our tree at home always had three or four strings of them. Some were just plain colored lights, red and blue and green. But there were three or four special ones that I looked forward to from year to year. One was milky white — round, with a grid on it like a globe, and little red fish behind the grid. There was another one that was a red cottage with snow on its roof. When just the lights of the tree were on, I liked to put my face up close to the globe with the fishes on it — and to the windows of the little red cottage. They were part of what I looked forward to at Christmas from one year to the next.

I understood that I couldn't complain about Billy Wynne's tree, and my mother kept remarking on how clever they were to make their own decorations the way they did. But I couldn't bring myself to say anything about it at all, so that everybody knew how I felt.

As the day wore on, the wind died down and it began to warm up, though the overcast didn't lift.

Just before noon, Aunt Sarah came in from the kitchen and told my father that William was out in the back yard with his family.

William was a Negro man who lived behind Aunt Sarah and Uncle Sam on a piece of land that had belonged to my grandfather at one time. In 1938 it had belonged to someone else for a number of years, and William farmed it on shares for whoever the owner was. But William had been born on that piece of land.

William Lawton was his name. He had simplified the spelling too, but his name was closer to the original than my own was.

Our family name had been "Laughton" until sometime in the eighteen nineties. My grandfather and his brothers had changed it to "Loftin" because the Negroes had all pronounced it like they were sight-reading it as two words: "laugh-ton." They pronounced it "Laeftin," or "Leftin."

Uncle Polk told me about the changing of the name. "Gene couldn't stand to hear the niggers call him 'Leftin.' He started all over again with the spelling."

No one ever remarked on the fact that the Negroes had decided what our name would be.

William was the same age as my father, and they had played together as children. He still did odd jobs for Aunt Sarah and Uncle Sam, and on Christmas they came to the house to exchange presents.

We went out onto the back porch and found William and his wife and children standing in a line in the back yard. His wife held a large brown paper bag that was tied at the neck with a piece of red string. William was holding his hat in his hand like it was a basket, and there were several smaller packages in it also. Tied up in brown paper with red string.

"Merry Christmas, William," said my father.

"Yas, sah," said William. He looked a little like my father, with a pale, coppery skin and light eyes. His wife's name was Octilla. She was a very thin woman who always wore a bandanna on her head. She stood extremely straight, but the shanks of her legs beneath her dress were bowed, and she was wearing a pair of men's brown cap-toed shoes.

My father went down the steps and walked up to William. William looked down at the ground. They didn't shake hands, though I had expected that they would.

"Is that Rufus?" My father nodded his head toward the oldest child. There were nine of them, standing in a line off Octilla's shoulder, stepping down from oldest to youngest. William stood at the end beside his wife.

"Sho is," said William. "He be done got some size on him."

"Going to outgrow you, William," said my father.

"Yas, sah," said William. He would speak only in response to my father.

My father reached into his pocket and took out a quarter, which he gave to Rufus. "Merry Christmas, Rufus," said my father. Rufus nodded his head, but didn't say anything.

There were six boys and three girls, and my father went down the line giving each one a quarter. The way he looked doing it was like a mechanic making some kind of minor adjustment on a row of machines. He spoke to each child in turn, but with some of the younger ones he couldn't recall the names. The boys all had their hair close cropped, with shaved-in part lines. The girls all had their hair done up in pigtails that stuck out from their heads in spikes, except the oldest, who wore a bandanna like her mother. The five youngest children were barefooted.

" 'Dethonia'? Where did you find a name like *Dethonia*, William?" said my father. The youngest child was a boy, about five years old.

William looked at his wife and nodded his head. "Octilla give them they names," he said.

Octilla had a pinch of snuff inside her lower lip. When William nodded at her, she leaned over behind his back and spit onto the ground. Then she straightened back up and stared straight ahead. "Hit's fambly," she said.

While they were talking about him, Dethonia put the quarter to his mouth, holding it with both hands. Then he put it into his mouth and swallowed it. It stuck in his throat and he fell down on the ground holding his neck in his hands.

"He swallowed it!" said my father. The line of blacks looked down at the small child on the ground. None of them made a move to help him. They didn't seem to be particularly interested in what was happening.

My father went over and picked Dethonia up. Then he put him over his knee and pounded him on the back three or four times. There was a gulping sound and Dethonia let out a yell. My father let him go, and he ran to his mother, burying his face in her skirt and hugging her legs.

"He swallowed it," said my father again, looking around on the ground where Dethonia had been.

"Hit'll pass," said William.

My father reached into his pocket and took out another quarter. "You keep it for him," he said, giving it to Octilla. She took it and rolled it in the corner of her apron.

"Much obliged," she said.

"You don't eat them, do you, William?" said my father, speaking to William.

"Don't get 'em to eat, Mr. Louis," he said.

My father blushed red when William said that, then he took out his billfold and gave William a five dollar bill. He looked at Octilla. "This is for you too," he said as he handed the bill to William.

William didn't look at it to see what it was. He took it and put it into his pocket. "Yas, sah," he said. "Much obliged, Mr. Louis."

Then Octilla handed William the paper bag with the red string on it, and William took the bag to the porch and gave it to Aunt Sarah.

"Sandy Claus," he said. He looked around. "For all you all," he said.

Every Christmas William and Octilla gave Aunt Sarah and Uncle Sam a ten pound bag of shelled pecans. The trees belonged to Aunt Sarah and Uncle Sam. Aunt Sarah and Uncle Sam gave William and his family their Christmas dinner as their present. Uncle Sam always raised four or five turkeys for Thanksgiving and Christmas, and they gave one to the Lawtons on those two holidays. Also Aunt Sarah set aside one of her fruit cakes for them when she did her Christmas baking.

William took the small brown packages out of his hat. "For the childruns," he said, giving them to my father to distribute. My father brought them to us where we were standing on the porch. Inside each package was a light bulb that had been painted red, with *"Mery X"* swirled in the wet paint with a finger before it dried. My sister was pleased with hers, but I didn't know what to say.

"Thank you," I said, speaking more to my father than to William.

Alice had gotten a tea set from Santa Claus, and she went into the house and came back with a place setting of the miniature knives and forks and spoons. She gave a piece to each of the three girls. While she was doing it, the boys all looked at her, and when she had finished, they all looked at me. I tried to think of something that I had six of that I could give them. I wanted to do it partly because I thought that it would wipe away the memory of the way I had acted the night before, but also I just *wanted* to do it. Only I didn't *have* six of anything. I had already gobbled up all the candy in my stocking.

I was wearing the new cowboy suit I had gotten from Santa Claus, and wished that at least I hadn't had that on. The boy who was nearest my age, was named Ligon. Sometimes I played with him when we would visit. Every time I looked at him, he would be looking at me — at my cowboy suit and the new Gene Autrey pistol I had gotten to go with it. He kept on looking at me, even after it became clear that I wasn't going to give them anything the way my sister had.

Aunt Sarah took the bag of pecans into the house, then Uncle Sam brought out the turkey, and she brought out the rest of the dinner on a tray with a white cloth over it.

Afterwards, Billy Wynne gave each of the children an orange out of a bag, and Leigh gave each of them an apple.

When Leigh got back onto the porch, William said, "Much obliged." Then he put his hat back onto his head, and they all faced right and marched out the back yard single file with the smallest child leading and Dethonia holding to his mother's skirt.

After they had gone, I held up the red light bulb and examined it all around. "What's it *for*?" I asked my mother.

"They made it for you," she said.

I didn't understand her answer. "Do they think it's beautiful?" I asked.

She looked at me. "*I* think it's beautiful," she said.

Later I tried my bulb in a lamp, but it didn't work. When I shook it beside my ear I could hear the filament rattling inside the globe.

As with Billy Wynne's Christmas tree, it took me years and years to see for myself how beautiful that painted light bulb was. I must have gotten at least two of all of the things I ever wanted. Over the course of my childhood I had more than a dozen Gene Autry cap pistols. But I only got one of the Lawton's painted Christmas light bulbs, and before Christmas week was over I had lost it.

We ate dinner in the living room where a table had been set up big enough for all of us to sit down at one time. Aunt Sarah told my father how William and his family were doing.

"He's a *good* colored man," she said. "Of course, Octilla's surly."

"Loft thinks we should have taken that colored boy from D. Ford Crowther," said my mother. "Because he remembers the way it was with William."

"What colored boy?" Aunt Sarah asked. I looked at my mother. I had never heard this story before.

"When Nate was born," she said. "D. Ford Crowther wanted to give Loft a colored boy to play with him."

"*Give* him one?" said Aunt Sarah.

"Can you imagine?" said my mother. "There were colored children all over D. Ford Crowther's place. Loft tried to talk me into it."

My father didn't say anything.

"It was going to be trouble later on," said my mother. "Just *think* about it. Loft really wanted me to take in that colored child. We were talking about it for two or three weeks."

I thought about Ligon, and how it would have been to have him for my very own, to play with all of the time.

"Did you *really* do that, Louis?" said Aunt Sarah, talking to my father.

"I didn't think about him having to stay in the house," said my father. "William was my best friend when I was a child."

"It's a good thing you knew what *you* were doing," said Aunt Sarah, talking to my mother.

Aunt Sarah looked at my father. "I can't imagine what you were thinking about, Louis," she said. "I can't imagine what in the *world* you were thinking about."

"Yes," said my father. "Well. Everything works out for the best."

When I went to bed that night, I lay awake thinking how it would have been if I could have had Ligon to play Tarzan with. Ligon was copper-colored like his father. He would have made a good Indian.

DONALD HALL

Christmas Snow

he real snows I remember are the snows of Christmas in New Hampshire. I was ten years old, and there was a night when I woke up to the sound of grownups talking. Slowly, I realized that it wasn't that at all; the mounds of my grandfather and grandmother lay still in their bed under many quilts in the cold room. It was rain falling and rubbing against the bushes outside my window. I sat up in bed, pulling the covers around me, and held the green shade out from the frosty pane. There were flakes of snow mixed into the rain — large, slow flakes fluttering down like wet leaves. I watched as long as I could, until the back of my neck hurt with the cold, while the flakes grew thicker and the snow took over the rain. When I looked up into the dark sky, just before lying back in my warm feather bed, the whole air was made of fine light shapes. I was happy in my own world of snow, as if I were living inside one of those glass paperweights that snow when you shake them, and I went back to sleep easily. In the morning, I looked out the window as soon as I woke. There were no more leaves, no more weeds turned brown by the frost, no sheds, no road, and no chicken coops. The sky was a dense mass of snowflakes, the ground covered in soft white curves.

It was the morning of Christmas Eve, 1938. The day before, we had driven north from Connecticut, and I had been disappointed to find that there was no snow on my grandfather's farm. On the trip up, I had not noticed the lack of snow, because I was too busy looking for hurricane damage. (September, 1938, was the time of the great New England hurricane.) Maples and oaks and elms were down everywhere. Huge roots stood up like dirt cliffs next to the road. On distant hillsides, whole stands of trees lay pointing in the same direction, like combed hair. Men were cutting the timber with double handsaws, their breaths blue-white in the cold. Ponds were already filling with logs — stored timber that would corduroy the surface of New Hampshire lakes for years. Here and there I saw a roof gone from a barn, or a tree leaning into a house.

We knew from letters that my grandfather's farmhouse was all right. I was excited to be going there, sitting in the front seat between my mother and father, with the heater blasting at my knees. Every summer, we drove the same route and I spent two weeks following my grandfather as he did chores, listening to his talk. The familiar road took shape again: Sunapee, Georges Mills, New London; then there was the shortcut along the bumpy Cilleyville Road.

We drove past the West Andover depot, past Henry's store and the big rock, and climbed the little hill by the Blasington's, and there, down the slope to the right, we saw the lights of the farmhouse. In a porch window I could see my small Christmas tree, with its own string of lights. It stood in the window next to the large one, where I could see it when we drove over the hill.

We stopped in the driveway and the kitchen door burst open. My grandfather was in his milking clothes, tall and bald and smiling broadly. He lifted me up, grunting at how big I was getting. Over his shoulder, which smelled happily of barn and tieup, I saw my grandmother in her best dress, waiting her turn and looking pleased.

As we stood outside in the cold, I looked around for signs of the hurricane. In the light from the kitchen window I could just see a stake with a rope tied to it that angled up into the tall elm by the shed. Then I remembered that my grandmother had written my mother about that tree. It had blown over, roots out of the ground, and Washington Woodward, a cousin of ours who lived on Ragged Mountain, was fixing it. The great tree was upright now.

My grandfather saw me looking at it. "Looks like it's going to work, don't it? Of course you can't tell until spring, and the leaves. A lot of the root must have gone." He shook his head. "Wash is a wonder," he said. "He winched that tree back upright in two days with a pulley on that oak." He pointed to a tree on the hill in back of the house. "I thought he was going to pull the oak clear out of the ground. Then he took that rock-moving machine of his" (I remembered that Wash had constructed a wooden tripod about fifteen feet high for moving rocks. I never understood how it worked, though I heard him explain it a hundred times. He moved rocks for fun mostly; it was his hobby) "and moved that boulder down from the pasture and set it there to keep the roots flat. It only took him five days in all, and I think he saved the tree."

It was when we moved back to the group around the car that I realized, with sudden disappointment, that there was no snow on the ground.

I turned from the window the next morning and looked over at my grandparents' bed. My grandmother was there, but the place beside her was empty. The clock on the bureau, among the snapshots and perfume bottles, said six o'clock. I heard my grandfather carrying wood into the living room. Logs crashed into the big, square stove. In a moment, I heard another sound I was listening for — a massive animal roar from the same stove. He had poured a tin can of kerosene on the old embers and the new logs. Then I heard him fix the kitchen stove and pause by the door to put on coats and scarves and a cap — his boots were in the shed — and then the door shut between kitchen and shed, and he had gone to milk the cows.

It was warm inside my bed. My grandmother stood up beside her bed, her gray hair down to her waist. "Good morning," she said. "You awake? We've had some snow. You go back to sleep while I make the doughnuts." That brought me out of bed quickly. I dressed next to the stove in the dark living room. The sides of the stove glowed red, and I kept my distance. The cold of the room almost visibly receded into the farther corners, there to dwindle into something the size of a pea.

My grandmother was fixing her hair in the warm kitchen, braiding it and winding it up on her head. She looked like my grandmother again. "Doughnuts won't be ready for a long time. The fat's got to heat. Why don't you have a slice of bread and go see Gramp in the tieup?"

I put peanut butter on the bread and bundled up with galoshes and a wool cap that I could pull over my ears. I stepped outside into the swirl of flakes, white against the gray of the early morning. It was my first snow of the year, and it set my heart pounding with pleasure. But even if it had snowed in Connecticut earlier, this would have been my first real snow. When it snowed in Connecticut, the snowplows heaped most of it in the gutters and the cars chewed the rest with chains and blackened it with oil. Here the snow turned the farm into a planet of its own, an undiscovered moon.

I walked past our Studebaker, which was humped already with two inches of snow. I reached down for a handful, to see if it would pack, but it was dry as cotton. The flakes, when I looked up into the endless flaking barrel of the sky, were fine and constant. It was going to snow all day. I climbed the hill to the barn without lifting my galoshes quite clear of the snow, and left two long trenches behind me. I raised the iron latch and went into the tieup, shaking my head and shoulders like a dog, making a little snowstorm inside.

My grandfather laughed. "It's really coming down," he said. "It'll be a white Christmas, you can be sure of that."

"I love it," I said.

"Can you make a snowman today?"

"It's dry snow," I said. "It won't pack."

"When it melts a little, you can roll away the top of it — I mean, tomorrow or the next day. I remember making a big one with my brother Fred when I was nine — no eight. Fred wasn't much bigger than a hoptoad then. I called him hoptoad when I wanted to make him mad, and my, you never saw such a red face. Well, we spent the whole day Saturday making this great creature. Borrowed a scarf and an old hat — it was a woman's hat, but we didn't mind — and a carrot from the cellar for the nose, and two little potatoes for the eyes. It was a fine thing, no doubt about it, and we showed your Aunt Lottie, who said it was the best one she ever saw. Then my father came out of the forge — putting things away for the Sabbath, you know, shutting things away — and he saw what we'd been up to and came over and stood in front of it. I can see him now, so tall, with his big brown beard. We were proud of that snowman, and I guess we were waiting for praise. 'Very good, boys,' he said." Here my grandfather's voice turned deep and impressive. " 'That's a fine snowman. It's too bad you put him in front of the shed. You can take him down now.' " My grandfather laughed. "Of course, we felt bad, but we felt silly, too. The back of that snowman was almost touching the carriage we drove to church in. We were tired with making it, and I guess we were tired when we came in for supper! I suppose that was the last snowman I ever made."

I loved him to tell his stories. His voice filled the white-washed, cobwebby tieup. I loved his imitations, and the glimpses of an old time. In this story I thought my great-grandfather sounded cruel; there must have been some *other* way to get to church. But I didn't really care. I never really got upset by my grandfather's stories, no matter what happened in them. All the characters were fabulous, and none more so than his strong blacksmith father, who had fought at Vicksburg.

My grandfather was milking now, not heavily dressed against the cold but most of the time wedged between the bodies of two huge Holsteins, which must have given off a good bit of heat. The alternate streams of milk went swush-swush from his fists into the pail, first making a tinny sound and then softening and becoming more liquid as the pail filled. When he wasn't speaking, he leaned his head on the rib cage of a cow, the visor of his cap turned around to the back like a baseball catcher's. When he spoke, he tilted his head back and turned toward me. He sat on an old easy chair with the legs cut off, while I had taken down a three-legged stool from a peg on the wall. We talked about the hurricane a bit, and he made jokes about "Harry Cane" and "Si Clone." Whenever the pail was full, he would take it to the milk room and strain it into the big milk can, which the truck would pick up later in the day. We went from cow to cow, from Sally to Spot to Betty to Alice Weaver. And then we were done. While the last milk strained into the big can, I helped my grandfather clean out the tieup, hoeing the cowflops through the floor and onto the manure heap under the barn. Then he fitted tops on the milk cans and craned them onto his wheelbarrow. I unlatched the door and we went out into the snow.

The trenches that I had scraped with my galoshes were filled in. The boulder that Washington Woodward had rolled over the roots of the elm wore a thick white cap; it looked like an enormous snowball. The air was a chaff of white motes, the tiny dry flakes. (I remembered last summer in the barn, sneezing with the fine dust while my grandfather pitched hay.) The iron wheel of the wheelbarrow made a narrow cut in the snow, and spun a long delicate arc of snow forward. Our four boots made a new trail. Crossing the road to the platform on the other side, we hardly knew where the road began and the ditch ended. We were all alone, with no trace of anything else in the world. We came back to the kitchen for breakfast, slapping our hands and stamping our feet, exhilarated with cold and with the first snow of the winter.

I smelled the doughnuts when we opened the door from the shed to the kitchen. My father was standing in the kitchen, wearing a light sweater over an open-neck shirt, smoking his before-breakfast cigarette. On the stove, the fat was bubbling, and I could see the circles of dough floating and turning brown. When she saw me, my grandmother tossed a few more doughnuts into the fat, and I watched them greedily as they floated among the bubbles. In a moment, my mother came downstairs, and we all ate doughnuts and drank milk and coffee.

"Is it going to snow all day?" my father asked my grandfather.

"It looks so," said my grandfather.

"I hope the girls can get through," said my grandmother. She always worried about things. My mother's schoolteacher sisters were expected that night.

"They will, Katie," said my grandfather.

"They have chains, I suppose," said my father.

"Oh, yes," said my grandfather, "and they're good drivers."

"Who else is coming?" I asked.

"Uncle Luther," said my grandfather, "and Wash. Wash will have to find his way down Ragged."

That morning after breakfast, my Aunt Caroline arrived, and before noon my Aunt Nan. Each of them talked with me for a while, and then each of them was absorbed by the kitchen and preparations for tomorrow's dinner. I kept looking at the presents under both trees — a pile for the grownups under the branches of the big tree, and almost as many under mine. After lunch, Nan drove up to "Sabine," a little house three-quarters of a mile north, and came back with Uncle Luther. He was my grandmother's older brother, a clergyman who had retired from his city parish and was preaching at the little South Danbury church that we went to in New Hampshire. My grandfather disappeared for a while — nobody would tell me where he was — and a little later my grandmother was plucking feathers from a hen named Old Rusty that had stopped laying eggs. Then my grandfather dressed up in a brown suit, because it was Christmas Eve, and read a novel by Kathleen Norris. My father read magazines or paced up and down with a cigarette. I must have seemed restless, because after a while my father plucked one of my presents from under my tree and told me to open it. It was a Hardy Boys mystery. I sat in the living room with my father and grandfather and read a Christmas book.

By four-thirty, it was perfectly dark, and the snow kept coming. When I looked out the sitting-room window, past the light the windows cast into the front yard, I saw darkness with shadows of snow upon it. Inside the cup of light, the snow floated like feathers. It piled high on the little round stones on each side of the path from the driveway. Farther on in the darkness I could see the dark toadstool of the birdbath weighted down under an enormous puff of whiteness. I went to the kitchen window to look at our car, but there was only a car-shaped drift of snow, with indentations for front windows.

It was time for milking again. My grandfather bundled up with extra socks and sweaters and scarves, and long boots over his suit trousers, and my grandmother pinned his coat around his neck with a huge safety pin. She always fretted about his health. She had also been fretting for an hour over Washington Woodward. (Wash had been sort of an older brother to her when she was a little girl; his family had been poor, and had farmed him out to the Keneston cousins.) My grandfather stepped out the shed door and sank into the snow. He started to take big steps toward the barn when suddenly he stopped and we heard him shout, "Katie, Donnie, Look!" Peering out the shed window, we could just see my grandfather in the reflected light from the kitchen. He was pointing past that light, and while we watched, a figure moved into it, pacing slowly with a shuffling sort of gait. Then the figure said, "Wesley!" and started talking, and we knew it was Wash.

It would have been hard to tell what it was if it hadn't talked. Wash looked as if he was wearing six coats, and the outermost was the pelt of a deer. He shot one every winter and dried its pelt on the side of his hut; I think the pelts served to keep out the wind, for one thing. His face was almost covered with horizontal brown strips of cloth, covered with snow now, leaving just a slit for the eyes. The same sort of strips, arranged vertically, fastened his cap to his head and tied under his chin.

When he shuffled up to the shed door, my grandmother opened it. "Snowshoes," she said. "I knew that's how you'd do it, maybe." She laughed — with relief I suppose, and also at Wash's appearance. Wash was talking, of course — he was always talking — but I didn't notice what he said. I was too busy watching him take off his snowshoeing clothes. First, standing in the doorway but still outside, he stripped three gloves from each hand and tossed them ahead of him into the shed. It was even cold for us to stand watching him in the open door, but Wash had to take off his showshoes before he could come inside. His thick, cold fingers fumbled among leather thongs. Finally, he stood out of them, banged them against the side of the house to shake the snow off them, and stepped inside. As we closed the shed door, I saw my grandfather trudge up the blue hill toward the barn.

A single naked light bulb burned at the roof of the shed. Wash stamped his feet and found his gloves and put them on a table. All the time, his voice went on and on. "About there, McKenzie's old place, my left shoe got loose. I had to stop there by the big rock and fix it. It took me a while, because I didn't have a good place to put my foot. Well, I was standing there pretty quiet, getting my breath, when a red fox came sniffing along. . . ."

Now he began taking off the layers of his clothing. He unknotted the brown bands around his face, and they turned into long socks. "How do you like these, Katie?" he interrupted himself. "You gave them to me last Christmas, and I hain't worn them yet." He went on with his story. When all the socks were peeled off, they revealed his beard. Beards were rare in 1938. I saw a few in New Hampshire, usually on old men. Washington shaved his beard every spring and grew it again in the fall, so I knew two Washington Woodwards — the summer one and the winter one. The beard was brown gray, and it served him most of the winter instead of a scarf. It was quite full already and it wagged as he talked. His eyes crinkled in the space left between the two masses of his beard and his hair. Wash never cut his hair in winter, either — also for the sake of warmth. He thought we should use the hair God gave us before we went to adding other things.

He unwound himself now, taking off the pelt of the deer, which was frozen and stiff, and then a series of coats and jackets. Then there was a pair of overalls, and then I saw that he had wrapped burlap bags around his shins and thighs, underneath the legs of the overalls, and tied them in place with bits of string. It took him a long time to undo the knots, but he refused to cut them away with a knife; that would have been a waste. Then he was down to his boots, his underneath overalls, his old much mended shirt, and a frail brown cardigan over it. He took off his boots, and we walked through the kitchen and into the living room.

Everyone welcomed Wash, and we heard him tell about his four-hour walk down Ragged on snowshoes, about the red fox and the car he saw abandoned. "Come to think of it," my father said, "I haven't heard any traffic going past."

Wash interrupted his own monologue. "Nothing can get through just now. It's a bad storm. I suppose Benjamin's plow broke down again. Leastways we're all here for the night."

"Snowbound," said my Uncle Luther.

"Got the wood in?" Washington asked my grandfather.

Aunt Nan recited:

> "Shut in from all the world without,
> We sat the clean-winged hearth about,
> Content to let the north-wind roar

In baffled rage at pane and door,
While the red logs before us beat
The frost-line back with tropic heat . . ."

She giggled when she was through.

Aunt Caroline said, "I remember when we had to learn that."

"Miss Headley," my mother said. She turned to me. "Do you have that in school? It's John Greenleaf Whittier, 'Snowbound.'"

"Are we really snowbound?" I said. I liked the idea of it. I felt cozy and protected, walled in by the snow. I wanted it to keep on snowing all winter, so that I wouldn't have to go back to Connecticut and school.

"If we have to get out, we'll get out," my father said quickly.

In a moment, my grandfather came in from milking, his cheeks red from the cold. My grandmother and her daughters went out to the kitchen, and the men added leaves to the dining-room table. We sat down to eat, and Uncle Luther said grace. On the table, the dishes were piled high with boiled potatoes and carrots and stringbeans, boiled beef, and white bread. Everyone passed plates to and fro and talked all at once. My two aunts vied over me, teasing and praising.

"How was the hurricane up your way?" I heard my father say to Wash. He had to interrupt Wash to say it, but it was the only way you could ever ask Wash a question.

As I'm sure my father expected, it got Wash started. "I was coming back from chasing some bees — I found a hive, all right, but I needed a ladder — and I saw the sky looking mighty peculiar down over South Pasture way, and . . ." He told every motion he made, and named every tree that fell on his land and the land of his neighbors. When he spoke about it, the hurricane took on a sort of malevolent personality, like someone cruel without reason.

The rest of the table talked hurricane, too. My grandfather told about a rowboat that somehow moved half a mile from its pond. My aunts talked about their towns, my father of how the tidal wave had wrecked his brother's island off the Connecticut coast. I told about walking home from school with a model airplane in my hand and how a gust of wind took it out of my hand and whirled it away and I never found it. (I didn't say that my father bought me another one the next day.) I had the sudden vision of all of us — the whole family, from Connecticut to New Hampshire — caught in the same storm. Suppose a huge wind had picked us up in its fists? . . . We might have met over Massachusetts.

After supper, we moved to the living room. In our family, the grownups had their presents on Christmas Eve and the children had Christmas morning all to themselves. (In 1938, I was the only child there was.) I was excited. The fire in the open stove burned hot, the draft ajar at the bottom and the flue open in the chimney. We heard the wind blowing outside in the darkness and saw white flakes of snow hurtle against the black windowpanes. We were warm.

I distributed the presents, reading the names on the tags and trying to keep them flowing evenly. Drifts of wrapping paper rose beside each chair, and on laps there were new Zane Grey books, toilet water, brown socks and work shirts, bars of soap, and bracelets and neckties. Sentences of package opening ("Now *what* could *this* be?") gave way to sentences of appreciation ("I certainly can use some handkerchiefs, Caroline!"). The bright packages were combed from the branches of the big tree, and the floor was bare underneath. My eyes kept moving toward a pile under and around the small tree.

"Do you remember the oranges, Katie?" said Uncle Luther.

My grandmother nodded. "Didn't they taste good!" she said. She giggled. "I can't think they taste like that anymore."

My grandfather said, "Christmas and town meeting, that's when we had them. The man came to town meeting and sold them there, too." He was talking to me. "They didn't have oranges much in those days," he said. "They were a great treat for the children at Christmas."

"Oranges and popcorn balls," said my grandmother.

"And clothes," said Uncle Luther. "Mittens and warm clothes."

My grandfather went out into the kitchen, and we heard him open the door. When he came back, he said, "It's snowing and blowing still. I reckon it's a blizzard, all right. It's starting to drift."

"It won't be like '88," Uncle Luther said. "It's too early in the year."

"What month was the blizzard of '88?" said my father.

Uncle Luther, my grandfather, and my grandmother all started to talk at once. Then my grandparents laughed and deferred to Uncle Luther. "March 11th to 14th," he said. "I guess Nannie would have remembered, all right." My great-aunt Nannie, who had died earlier that year, was a sister of Uncle Luther and my grandmother.

"Why?" said my father.

"She was teaching school, a little school back of Grafton, in the hills. She used to tell this story every time it started to snow, and we teased her for saying it so much. It snowed so hard and drifted so deep Nannie wouldn't let her scholars go home. All of them, and Nannie, too, had to spend the night. They ran out of wood for the stove, and she wouldn't let anyone go outside to get more wood — she was afraid he'd get lost in the snow and the dark — so they broke up three desks, the old-fashioned kind they used to have in those old schoolhouses. She said those boys really loved to break up those desks and see them burn. In the morning, some of the farmers came and got them out."

For a moment, everyone was quiet — I suppose, thinking of Nannie. Then my father — my young father, who is dead now — spoke up: "My father likes to tell about the blizzard of '88, too. They have a club down in Connecticut that meets once a year and swaps stories about it. He was a boy on the farm out in Hamden, and they drove the sleigh all the way into New Haven the next day. The whole country was nothing but snow. They never knew whether they were on a road or not. They went right across Lake Whitney, on top of fences and all. It took them eight hours to go the four miles."

"We just used to call it the big snow," said my grandmother. "Papa was down in Danbury for town meeting. Everybody was gone away from home overnight, because it was town meeting everyplace. Then in the morning he came back on a wild engine."

I looked at my grandfather.

"An engine that's loose — that's not pulling anything," he explained.

"It stopped to let him off right down there," my grandmother continued. She pointed through the parlor, toward the front door and across the road and past the chickens and sheep, to the railroad track a hundred yards away. "In back of the sheep barn. Just for him. We were excited about him riding the wild engine."

"My father had been to town meeting, too," said my grandfather. "He tried to walk home along the flats and the meadow, but he had to turn back. When it was done, my brothers and I walked to town on the tops of stone walls. You couldn't see the stones, but you could tell from how the snow lay." Suddenly I could see the three young men, my grandfather in the lead, single-filing through the snow, bundled up and their arms outstretched, balancing like tightrope walkers.

Washington spoke, and made it obvious that he had been listening. He had broken his monologue to hear. "I remember that snow," he said.

I settled down for the interminable story. It was late and I was sleepy. I knew that soon the grownups would notice me and pack me off to bed.

"I remember it because it was the worst day of my life," said Wash.

"What?" said my father. He only spoke in surprise. No one expected anything from Wash but harangues of process — how I moved the rock, how I shot the bear, how I snowshoed down Ragged.

"It was my father," said Wash. "He hated me." (Then I remembered, dimly, hearing that Wash's father was a cruel man. The world of cruel fathers was as far from me as the world of stepmothers who fed poisoned apples to stepdaughters.) "He hated me from the day I was born."

"He wasn't a good man, Wash," said my grandmother. She always understated everything, but this time I saw her eyes flick over me, and I realized that she was afraid for me — for my innocence, I suppose. Then I looked around the room and saw that all eyes except Washington's were glancing at me.

"That Christmas, '87," Washington said, "the Kenestons' folks" (he meant my grandmother's family) "gave me skates. I'd never had any before. And they were the good, new, steel kind, not the old iron ones where you had to have an iron plate fixed to your shoe. There were screws on these, and you just clamped them to your shoes. I was fifteen years old."

"I remember," said Uncle Luther. "They were my skates, and then I broke my kneecap and I couldn't skate anymore. I can almost remember the name."

"Peck & Snider," said Wash. "They were Peck & Snider skates. I skated whenever I didn't have chores. That March 10th, I skated for maybe I thought the last time that year, and I hung them on a nail over my bed in the loft when I got home. I was skating late, by the moon, after chores. My legs were good then. In the morning, I slept late — I was tired — and my father took my skates away because I was late for chores. That was the day it started to snow."

"What a terrible thing to do," said my grandfather.

"He took them out to the pond where I skated," said Wash, "and he made me watch. He cut a hole in the ice with his hatchet. It was snowing already. I begged him not to, but he dropped those Peck & Snider skates into the water, right down out of sight into Eagle Pond."

Uncle Luther shook his head. No one said anything. My father looked at the floor.

Washington was staring straight ahead, fifteen years old again and full of hatred. I could see his mouth moving inside the gray-brown beard. "We stayed inside for four days. Couldn't open a door for the snow. I always hated the snow. I had to keep looking at him."

After a minute when no one spoke, Aunt Caroline turned to me and talked about the presents under my tree, making silly guesses: "I bet that's a doll." I recognized diversionary tactics. Other voices took up separate conversations around the room. Then my mother leaped upon me, saying it was *two hours* past my bedtime, and in five minutes I was warming my feather bed, hearing the grown-up voices dim and far away like wind, like the wind and snow outside my window.

LINDA GRACE HOYER

Solace

Ada dropped a lighted match into the heap of Christmas paper at the edge of her woods and watched its flame consume the red tissue in which one of several gifts from her son, Christopher, had been wrapped. It was a clear day, with a stiff breeze from the northwest. She wore faded bluejeans with unravelling cuffs and a red mackinaw that had belonged to her husband, Marty. An inch of snow had fallen during the night and, against a cloudless sky, the balsam fir that Ada's mother had planted to add a touch of green to the gray woods in winter gently waved its wide branches. With snow on the ground and the wind coming the way it was, the risk of setting fire to the woods was minimal, Ada thought. But even while she prodded the pile of paper with a staff she sometimes used to steady her steps when walking outdoors, a green pickup truck turned in to her yard and Mr. Murdough, her nearest neighbor, jumped from the cab.

"I saw your fire," he said, "and thought it might be the woods."

"Oh, no, this is where I always burn the paper — very carefully," Ada said, and she turned to the youthful tricolored collie that earlier in the year she had bought from the custodian of the local animal shelter. "We love that woods, don't we, Peter Pup?"

"You know that woods has no fire lanes and there'd be no way for us to bring in a fire engine," Mr. Murdough said.

"I know that," Ada said. Mr. Murdough's unexpected arrival implied a need for his presence that Ada had not felt, and she did not smile.

"If you tell me where to find a bucket, I'll bring water from your spring, to douse the fire when you leave."

Though Ada previously had been unaware of Mr. Murdough's resemblance to her late husband, she noticed it now. Their straight blond hair, their deep-set hazel eyes and jutting jaws were similar. Especially like Marty was Mr. Murdough's determination to *help*.

The April that followed Marty's death, Mr. Murdough had driven his tractor into a field where Ada was hand-raking newly turned ground prior to planting peas in it and, above the roar of the engine, shouted, "That's not the kind of work you should be doing. It's too hard for you." There had been no time for Ada to explain that on account of a recent thunderstorm the soil was too wet to be worked any way but by hand. Looking as determined as Marty might have under the same circumstances, Mr. Murdough had sent the tractor careering back and forth, while she stood by and saw her garden ruined. Then, without speaking, Mr. Murdough had driven away, and Ada, rake in hand, had retired from the field. To this winter day, eight and a half years later, Ada had not returned to plant peas, though in summer she drove her own tractor-drawn mower into that field to cut a tangle of red clover and Queen Anne's lace that grew where peas might have grown.

In the face of Mr. Murdough's present determination, Ada managed a smile that felt dry, if not actually forced. "The spring is so close," she said. "I'll douse the fire, if necessary."

"Are you alone, Ada?"

"Yes, Mr. Murdough. I'm alone."

"I thought Christopher might've come. For Christmas."

"It's a long way for him to come, and I don't mind being alone on Christmas — or any day. In fact, I enjoy being alone. After all, we'll all be alone in our caskets."

"I've never thought of that, Ada, and I'm not sure that you should have."

"I often attend my funeral in imagination. It can make Christmas alone seem happy."

"I'll suggest it as an exercise for my mother the next time she complains of being left alone. My father, as you know, was no saint."

"And now she thinks he was? A saint?"

"Yes."

"I know how that is."

"But Marty *was* a saint."

"Not quite," Ada said.

"I never heard him say an unkind word about anybody."

"I did."

"He was a great man."

"He was a singular man, with the ability to lead his students and acquaintances to accept their own singularity. That is a rare gift."

"Mother worries about you — all alone."

"Tell her not to worry. The Wertz sisters have invited me to share their Christmas dinner. And tell her to be glad that her son lives so close."

"Be careful when you drive today. There's ice under the snow."

"You take care, and have a merry Christmas."

"A merry Christmas to you, too." Briskly, Mr. Murdough returned to his truck and started in the direction of his mother's house with Peter Pup barking, leading the way.

A family of yellow jackets had nested during the summer in the ground not far from where Ada stood with her back to the fire, and the sharp stinging pain in her right ankle recalled summer's several clashes with its members; indeed, Ada would have been no more surprised to see a yellow jacket taking leave of her than she had been by Mr. Murdough's arrival a few minutes earlier. Widowhood, it seemed to her, was more surprising than her marriage had ever been.

What Ada saw when she looked down was not an angry yellow jacket but a fringe of flame where the right cuff of her bluejeans had been.

To Marty, an unexpectedly painful happening had been either "a new experience," and therefore a kind of "blessed event," or, as the blooming rhodora had been for Emerson, "its own excuse for being." Though disinclined to share Marty's stoical acceptance of surprises, Ada managed to bow from the waist and, with callused hands and a wry smile, stifle the flame. That done, she called the dog and went into the house with him. At this point, as she saw it, there was no need to douse the trash pile.

After her father's death, Ada had carried upstairs the cushioned maple chair she had given him for Christmas in 1934 and set it at the head of Christopher's bed. Abandoned, the bed and chair waited with an expectant air in the bedroom where Christopher had slept. Actually, they had the look Ada saw, on her way down the hall, reflected in her bathroom mirror. It was the look of a person who, although obviously of less use than she formerly was, continued to expect well of the future. Holding the medicine-cabinet door open, Ada was relieved to see that a magazine clipping Marty had pasted inside long ago was still there. She read it aloud while Peter Pup listened: " 'Whether caused by flame or chemicals, a burn should be flooded with water immediately for approximately fifteen minutes. A burn caused by chemicals should be examined by a doctor as soon as possible.'

"The treatment will be simple as taking a bath," he said, and, having closed the medicine-cabinet door, she opened both spigots of the bathtub. Much simpler, surely, than the application of apple butter and sliced raw potatoes, tied on with strips of an old sheet, that her mother had used when Ada had burned her arms in hot corn mush. How old had she been at the time? Three, perhaps? Ada remembered, as though it had happened today, the corn's color — pure gold — in an iron kettle on the arrow-backed chair. She remembered, too, how, after an awkward struggle with the bandages, her mother, who seldom had time to hold her, had taken her onto her lap and held her there until the pain was gone. Compared with that pain, the pricklings Ada felt while bathing her ankle were a discomfort, nothing more.

Ada was in the tub when the phone rang. "That's Lucy Wertz calling to say, 'Are you still alive?'" Ada told Peter Pup. And when, nude and waterlogged, she climbed from the tub and crossed the hall to answer the phone, she found that the caller was indeed Lucy Wertz.

"Were you at the barn?" said Lucy.

"No, I was taking a bath."

"In that case, you should have your breathing fixed, Ada."

"After the pulmonary lab tests, Dr. Hutchinson told me not to worry about my slight emphysema."

"Then perhaps you need an evaluation of your heart."

"Have you forgotten the Holter monitor I wore for one whole day last year, and the digitalis Dr. Razzano prescribed?"

"You may need another prescription."

"Right now what I need is a towel."

"You are coming to have dinner with us, aren't you?"

"Yes, after I'm dressed. If I'm not there by twelve, start dinner without me. Mr. Murdough was here and said there are patches of ice under the blowing snow."

"We've seen a car go by the house this morning. The road is open."

Ada didn't argue with her. Never having learned to drive, the Wertz sisters had sold their husbands' automobiles and forgotten the difficulties of driving in wintertime completely, so that nothing Ada might have said on that subject would have been useful.

"We'll pray that you have a safe trip," Lucy said, adding, "Jane's hungry."

"I'll try to be there by twelve," Ada said.

At ten minutes before twelve, Lucy Wertz, seeing Ada's blue compact in the snow-covered driveway beside the house, opened the back door and, with a delight so shrill that a stranger unaccustomed to Lucy's way of greeting visitors might have fled to the safety of the woods, said, "Merry Christmas, Ada. It's good to see you."

Familiar though Ada was with Lucy's greetings, they surprised her, so that without a word she followed Lucy into the kitchen, where Jane was turning the yams in a glaze of butter and sugar.

There, in the voice that a moment before had welcomed Ada, Lucy said, "Go on into the living room and wait until dinner is ready." To reinforce her command, Lucy led the way and, from the center of the room, said, "Sit down and *read* until I call you."

"In which one of the chairs would you like me to sit?" Ada asked, remembering Marty's saying to her, "You can take the girl out of the country, but you can't take the country out of the girl." Lucy, Baltimore-born and for forty years a teacher in the public schools of that city, was trying to take the country out of the girl Ada no longer was.

Lucy said, "You may sit wherever you like."

But, of course, nothing could have been less true. If given her own choice of a place to sit, Ada would have stayed in the kitchen, where Jane was turning the yams in their glaze of butter and sugar.

"Then I'll sit here," Ada said, moving toward a very old Windsor chair with the patina of age and its frailty.

"That will be all right." The words came slowly, as though Lucy, knowing Ada's weight, would have preferred to have her sit on the davenport. But then, speaking crisply, she said, *"Read this,"* and left Ada on her own.

The magazine that Lucy handed to Ada was a monthly publication intended to advertise the virtues of that branch of Protestantism of which the Wertz sisters were members, and Ada dropped it, unopened, on the neat pile of magazines from which Lucy had taken it. That done, she sat down in the old Windsor chair and turned a critical eye on her surroundings.

The room was one she had known in childhood and remembered with great affection, because at that time a favorite aunt and uncle had owned the house and during her mother's illnesses had offered Ada the solace she needed. Later, when her mother had recovered, Ada went to visit Uncle Nathan and Aunt Elizabeth with her parents. On those festive occasions, she had been allowed to stay in the kitchen while meals were being prepared and, best of all, encouraged to feel that her being there was *helpful.* "Will you bring the balloon-backed chairs from the parlor?" Aunt Elizabeth would say if her sons were at home from the city and extra chairs were needed for the table. Or in warm weather, when milk and butter had to be refrigerated in the spring ditch, she would say, "Run for the butter and cream, Ada. The dinner is almost ready."

It seemed to Ada that all that was bright and warm in her memories of childhood had happened in this room. Now the room — with its newly plastered white walls and precious Persian rug — was bright without being warm. It was extraordinarily neat. But, remembering it as it had been seventy years ago, she resented this neatness. Both the piano and the bookcase were gone, along with Uncle Nathan's Boston rocker, where Aunt Elizabeth sat to mend his socks by the light of a huge kerosene lamp. Gone, too, was the horsehair sofa — that wonder of slippery elegance — where Ada herself sat while her cousin Mordecai played the piano. The room had held a round stove, with nickel-plated extensions to warm cold feet. And Ada had not wanted to be in the kitchen.

Her wait, happily, was not long, and when she joined Lucy and Jane in the dining room her plate had been filled.

"We prefer chicken to turkey," Jane said. "We hope you do, too."

"I like both. And this looks lovely," Ada said.

"Harvey liked ham," Lucy said. "What did Marty like?"

"Hamburger with cream sauce," Ada said.

"Bless his heart."

Seeing that the sisters had closed their eyes and bowed their heads in the silent blessing ordinarily asked by them, Ada inaudibly said, "Dear Lord, bless this house and help me to get home."

When their plates were as clean as good appetites could make them, Jane passed the fruitcake and Christmas cookies, while Lucy brought hot water to make instant coffee in their expectant cups. Meanwhile, Ada wondered who now alive in this world could bake mince pie the way her mother had.

Later, when the table had been cleared and Ada spoke of leaving, Lucy said, "Why, child? You've hardly said a word. You must tell us how Peter Pup is."

"Peter Pup is fine."

"And you?"

"I'm lucky to be here."

"Aren't we all?" Lucy said. "It's so *beautiful* here."

Jane, with a faraway look in her eyes, agreed, and said, "Yes, it is beautiful here. I was born in the middle class and expect to stay in it."

Taken by surprise, Ada laughed. "Middle class" was a term she seldom used, and if anyone had asked her where in America's complicated society she belonged, she almost certainly would have said, "I don't know."

Once, years ago, at a picnic on the church lawn, after telling Ada that both of her parents had migrated from Berlin to Baltimore, Lucy asked, with an anxious look, "You are *German*, aren't you?"

Ada said, "My father told me that we can't measure a snake while it's running." Remembering her rudeness on that occasion and hoping to make amends now, Ada said to Lucy, "I caught fire this morning."

"How, child?" Lucy and Jane said together.

"I was burning trash where I always do, and watching Peter Pup herding Mr. Murdough into his truck, when the fire took hold of my jeans."

"What did you do? Did you roll on the ground? Did you call Mr. Murdough?" They spoke as one person and that one Lucy.

"I smothered the flame with my hands."

"How could you?"

"Easily. It was a small flame, and I was lucky."

"Yes, you were lucky."

"And now I really must be going. I'm expecting Christopher to call."

"We'll call tonight to see how you are."

Ada wanted to tell Lucy that another interrogation on the subject of her health would be an invasion of privacy but found herself saying, "Thanks for the lovely dinner. It made a perfect day."

"Come back soon," Lucy said. "Be sure to drive carefully."

On the ice of the Wertz sisters' driveway the wheels of Ada's car spun for some time before she reached the sun-dried road. She was still ten miles from home and knew that snow had drifted into the road along the way. There was one small plain where, having had previous experiences with snowdrifts, Ada expected her car to stall, but when she got there, instead of a snowdrift she found two neat piles of snow, with the road, clear as could be, between them.

Seeing the green truck up the road, she knew that the man leaning on his shovel in the truck's shadow was Mr. Murdough. He was smiling in the complacent way that Marty smiled when, another day of teaching behind him, he walked from his parked car across the lawn toward their back porch.

Ada stopped her car. "What do I owe you, Mr. Murdough, for opening the road?" she asked.

"That's what neighbors are for."

"In that case, thank you *very* much. I want to be home by the time Christopher calls."

"You'll have no trouble from here on."

"You're a saint."

"Any time you need help — day or night — call me," Mr. Murdough said as Ada's car gathered speed.

Words like "That's what neighbors are for" were part of the local language and not to be taken without a grain of salt. They were, however, a comfort to hear. At home, Peter Pup would be waiting, and that, too, was a solacing thought.

When Christopher called, Ada was resting in the kitchen with the dog. When she told Christopher that on that very day both Mr. Murdough and a fire had visited her, he asked, "Was the fire Mr. Murdough's fault? Did he push you toward the trash pile?" Christopher's voice suggested a blend of genuine concern and amusement.

This was a form of banter she had used when Christopher was a child and he, out of a sense of loyalty — or was it fear? — still used.

"Have you seen a doctor?" Christopher wanted to know.

"On Christmas?"

"How *is* your health, Mother?"

"You know my heart is damaged?"

"I know. Dr. Hutchinson told me."

"And there is lung damage, too, and a considerable loss of memory."

"The way you describe it, it almost sounds like fun."

"But none of my doctors look amused when they see me. Have I lived too long?"

"Certainly not," Christopher said with conviction.

"That's *nice* to know."

"We'll talk again on New Year's Day, Mother. In the meantime, don't stand too close to the fire."

"Thanks for being a good boy, Christopher," Ada said, and settled the receiver back in its cradle.

Peter Pup, relieved of the obligation to eavesdrop, went to his nest and, with a deep sigh, curled up to sleep. Ada, after going to the window and making certain that it was the evening sun and not a brush fire burning among the gray trees beyond the old fir, turned on her radio and sat down to hear the last of the Christmas music. A shadow of the barn lay on the field, where fringes of dry buck grass moved like the gentle flame that had felt like the sting of a yellow jacket and, like the pain of a yellow jacket's sting, was soon gone.

WILL STANTON

The Trail of Ernestine

lthough there isn't a name for them they make up a distinct species — small, but once you've been exposed to them, unmistakable.

They are the lost ones — women alone who drive an old car and have come to stay.

Their clothes are strange and somewhat tacky, but nobody minds because they got them in Brussels and Guatemala. They have the scent of sandalwood and faraway places. They find beauty in stones.

They are disdainful of material things, their paths marked by a comet's tail of possessions left behind, so months — years — after their passing, people find themselves packing a Mexican loom to mail.

Friends of some relative, they wander into your life as

casually as a stray pup and as easily capture the hearts of the young. Then — equally casual — they wander away. The one who wandered into our life was named Ernestine.

"After all, it's Christmas," Dolores said, "and we have the station wagon." I didn't argue.

"Christmas," I said, "by George, you're right. It's this month, isn't it?"

Dolores had a cookbook open on the kitchen table and little packages of green and red things spread around. Candied something or other.

"I'd go myself," Dolores said, "but it's only four days to Christmas and you can see what I still have to do."

I got up. "If I've got to go all the way to Titusville, I'd better get started."

It was the day of the big game on TV, but I didn't mention it. I expect a lot of men would have made a big thing out of it — let their wives know they'd spoiled the whole day for them — but I like to think I'm a little above that. I went upstairs to put on some shoes. No — I'd go without a word. It would be my little Christmas present to Dolores.

When I came downstairs Paula was there from next door.

"Well," she said, "you all set? Your present for Dolores all picked out?"

"Since last August," I said.

Dolores dropped her cookbook. "Since when?"

"You remember," I said, "when the washer was acting up and I said we couldn't afford a new one. And you said —"

"I said we could charge the washer and call it my Christmas present. And here I was afraid you'd forgotten."

"Look," I said, "do you want me to go or don't you?"

Paula took up an apple and took a bite. "Where are you going?"

"Titusville," I said. "A seventy-mile round trip to pick up a whatnot left there by a woman that called me a mercenary —"

"Ernestine," Paula said, looking pleased, "for heaven's sake, where is she? I haven't thought of her in ages."

"She's staying with this elderly couple in Elmhurst," Dolores said, "and she wanted to make it a nice Christmas for them — Pursefolder, Pennyfoot — it's sort of a strange name."

"Pursefolder?" I said, "what's strange about that?"

"Please shut up," Dolores said. "Anyhow, Ernestine had all these Christmas decorations and other things that she took to Titusville when she left here. And when she left Titusville it was in the middle of the night and she only took what she could carry — two suitcases and the cat."

"Is that the same cat she had when she was here?" Paula asked. "The one that bit Avery?"

"It wasn't the cat that bit Avery," Dolores said, "it was the parrot. The one she was keeping for that woman from West Virginia."

"Oh, for god's sake," I said. There were probably a dozen people engaged in shifting around Ernestine's possessions in a never ending chess game.

"There's no need for such a mood," Dolores said, "just because I asked you to do something. Besides there's a special satisfaction that comes from giving of yourself so here's your chance."

"Didn't I say I'd do it?"

"Yes, but you don't want to."

"That makes it even better."

She said I had no idea of the Christmas spirit.

"Look," I said, "you take a fellow that's got better things to do — watching a special football game or whatever — but he goes anyhow. That's what you call giving of yourself."

She looked over at Paula shaking her head. "Lucy wants to go along," she said to me. "I have a whole list of errands and I've gone over it with her so she knows all the details. Besides, she wants to see Ernestine."

"Wouldn't Lucy rather stay home?" I asked. "She was saying she had all these exams —"

"That was in November," she said. "What you're saying is you don't want to spend the afternoon with your own daughter."

When we stopped for gas, Lucy asked if she could have a soda. "You just finished your lunch," I said, "for heaven's sake. It's going to be a long ride and I'm not going to buy you something to eat or drink every time we stop." She said she had her own money.

"You can have a soda and that's it," I said. "Don't ask for anything else."

The man at the station said the oil was down two quarts. "You're overdue for a change," he said. I told him to put in one quart. The cheapest.

I walked back and kicked the rear tire. I could feel the slush seeping through my shoes and suddenly, for the first time, it really seemed like Christmas. The torn banner flapping over the station, the woodsy scent of antifreeze as the out-of-state cars got their radiators topped off. The memories came flooding back like the ghost of Christmas Past — standing in slush with barely enough money to cover my shopping list and having somebody tell me I needed an oil change — a new battery.

Of course there was something special about the old-time Christmas. We kids used to love to hear my grandmother tell about cutting down their own tree and decorating it with real candles. But any time I start telling the kids about the old days, Lucy picks up a magazine and Avery starts to scratch.

The back seat was full of packages. Lucy had the list of what went where and how to get there. She had one package all wrapped up that she was holding. For Ernestine she said.

"You were pretty fond of her I guess."

"She was nice." Lucy smiled at the package, straightening the ribbon. "I used to go down to her room in the evening and we'd talk — about art, nature — I don't know. She made it seem like everything in life could be so much more exciting — more fun."

She could make things look good, I'll say that. We'd met her through Dolores' cousin — she didn't have any place to stay and we had room, so there was that to start with. She was going to teach the kids Spanish and art and look after the house while Dolores worked at the gift shop.

Then — well, I had to lend her money to have her things shipped in from Indiana. And it turned out she didn't know any more Spanish than I did. She turned on the broiler to warm the cat's food and left it on all day. Etc.

Lucy was gazing out the window. "She taught me to see things I'd never seen before. She put up a bird feeder outside the window and got notebooks for Avery and I to write down all the different kinds. I had eleven names and then you tore the feeder down."

The thing was Ernestine had gotten interested in making pottery and stopped putting out bird food. I bought it and left the bag in plain sight, but I'd come home from work and the birds would be there in the feeder pecking at the bare boards and looking in the window. I fed them when I could, but when I couldn't get home in time I'd picture them sitting there, waiting. So I took the feeder down. By then my reputation was beyond repair.

We located the Winkler house and I let Lucy run in with a basket of preserves. Mrs. Winkler called to me from the porch, "If you two aren't a couple of Santa's helpers," she said, "coming all the way out here to see an old lady." I told her we were just passing by, but she didn't seem to hear.

Back in the car Lucy gave a satisfied sigh. "I think that's the best part of Christmas — giving things to people who really appreciate them."

"It's always nice to be appreciated."

She looked at me. "You don't have any Christmas spirit at all, do you?"

"It doesn't make any difference," I said, "as long as I deliver the goods — get the job done."

"Oh sure," she said. "You had to buy a new washing machine anyway, so you call it Mom's Christmas present." I wasn't expecting flattery. Lucy never approved of anything I did.

"How many more stops?" I asked.

"There's the difference," she said. "To you this is just a chore. To Mom it's fun getting together things to give others — a privilege." She was staring out at the passing billboards. "There are two kinds of people in the world," she observed, "those who put up bird feeders and those who tear them down." Her voice had the self-satisfied note of one who has just originated a quotation.

"That package you've got," I said, "something special for Ernestine?"

"Special?" she asked, "I guess. Last year she gave me a locket of hers — a family heirloom. And I gave her a hundred-year-old pewter candlestick."

I gave a whistle. "A hundred years — that's a real antique."

"She seemed real pleased — said she'd keep it with her very special keepsakes. But then she said it wasn't being old that made it so special, it was because I had picked it out. It wasn't the gift, she said, it was the thought behind it."

"Very true," I said. This was an expression like "after all it's Christmas," that covered many bad guesses. It was the three wise men that started it when they decided that frankincense and myrrh would be just the ticket for a newborn babe. As they said, it wasn't the gift. Matter of fact the thought behind it wouldn't have taken any prizes either. But it was the start of a tradition. I've never received any frankincense or myrrh, but I've gotten a lot of presents just about that handy.

"By the way," I said, "about the washer — I don't want you to get the idea that's the only present Mom's getting."

"You mean the stationery, the candy and bath salts?"

I turned to look at her. "How did you know about those?"

"It's what you give her every year."

"All right, that's sort of a tradition," I said, "but it so happens I'm giving her something special. A new percolator."

"Oh wow," Lucy said.

"Oh wow, my elbow," I said. "Do you happen to know what a fully-automatic electric percolator costs these days?"

"That's your answer to every question," she said, "always money."

"If you can get other people to change the questions," I said, "I'll be happy to change the answers."

"Ernestine never made more than $1,000 a year in her life. But she didn't consider that a handicap. It never stopped her from doing things for others."

"That's great," I said. "Anybody that can get along without money these days can teach us all something." Ernestine didn't have groceries to buy or a phone bill to pay. Not that she didn't use the phone — it seemed all her friends were in places like Arkansas and Utah. And if I said anything about the bill that was like one vote against friendship.

Lucy was gazing ahead. "She showed me how you could find beauty wherever you looked."

"Couldn't agree with you more."

"It's easy for you to say it," Lucy told me, "living it is something else."

This was one reason I was never real eager to go riding with Lucy. I had to spend all my time defending myself and kept running stop signs.

"She made me feel special. She always told me to walk proud."

"I've told you the same thing."

"You tell me not to slouch," she said, "it isn't the same thing."

Every so often the woman would turn out to be right. It was one of her most maddening qualities. A person who's always wrong is easier to forgive.

We found the Schaeffer house without any trouble. "And what is Ernestine up to these days?" Mrs. Schaeffer asked.

I said we didn't know. "We haven't seen her in a year. We just came to get her things."

"Good." She turned to Lucy. "And this must be Caroline." No Lucy said thinly, she wasn't.

"Oh. Well, you'll have to meet my Babs. She and Ernestine were real close. At the first, anyhow." She went to the stairway and called. Babs was a bulky, unblinking child with thick braids.

"Ernestine and I had a secret code," she told Lucy, "did she teach it to you?" Lucy said no. "That's what I thought."

Ernestine's things were in her room over the garage — a rocker, the decorations and the what-not. In one corner was a contraption that turned out to be a puppet theater. There had been some effort to decorate the room, spruce it up and make it look less like a garage.

"We were going to have a puppet theater," Babs said, "like a club. Some were working on costumes and scenery and I was writing a play. But she left before it was finished."

"There must be books on puppets," I said. "No reason you couldn't go ahead with your show."

"Who cares?"

Driving away I noticed that Lucy seemed unusually silent. "Too bad they never got that puppet theater finished," I said. "I was thinking our basement would be a great place for one."

Lucy wasn't thinking about puppets. "Ernestine called her Princess," she said. "That girl. She showed me a card from her — a birthday card."

"She have any special name for you?" I asked.

After a minute she said: "Lucia."

"Say," I said, "I like that. Loo-chee-a. Got a good classy ring to it." She didn't say anything. "People name their cats Princess," I said. She still didn't say anything, but after a minute I glanced over and she was smiling.

"To you," I said, "maybe a percolator doesn't seem like much of a present. But the one we've got doesn't shut off — keeps on boiling the coffee. And the handle's all wired together."

She was looking at the windshield but seeing far beyond. "Ernestine said you should never give a wedding present that somebody might buy anyway — like for the house. Give something that speaks from the heart — a flower — a single pearl."

"That handle," I said, "I bet your mother's burned herself many times."

We found the Elmhurst address with no trouble and the old couple were home. Mr. and Mrs. Prufrock.

"Well, isn't it a shame," Mrs. Prufrock said, "going to all that trouble and now Ernestine isn't here."

I asked where she was. "Santa Fe," Mr. Prufrock said.

"We had the guest room all fixed up," Mrs. Prufrock said, "and then she got a phone call. She just packed up and left — two suitcases and a cardboard box. As if she'd never been here."

"Borrowed four dollars from me," Mr. Prufrock said.

"She left a magazine rack with a whole raft of magazines — a pair of arctics, African violets — "

"Cabbage slicer," Mr. Prufrock said.

"A cabbage slicer," she said, "and I don't know what all. That candlestick there on the table."

"And here we come with a whole lot more," I said. They didn't mind though, they had plenty of storage space. Mrs. Prufrock admired the rocker, said it was the very image of the one her Aunt Julia had.

"Might as well enjoy it," I said. "And here's a waffle iron — good as new. She left it behind and the people there didn't want it."

You would have thought I'd given them something precious. "We'll think of you whenever we use it," she said. I told her that wasn't necessary.

"Here," Lucy held out her package, "this is for you."

"Well now," Mrs. Prufrock said, "forever more." She turned to her husband. "Did you ever?" He said no. We all said Merry Christmas a few times and left.

There was no conversation for the first few miles. Then I said, "That was real nice — giving them that present."

"I hope they like it," Lucy said, "the candlestick too."

I'd spotted the candlestick the minute we'd stepped into the room, but I'd hoped Lucy might not notice.

She was looking down at her hands. "I only wish Ernestine had been there when I gave it to them — so she could see I didn't care. Not a bit."

"I know."

She shook her head. "Boy, how dumb can you get? I kept thinking of the time she was with us as something special — like Camelot sort of. And now —"

"No reason for you to think any different," I said. "The things about Ernestine that you liked haven't changed."

"I don't know why you're sticking up for her; you never did like her."

True. And at that point I liked her even less. Still there were the feelings she'd brought out in Lucy — her affection

— her loyalty — these seemed sort of precious to me. I didn't want to see them scrapped. "When Ernestine came to stay with us," I said, "she didn't have any people or any place to go. We took her in and you were her friend. Now she's on a bus somewhere with a couple of suitcases and a cardboard box, going to move in with somebody else — hoping to find another friend. And I think if she finds as good a friend as you were, she'll be pretty lucky."

After a moment she looked up at me. "Sometimes it's hard to tell whose side you're on."

"Sometimes it's hard for me too." I pulled up in front of a drugstore. "I want to get a paper — why don't you come in and we'll have a soda?"

She was starting to get out when she noticed the neon of the bar next door. "You never drink soda," she said. "Why don't you have a beer? I don't mind waiting in the car."

"I'm not in the habit of letting my dates wait in the car," I said.

"I'm sorry," Dolores said. "I had no idea it would take you so long."

"We would have been earlier," I said, "only Lucy and I stopped in a bar."

Dolores grinned. "That'll be the day." She turned to Lucy who had just come in. "Hi! Dinner won't be for a while — why don't you have a soda or something?"

"No thanks," Lucy started upstairs. "Dad and I stopped in a bar."

After a moment Dolores started nodding her head. Very slowly. "There was a football game on TV," she said, "a playoff. I made you miss it."

"I put oil in the car."

"I made you drive all over," she said, "on a wild goose chase, and you don't even act mad."

"After all," I said, "it's Christmas."

"And now —"

"It comes but once a year."

"I know," she said. "You take your daughter into a saloon —"

"We had a nice talk. She helped me decide on your present."

"My present —"

"It isn't the gift," I said, "it's the thought behind it."

She came over and took me by the shoulders, resting her head against me. "I can't get over this feeling," she said, "that the things I've always counted on are all crumbling down around me."

She was joking of course. Still, I know what she meant. We like to feel secure — to know the people around us will always stay just the way they are.

On the other hand, a little change is sometimes a good thing. Which is why I decided to surprise Dolores for Christmas. After I'd bought the stationery and the bath salts, I recalled what Lucy had said about a present that speaks from the heart. So I searched around and bought her a single perfect red rose. I put it inside the percolator.

ANNIE DILLARD

Feast Days: Christmas

Let me mention
one or two things about Christmas.
Of course, you've all heard
that the animals talk
at midnight:
a particular elk, for instance,
kneeling at night to drink,
leaning tall to pull leaves
with his soft lips,
says, alleluia.

That the soil and freshwater lakes
also rejoice,
as do products

such as sweaters
(nor are plastics excluded
from grace),
is less well known.
Further:
the reason
for some silly-looking fishes,
for the bizarre mating
of certain adult insects,
or the sprouting, say,
in a snow tire
of a Rocky Mountain grass,
is that the universal
loves the particular,
that freedom loves to live
and live fleshed full,
intricate, and in detail.

God empties himself
into the earth like a cloud.
God takes the substance, contours
of a man, and keeps them,
dying, rising, walking
and still walking
wherever there is motion.

At night in the ocean
the sponges are secretly building.
Once, on the Musselshell,
I regenerated an arm!
Shake hands. When I stand
the blood runs up.

On what bright wind
did God walk down?
Swaying under the snow,
reeling minutely,
revels the star-moss,
pleased.

C. TERRY CLINE, JR.

Epiphany

He was on Fifth Avenue because he had nowhere to go, walking to keep warm, alone in a crowd. George Harcourt caught a glimpse of himself in a pane of glass and the visage made him halt, staring at the residue of a man he had become. Beyond his image, in the department store window, a North Pole scene with Santa and his elves fashioning toys for good girls and boys.

Christmas.

Once a year it came to remind him of eleven months of failure. The times he'd had money on the eve of Christmas were so few he could remember them vividly.

Well, *not vividly*. But he remembered them.

One year before Elaine died, he managed to give her

everything she wanted — every tiny gift on her list.

By that time, of course, she wanted considerably less. She no longer jokingly asked for trips around the world or expensive furs and automobiles. The reality of his failures and her illness had reduced her wish list to nightgowns, slippers, roses in December.

He twisted away from the memory without moving a muscle. His insides contorted as he watched the robot Santa and the fixed smiles of the mannequin elves responding to some mechanical turn.

In the window he saw the reflection of sixty-eight years of Christmas. Sixty-eight years. His form was bent, the tattered coat collar turned up against bitter cold, his worn muffler wrapped around his neck so only his eyes and forehead showed. Beside him, a child squealed with glee, pointing at the Santa Claus laughing as he held his belly, the happy elves at work by rote, hammering, sawing. A red cellophane fire in a mock hearth gave warmth to the scene.

Somewhere amid the crowd of last minute shoppers, another Santa, this one the supplicant, rang his bell in hopes of attracting coins for his kettle.

When the wind came up the man-made canyon of tall buildings, it brought snow in swirls that burned the flesh and dried the eyes. Icy particles nipped his ears despite the scarf. His breath had condensed in the wool, frozen only to thaw with his exhalations, giving a frosty beard to the fabric covering his mouth and chin.

"Coldest night this year," someone said, in passing.

"Merry Christmas!"

Tinkling bells jingled over hurried passersby; only a few paused to watch, along with George, the artificial fire and laboring elves.

He shuffled his feet, bones aching with that arthritic thrum that comes in winter. An exposed nail in the sole of his shoe rasped concrete as he moved. He wrapped his coat more tightly, preserving the last warm blood he had.

"Merry Christmas!"

It had never been. Except the few times he had money. *Precious few.*

Things might've been different if he'd married Janet Longstreet. Her laughing blue eyes and radiant smile would have been bestowed upon children — they would've lived in a house in a neighborhood filled with laughing eyes and radiant smiles.

Her parents forbade it. He never saw her again. Then, when he married Elaine, it was for the practical matter of doing what was right, nothing concerning the heart.

The irony was, the baby died.

"But I do love you, George," she sometimes pressed.

Him? The failure, repeated failure that he was?

He lingered at the department store entrance, warm air purling around his body, a delicious aroma emerging through revolving doors. The smells of Christmas! Roasted nuts in a specialty shop. The rich Caribbean scent of coffee in another shop next door. The tantalizing fragrance from a delicatessen; the smell of the people — powdered and perfumed and cleansed for the holidays; lotions and musks, creams and oils to soften chafed flesh and smooth the tone of skin.

"Buy you a cup of coffee, old timer?"

He turned with two small steps to gaze at a stranger. *A dollar.* "God bless, sir."

"Merry Christmas."

He called after the donor, "God bless, sir!"

A moment later the doorman of the department store came forward, insisting, "Move along, move along."

So he did. Feet shuffling, the snow rising in tiny white tornadoes, the street glistening with the melt, lights glowing through the corona of icy precipitation.

The sounds of Christmas: taxi tires singing, the occasional toot of a horn, the babble of a million voices rising in a constant drone from avenues and streets, from markets and sidewalks. "Merry Christmas!" some called. "Season's Greetings!" the reply.

Sleigh bells and church chimes and theatrical organs segued from one carol to the next, "Jingle bells . . . Jingle bells . . ."

He couldn't blame Elaine for this. He couldn't blame anyone, but himself. Although he tried. The banker who would not refinance loans, forcing him to insolvency, the broker who defaulted on his debts to George; the vagaries of business, the demands upon a gentle soul in a commercial sea of sharks.

"You keep doing what you hate, George," Elaine would reason. "Do what you most want to do — then, even if you fail, you will have enjoyed it. Life is too short, George — too short."

Sixty-eight years.

Too short. Elaine was right. Too brief.

He moved away from the bright lights of window displays, taking a cross street toward the bus terminal where a dollar would buy two donuts and a cup of coffee, refill free. It was one of the few places that tolerated him for the time it took to spend the money he had.

His hands were so cold, he lifted one clenched fist to see, for certain, the crumpled dollar was still there.

"Merry Christmas!" a youthful choir seemed to tumble around him, faces burnished by clime and time, cheeks red, eyes alight. They said to everyone, "Merry Christmas!"

In lieu of children, since there were none, Elaine had taken to her breast the curs and mongrels of the world, their house overflowing with abandoned pets under her charge. She decked the tree and decorated the house, wreaths on the door and seraphs hung by threads from the chandelier and fireplace mantel.

"Christmas is for sharing, George," she would explain. "We have no one to share with, except these unfortunate animals."

She shared with people too. Half of the pitiful little they possessed, Elaine would share when need was known.

When he reached Broadway, a small band from the Salvation Army played to the moving crowd as if it were a river flowing around the musicians, too busy to stop, caught in currents of time and preoccupation. George waited for their next selection. A young woman in the Army uniform warmed a brass mouthpiece under one arm so the metal would not stick to her lips when next she played.

Silent night . . .

He had an instant memory of childhood: Mama delivering a turkey from the oven, juices flowing, the kitchen redolent with cinnamon and cranberries, mincemeat pies and pineapple used to garnish a baking ham.

Holy night . . .

In the living room, Papa always set up a manger with the Christ child in swaddling clothing, the figures of Joseph and Mary a prized family possession since grandfather brought them from England a generation ago.

All is calm . . .

That sudden still that came over a boisterous gathering, everybody holding hands, heads down, thankful for peace, health, and family.

All is bright . . .

Who could say then, in those golden days of youth, the cruelties life held for people who endured long enough? His brothers, Charles and Raymond, to die on opposite sides of a world at war, Mama and Papa, sister JoAnna.

Round yon virgin, mother and child . . .

Tears stung his eyes, listening, remembering Papa's sonorous prayer filled with thanks, "For us being together," he would pray, "for having one another," he would say.

Holy infant, so tender and mild . . .

The Nativity seemed to breathe in that moment long ago, the carved wooden faces reflecting the flicker of firelight. The crackle of logs a comforting snap and sizzle, the smell of burning wood a rapture to the nostrils.

Sleep in heavenly peace . . .

He tore himself away with a lurch, stumbling past the band, pushing through the hurried mass of people, his throat seared by sub-zero cold, the freezing tears forming lachrymal icicles in his woolen muffler.

How had he come to this? A bum, a worthless, penniless, unproductive bum! He had nobody — all dead, those related by blood, all estranged, those he'd once called friends.

He'd never had children, not after the first one died in birth, leaving him with Elaine who married him because it was "right" and not for love.

"Having children is an act of sharing," she would reason, but he could never afford it.

"It is the making of forever, George. It is the only hope of seeing the future, through the eyes of children."

He could scarcely support her. How could he support children?

She fed the dogs and cats, sang her Noëls to them. Yuletide greetings to birds in the feeder!

He reeled across the street, tires screeched, an angry voice cursed him, but he staggered on, between parked cars, onto the sidewalk, and leaned against a wall, weeping.

How had he come to this?

Christmas was the annual reminder of all he had failed to accomplish. He had always dreaded going home to Elaine, admitting once again he had nothing to give her. So he went to the bars and drank with like men of similar talent. After a few years, Elaine didn't miss him, dreaded to see him, and she hummed her Christmas tunes to canine and feline and tended her window aviary.

Damn him. Damn him!

He put a trembling hand to his face, his fingers so numb they felt alien wiping his eyes.

The dollar!

He turned the hand, looking, spun and retraced his steps. The dollar — gone!

"Merry Christmas!" a shout from passing smiling faces. "Merry Christmas!"

He hated it, hated the joyful voices, the tinkling bells, the lift in their steps, the light in children's eyes filled with hope and excitement! He loathed the exchange of gifts he'd never been able to give, the false surprise of a disappointed recipient as she unwrapped them — trifling — *damn him!*

The dollar was gone. In the halflight of midstreet he could not see even had it been there. Like everything else in life, he'd let it slip away.

The fall of snow was heavier, the hour later, people vanishing into buses, subways, taxis and automobiles.

Going home. With their gifts, to their loved ones. Going home.

He blew through his scarf into the curled fingers that had lost the dollar, trying to warm them.

Round walls and through the mesh of fire escapes came wind that seemed to whisper, *Silent night . . .*

He hugged the walls, feet scuffing, the exposed nail scratching the sidewalk. He had a favored grill several blocks from here. Out of the underground rose warm air currents that wrapped him in blankets of heat. He would sleep there tonight and, soon enough, Christmas would be gone for another year.

Holy night . . .

He gathered cardboard boxes from trash bins, dragging the larger of these to the latticework metal bed of his choosing.

All is calm, all is bright. . .

He constructed a tent of corrugated pressed board, two layers beneath and one above, surrounding himself with a teepee of boxes. Somewhere below, the subway trains rumbled and heat curled around him as he pulled the crates nearer, sheltering himself against the whining wind and whipping snow.

So cold. So achingly cold.

Sleep . . . in heavenly peace . . .

"Hello? Anybody in there? Hello?"

He pushed back boxes and looked up. *A woman.*

"Sir, we'd like you to come spend Christmas with us."

"Who?" he asked.

"It'll be warm," she promised. "There'll be all the food you want — come with me —"

He blinked against sleep, trying to see her better. The full moon was behind her head and — he laughed —

"You look as though you have a halo," he said.

She laughed, too, extending a hand. "Come have Christmas with us."

At curbside, an automobile rumbled softly, the exhaust making tiny puffs that wafted away and disappeared.

"Warmth," she coaxed, teasingly, "food, friends."

"I — my clothes — I'm not dressed for . . ."

"It doesn't matter," she said. "Come with me."

He shoved aside boxes and fearing her distaste, he wouldn't touch the hand she held out to him. He managed to get to his feet and into the front seat of the warm car, heat soothing his ankles, easing the ache of muscles.

He could see her no better by the dim green illumination of the dashboard, but to his eyes she was indeed an angel.

They crossed town, through a tunnel, into the countryside. George held his hands down to the auto heater, flexing his fingers.

"Where are we going?" he questioned.

Her smile *was* radiant. "You'll see."

Headlights brought passing scenes to brief display, snow giving the hills and valleys cleanliness and purity.

"How far is it?" he inquired.

She smiled again. Like all angels, she seemed familiar in her own cleanliness and purity.

"I'm so pleased I found you, George. Don't you remember me?"

His heart rose in a halting beat. "Remember?"

"My parents said we could not marry, George."

"Janet? Janet Longstreet?"

"We were so young, George. You know they were right. We would have destroyed ourselves had we married. But I've thought of you often."

"Janet, I — my clothes — the reason I look like this . . ."

"It doesn't matter, George," she said, and somehow the way she said it made it seem true.

"When we didn't marry, I met Elaine . . ."

"Was she a good wife?"

Good? She was never unfaithful. She stood by him when he failed. She urged him to try again, always. She forgave his weaknesses, suffered his remorse.

"Yes," he said. "She was a good wife."

"Then you must have been a good husband, George."

"I never could give her what she deserved."

"You gave yourself. That's all anyone wants of another."

"I meant . . ."

"I know what you meant," she smiled, beautiful as always.

"And, and, and you, Janet?"

"I'm pleased I found you, George."

She turned off the highway, taking a roadway that seemed vaguely reminiscent despite the humps and mounds of drifted snow cloaking everything.

"Here we are," she said, stopping the car. She bathed him in a smile. "They're expecting you, George."

"Who?" He wiped condensation from a window with one ragged sleeve, trying to see.

"Go on in, George. They're waiting."

"Who? Who is waiting?"

He heard laughter, a man's voice, and the car door flew open.

Charles? His brother, Charles?

Impossible! Charles died at Tarawa.

"Get out, come in!" his brother yelled. Charles always yelled when he was happy. He pulled George to his feet, rocking him in a hug. "Merry Christmas, George!"

Flustered, George turned to question Janet, but the car was driving away.

Home? This was home?

Charles held him with an arm around his shoulder, "Mom has a turkey you won't believe, George. It must weigh forty or fifty pounds."

"Mama? But — I can't go in like this."

"Like what?" Charles held him back, examining the tattered coat, the worn shoes.

"Mama to see me this way? I can't go in there."

"George, George," Charles laughed, that barrel-chested rumble of pleasure that was so uniquely his, "you never have understood, have you? It's you we want to share, George. Now come on in where it's warm."

"Mama!" his sister JoAnna's voice rose to a shrill and she leaped for him, swinging from his neck as she had as a child. "Mama! Come see who's here!"

"JoAnna, how? I don't understand."

The pungency of freshly cut fir made him take a quick breath. The Nativity scene was there, beside the tree, the fire crackling, a sputter of sap sizzling.

"Oh, George!" Mama and Papa, she with apron in hand, rushing to enfold him.

"Mama, about my clothes — let me explain —"

"George, do you think it matters?" Papa chided. "Come, come, now. This is Christmas. We thank God we can share."

Raymond — dead in France, 1944 — but there he was, holding George, the two of them crying, everybody watching, all forgiving.

"I didn't bring anything to give," George sobbed.

"You're here. *You*, George. That's enough."

The table was laden with delicacies, ham, turkey and dressing ready for ladles of mushroom sauce, cranberry relish being delivered by — "Elaine?"

"Yes, George. Look, we're together. Isn't it nice?"

"Yes, but how?"

She looked wonderful, slipping her arm around him as she always did when she had a secret to reveal.

"Your mother and I prepared your favorite dessert, George. See — mincemeat pie."

"Elaine, I would be wiser if we could, somehow, begin again. I know more about business, even in failure . . ."

She put a finger to his lips, quelling the thought.

They were a circle around him, the table waiting, logs in the fireplace sputtering with an escape of gases.

"This is what Christmas is all about," Mama said. "Being together with those we remember."

Without command, they linked hands and Papa bent his head in prayer.

". . . for health, for family, for peace . . ."

. . . heavenly peace . . .

"For one another," Papa said, "we give thanks."

. . . sleep . . . in heavenly . . . peace . . .

The growl of gears and a hiss of pneumatic brakes seared the clear morning air. Voices afar, the shudder of an engine, the slam of metal doors echoed against the walls of buildings.

"I hate these Christmas morning pickups," the attendant said, rolling the body off cardboard, onto a stretcher. "These poor bums, alone, freezing to death. It's depressing."

His companion, the driver, helped push the stretcher into the ambulance, and they shut the doors.

"Christmas Day. It shouldn't be so." They got into the vehicle.

The driver glanced back at the covered form.

"I like to think," he said, "it isn't bad. I like to think they've gone home for Christmas."

Sleep . . .

In heavenly peace . . .

Sleep.

TILLIE OLSEN

Dream-Vision

In the winter of 1955, in her last weeks of life, my mother — so much of whose waking life had been a nightmare, that common everyday nightmare of hardship, limitation, longing; of baffling struggle to raise six children in a world hostile to human unfolding — my mother, dying of cancer, had beautiful dream-visions — in color.

Already beyond calendar time, she could not have known that the last dream she had breath to tell came to her on Christmas Eve. Nor, concious, would she have named it so. As a girl in long ago Czarist Russia, she had sternly broken with all observances of organized religion, associating it with pogroms and wars; "mind forg'd manacles''; a repressive state. We did not observe religious holidays in her house.

Perhaps, in her last consciousness, she *did* know that the year was drawing towards that solstice time of the shortest light, the longest dark, the cruellest cold, when — as she had explained to us as children — poorly sheltered ancient peoples in northern climes had summoned their resources to make out of song, light, food, expressions of human love — festivals of courage, hope, warmth, belief.

It seemed to her that there was a knocking at her door. Even as she rose to open it, she guessed who would be there, for she heard the neighing of camels. (I did not say to her: "Ma, camels don't neigh.") Against the frosty lights of a far city she had never seen, "a city holy to three faiths," she said, the three wise men stood: magnificent in jewelled robes of crimson, of gold, of royal blue.

"Have you lost your way?" she asked, "Else, why do you come to me? I am not religious, I am not a believer."

"To talk with *you*, we came," the wise man whose skin was black and robe crimson, assured her, "to talk of whys, of wisdom."

"Come in then, come in and be warm — and welcome. I have starved for such talk."

But as they began to talk, she saw that they were not men, but women:

That they were not dressed in jewelled robes, but in the coarse everyday shifts and shawls of the old country women of her childhood, their feet wrapped round and round with rags for lack of boots; snow now sifting into the room;

That their speech was not highflown, but homilies; their bodies not lordly in bearing, magnificent, but stunted, misshapen — used all their lives as a beast of burden is used;

That the camels were not camels, but farm beasts, such as were kept in the house all winter, their white cow breaths steaming into the cold.

And now it was many women, a babble.

One old woman, seamed and bent, began to sing. Swaying, the others joined her, their faces and voices transfiguring as they sang; my mother, through cracked lips, singing too — a lullaby.

For in the shining cloud of their breaths, a baby lay, breathing the universal sounds every human baby makes, sounds out of which are made all the separate languages of the world.

Singing, one by one the women cradled and sheltered the baby.

"The joy, the reason to believe," my mother said, "the hope for the world, the baby, holy with possibility, that is all of us at birth." And she began to cry, out of the dream and its telling now.

"Still I feel the baby in my arms, the human baby," crying now so I could scarcely make out the words, "the human baby, before we are misshapen; crucified into a sex, a color, a walk of life, a nationality . . . and the world yet warrings and winter.

I had seen my mother but three times in my adult life, separated as we were by the continent between, by lack of means, by jobs I had to keep and by the needs of my four children. She could scarcely write English — her only education in this country a few months of night school. When at last I flew to her, it was in the last days she had language at all. Too late to talk with her of what was in our hearts; or of harms and crucifying and strengths as she had known and experienced them; or of whys and knowledge, of wisdom. She died a few weeks later.

She, who had no worldly goods to leave, yet left to me an inexhaustible legacy. Inherent in it, this heritage of summoning resources to make — out of song, food, warmth, expressions of human love — courage, hope, resistance, belief; this vision of universality, before the lessenings, harms, divisions of the world are visited upon it.

She sheltered and carried that belief, that wisdom — as she sheltered and carried us, and others — throughout a lifetime lived in a world whose season was, as still it is, a time of winter.

HELEN NORRIS

The Christmas Wife

His name was Tanner, a reasonable man in his early sixties, desiring peace, a measure of joy, and reassurance. All that was submerged. The tip of the iceberg was a seasoned smile that discouraged excesses and a way of looking, "That's fine but not today." His marriage had fitted him like a glove, but now his wife Florence was dead for three years. And so it came to pass that Christmas was a problem.

Not a large problem, but one that niggled when the weather turned and got a little worse with blackbirds swarming in the elm trees, on the move. And here he was looking out at the falling leaves, chewing his November turkey in a restaurant down the block, and going nowhere. Except to his son's in California (Christmas with palm trees!), to his daughter-in-law with the fugitive eyes and his grandsons bent on concussions, riding their wagons down the stairs at dawn, whaling the daylights out of their toys. During the long, safe years of his marriage his hand had been firmly, as they say, on the helm. He had been in control. It alarmed him that now he was not in control, even of his holidays, especially of Christmas. A courtly man with a sense of tradition, he liked his Christmases cast in the mold, which is to say he liked them the way they had always been.

Now, the best thing about Thanksgiving was its not being Christmas. It held Christmas at bay. But then the days shortened and the wind swept them into the gutter along with the leaves. And it rained December . . .

He had seen the advertisement several times that fall, a modest thing near the real-estate ads in the Sunday paper, the boxed-in words: "Social Arrangements," and underneath in a smaller type: "Of All Kinds." He had thought it amusing. At the bottom a phone number and then an address.

Actually the address was a little elusive. He passed it twice without seeing the sign. It would have been better perhaps to have phoned, but he wanted to maintain a prudent flexibility. Inside, the lighting was dim and decidedly pink. It proceeded, he saw, from a large hanging lamp that swung from the ceiling, an opulent relic with a porcelain globe painted over with roses. The wind of his entrance had set it in motion and he stood in the rosy bloom of its shadows. He was conscious of pictures in massive frames — one directly before him, a half-draped woman with one raised foot stepping out of something, perhaps a pool — a carpet eroded slightly with wear, a faint sweetish smell of baking food. To his left a man was bent over a desk. Incredibly he seemed to be mending his shoe. Filing cabinets flanked him on either side. For a silent moment they studied each other. What Tanner observed was a dark, smallish face of uncertain age, possibly foreign, with a dusting of beard, a receding hairline, and rimless glasses with one frosted lens. He managed some irony: "Are you the social arranger?"

"I am at your service." The man swept the shoe neatly into his lap, and then he repeated, "I am at your service."

"Yes," Tanner said. "Your ad is tantalizing but a little unclear. The scope of your service . . ."

The man interrupted. "It is very clear. We make social arrangements of all kinds."

"Splendid! Then perhaps I can rely on you."

"We are discreet."

"Oh, I assure you, no call for discretion." Then he laid it before them both, making it seem a spontaneous thing, almost as if the occasion inspired it. The arranger clearly was not deceived. With his unfrosted lens he seemed to perceive how long it had lain on the floor of the mind, how a little each day it had taken its shape and resisted being swept with the leaves to the gutter.

"I am by nature a sociable man." The arranger inclined his head with enthusiasm. "I live alone. My wife is dead. Christmas has become . . . What I require is a Christmas companion. A lady of my age or a little younger. Not handsome or charming. But simply . . . agreeable. Reasonable health. A good digestion, since I shall look forward to cooking for the occasion."

The other was making notes on the back of an envelope. "My secretary," he said, "is out with the flu. An inconvenience." Then he looked up and past Tanner's head. "Overnight, I presume?"

Tanner said lightly, "I've consulted the calendar. Christmas arrives this year on a Saturday. Actually I should prefer the lady for the weekend. But I wish it to be most clearly understood: the bedrooms are separate."

The arranger put down his pencil and adjusted the frosted, then the unfrosted lens. He propelled his chair backward ever so slightly into the burning heart of his files.

"There is a difficulty?" Tanner asked, concealing his unease. "Christmas, I'm sure, is a difficult time. But there must be a few in your files who live alone and would welcome a pleasant holiday with no strings attached." He stared with some irony at the array of cabinets.

"My secretary at the moment . . . Your request is reasonable. We shall consult our files. There is the matter of the fee."

Tanner was ready. "I am prepared to pay a fee of five hundred dollars for a suitable person. And, I may add, a bonus of one hundred to be paid in advance to the lady herself in case she wishes to make some holiday preparation." He had made an impression. He saw it at once. And then, without really intending it, he explained, "I arrive at these figures by checking the cost of a trip to my son's and concluding that this would serve almost as well and be on the whole a great deal more convenient." He turned to go. "In the meantime I shall check on your agency."

"Of course. It is welcomed. Your name and number? A few facts for the files."

"I shall drop by again."

"But your telephone number?"

"I shall be in touch." He left at once. He was again in control of his life, his seasons. The knowledge exhilarated him. He took a deep breath of the chilly air. Halfway down the block he stopped before a store window and studied the objects on display with care. Some plumbing equipment, secondhand it seemed. He was not after all in the best part of town. The bowl of a lavatory brimmed with live holly. In the mirror above it his own face was smiling.

As he moved away he played with the idea of stopping it there, of letting the plan of it be the whole. He sniffed at the edges. The scent of it, crisp, indefinable, a little exotic, was in the wind as he turned the corner.

Before a profitable sale of his business had left him retired and now, as he told himself, dangerously free, he had been an architect. A few years ago he had built for a friend a small vacation house back in the mountains, a comfortable distance away from the city. It was quite the nicest thing of its kind he had done. "Do me something you'd like for yourself." With such an order how could he resist giving all of its contours his gravest attention? He recalled it now with a growing pleasure, how it made its alliance with rock and sky. It was in the year after Florence died, and perhaps it was some of his lost communion that he poured without knowing it into the house.

When he returned to the tiny apartment, haunted with furniture, where he had lived since the death of his wife, he looked at it with a critical eye and found it hostile to holiday cheer. He rang up his friend, who was now in Chicago. What about the house? Using it for the holiday? Well, would you mind . . . ? Well, of course he wouldn't mind.

When the key arrived in the mail he put it into his pocket and went for a walk. He watched the gray squirrels loitering in the park and the leaves crusting the benches and the sun going down through a network of fog. He reminded himself that what he wanted was the mountain air like a ripening plum and the smell of burning wood in the morning. He wanted the cooking. He wanted the house he had made and loved and the presence of a woman, simply her presence, to give it the seal of a Christmas past. There was no woman of his acquaintance whom he could ask to cancel her plans and give him a Christmas out of her life. In return for what? With a woman he knew, there would be the question, the expectation, the where-are-we-going? to spoil the fine bouquet of the season. In the morning he drove to the arranger.

Actually he had meant to check on the agency, but then it had come to seem that part of the adventure, perhaps the whole of the adventure, was not to do so. So that now the unlikely aspect of the office, with its lamp and the rocking circles of light and its unpleasant piney odor of cleanser, and of the arranger, today without tie and faintly disheveled, did not disturb but even elated him. He was startled and then amused to observe that one of the pictures on the wall had been changed. The one he had particularly noted before of the woman emerging half-draped from a pool had now been replaced by a pasture with cows.

"It occurs to me," said Tanner, "that I don't know your name."

"I have a card somewhere." The arranger rummaged, overturning a vase full of pencils. He was looking flushed, even feverish, but perhaps it was only the rosy light. "My secretary is out . . ." He abandoned the search. "But your name . . . we don't have it. Do we have your name? We require references for the protection of all."

"You have found someone for me?"

The arranger fixed him with the unfrosted eye and gave his desk chair a provocative swivel and coughed for a while. "I believe," he said, "we have just the party." After a pause he propelled himself backward into his files. He caressed the drawers lightly with delicate fingers and opened one with an air of cunning. And swiftly removing a card, he called out: "I think, I do think, this is what you require. I shall read you details, and then of course you can judge for yourself."

Tanner said firmly, "I don't at all wish to know the details. I rely on your judgment." It seemed to him suddenly to spoil the occasion to have the woman read out like a bill of fare.

The arranger was visibly disappointed, as if he had suffered a rejection of sorts. But presently he shrugged and closed the drawer carefully. Still holding the card, he propelled himself forward and into his desk.

Tanner said, "I have here a list of my own: pertinent facts, a reference or two."

The arranger took it and scanned it slowly. Then very quickly the matter was concluded. Tanner was handed a map of the city marked with an X where he was to wait for the lady in question to step from the 2:20 bus on the afternoon of the day before Christmas.

"But I should be happy . . ."

"She wishes it so," said the arranger reverently. And as Tanner was leaving, he called out gravely, "She is one who has recently entered my files. A rare acquisition."

Tanner bowed. "I shall treat her accordingly."

It had occurred to him of course — how could it not have? — that the whole thing could well be a jolly rip-off.

While he waited with his car packed with holiday treats, no woman at all would emerge from that bus or the next or the next. The phone would ring on in an empty office. I'm sorry, the number is no longer in use. But because he so richly deserved this Christmas he could not believe it would really be so. And if it were . . . then he would drive slowly and quietly home and slowly and quietly get Christmas drunk. Part of the reward of growing older was precisely this trick one seemed to acquire of holding two possible futures in mind, of preferring one while allowing the other.

He found, on the whole, in the days that followed that it was best to assume that the lady would appear and to give his attention to preparation: a miniature tree, a wreath for the mantel, the mincemeat pies on which he prided himself, the small turkey stuffed with his own invention, the imported Chablis. He had always done most of the holiday meal when Florence was alive. He spent a great deal of time on the gifts, one nice one for her and several smaller things (he wished now that he had permitted himself a few details such as height and weight), a gift for himself in case she failed him in that department.

And of course the day came and the hour struck. With the trunk of his car neatly loaded, he was waiting by the curb. When he saw the bus coming he got out of the car. And there she was, the last to descend, as if she had lingered to look him over. Clutching a small bag, she stood alone looking down at the pavement and then up at him, the winter sun in her narrowed eyes. And she was so unmistakably what she was, a bit of merchandise sent out on approval, that he knew her at once with a catch in his throat and a small despair.

"I'm John Tanner," he offered and gave her his arm, and then as he assisted her into the car, "I've been looking forward to this for days." She wanly smiled.

After that as he drove and kept up a patter of talk to put them both at ease, he remembered how she looked, without looking at her: sand-colored hair (he guessed it was dyed), colorless eyes, a small thin face. He thought she could be in her middle fifties. She rarely spoke, and when she did her voice had a breathless hesitation — very soft, so low that he scarcely heard her.

So he said to her: "Don't be uneasy. I'm really a very comfortable person. This is new to me too. But I said to myself, why not, why not."

She coughed a little.

Then they were climbing into the mountains and the air became damp with fallen leaves and notably colder. When they reached the road that led to the house already the dark was lapping at the trees in the valley below. And around the curve was the house before him exactly as he had made it to be — clean-lined, beached on the rock with pines leaning into it, breasting the wave of sweet gums and oaks that foamed at its base.

He thought how much he had always liked it. "I built it," he said to her. "Not with my hands. Perhaps you were told I'm an architect by trade." He wondered suddenly what she had been told and if it had made her decide to come, or if after all the money was the whole of it.

"I'll go first," he said. "The steps are narrow." With a shyness he had not expected to feel, he climbed through a thicket of wild young shrubs that had marched through the summer to take the stairs. Her plaintive cough like the cry of a bird pursued him into the dusk that gathered about the door. It summoned the longing out of his soul. At that moment he wished that this Christmas were past, over and done with along with the rest. His hands were trembling when he turned the key.

Inside it was dark, with a faint little warmth from the windows that lately had drunk up the sun. He switched on the light and paused to see the great curving room spring to greet and enfold him, exactly as he had created it to do, all the sweeping half-circle of wood and stone, brown, rose, and gray. It calmed and restored him as it always had. He noted the lovely stone curve of the mantel and below it the faggots laid ready to light. Beneath his match they sprang into bloom. And when he turned round the fireshine was kindling the great tile stove, the hub of the wheel, the heart of the house, with its own special curve like a hive of bees. How he loved that stove! He had found it in an old hunting lodge near Vienna where he went for a week after Florence had died. He had bought it and had it dismantled with care and shipped to this place, then reassembled, while he ordered and implored, agonized and exulted, till again every tile was exactly in place — only one of them cracked and that still mourned and unspoken like a guilty secret.

He turned to share it all with the woman behind him, but she was warming her hands in the blaze of the fire. So now he would fill the hive with good oak and a little pine for the seethe and flair. Till the translucent bricks that encircled its base would be gemmed and ringed into amber and garnet. The hunting scenes on the creamy tiles would shimmer and glow and appear to change from moment to moment — the deer and the boar, the flowers, the trees, all richly orange and yellow and brown, as if honey had seeped through the hive to stain them. And the circle of the house would draw close and warm. Guests had always exclaimed: But where, but how? The children accepted without a word. They ran to embrace it and warm their faces. When something is right the children will know it.

He drew the curtains against the night. Then he showed her her room done neatly in white, and assured her the chill would be gone in an hour. While the daylight held he loaded the stove with wood from the generous pile banked against the rock outside. He unloaded food from the trunk of his car and all the rest. He busied himself and refused to think beyond the task at hand. He could hear her coughing in a stifled way.

While he was checking the fire in the stove he recalled with a start and a sense of shame that he had not asked or been told her name. Again she was warming her hands by the hearth. He stood behind her with an armful of wood. "What shall I call you? You must tell me your name." He made it sound as gracious and easy as possible.

She turned to him then. "My name is Cherry."

He found it a fatuous, unlikely name for the woman before him. He wondered if it had been invented for him. He would not trust himself to repeat it. He said instead, "Please call me John."

Her eyes were colorless, he observed again, and reflected the fire, the room, himself. He could find in them nothing of the woman behind them. They seemed in a strange way not to see him. The flesh beneath them looked faintly bruised. The cheekbones were firm and slightly rouged. There were small, parenthetical lines at the corners of a thin and somber mouth, which he noted with relief was free of rouge. He said to her kindly, "You seem to be coughing. Perhaps we have something here that would help."

She withdrew from him then. Her eyes shut him out. "Oh, no, I'm fine. It's just . . . well, I had the flu but I'm over it now. But when night comes on . . . I cough just a little."

He reassured her. "The flu is everywhere. I've really remarkable resistance to it."

"I'm really quite well."

"Of course," he said and winced to recall that clearly he had specified reasonable health. He could explain now her stifled voice in the car. "I've made a little light chowder for supper. Something very light. It will warm you up and be just the thing. I've always made it for Christmas Eve."

"That would be nice. I can help you with it."

But he would not have it. He placed her in a chair before the fire with a throw from the sofa around her shoulders and told her to rest her voice and be still. Then to get her into the spirit of things he found the wreath made of ribbon and holly and balanced it on the mantel before her. And he added a length of pine to the stove. He opened the vents to make it hum for her like a hiveful of bees in the manner its maker had meant it to do — a trick of construction he had never fathomed. The tiles had taken on a splendid sheen. He wanted to tell her to turn and watch.

While he was warming their supper in the kitchen, she came and stood in the archway, her eyes pale as glass, her hands, transparent with blue veins, clutching the sill like roots. He had put on his dark-rimmed glasses for the work. She looked at him with a kind of alarm as if he became even more the stranger, almost as if she surprised an intruder. But he led her back to the chair by the fire. He scolded her heartily, "I want you well by Christmas." The words and the gestures sprang naturally out of the last years with Florence.

He served them both from trays by the fire, making it all seem easy and festive. She ate very little. He poured her a glass of Tokay, and while she sipped it, her face now pink from the fire, he got out the tree and began to trim it with the tiny carved figures he and Florence had found in a shop in Munich before their son was born. He told her about them. She put down her glass and began to help. One of the small figures slipped from her fingers. When he bent to retrieve it he saw that her eyes were swimming in tears. "Don't worry," he said. "They're quite indestructible."

She fought for control. "It's my glasses," she said. "I don't see without them."

"Of course. Where are they? I'll get them for you." He rose at once.

She drew in her breath. "I forgot to bring them."

Or had she thought he would find them unpleasing? He was really impatient. Should he have specified in the beginning that he wanted a woman who could manage to see?

Finally he asked, "Shall I put on some music? Or would you just rather call it a day?" He did not like to say "go to bed," an innocent phrase that had been corrupted.

"It's what you want."

"It's what you want too."

But she shook her head. She was paid to pleasure him, to enjoy what he offered. He was suddenly struck with how easily the shape of a thing could change and take on the color of prostitution. A practiced woman would take care to conceal it, but in her innocence she underlined it. He rose and removed the throw he had placed on her shoulders.

His voice was grave. "If I'm to have my way . . . I want you to have a good night's sleep."

The evening was gone. He could not retrieve it, nor would he have done so. His heart was heavy. He lowered the lights. Her face was uncertain but she moved away past the stove that sang softly like a bird in the dusk, throwing its shadows on floor and wall. She looked at it briefly and passed without comment. Perhaps she could scarcely see it at all. Her gesture summed up for him the failure of the day.

He tried to sleep. The wind had risen. The pines above his bedroom were stroking the roof. In the room beyond he could hear her coughing. Wasn't she after all what he had ordered — a nothing who would not intrude or assert or assess or be?

He tossed in despair. Christmas is dangerous, it's too hot to handle, it's a handful of roots breeding — what did the poem say? — memory and desire. Get another day. Fourth of July, Labor Day. Don't pit yourself against Christmas. You lose. You can't contain it. It runs backward into a shop in Munich. It echoes . . . It's calling your own name down a well.

He slept a little. And in his dream the social arranger took off his glasses and lo, behind them his eyes were laughing. The eye once hidden by the frosted lens was crinkled with laughter. Why are you laughing? Tanner approached him and saw, peering, that the eye was a stone and cracked into pieces.

He awoke, dispossessed. The dark ran liquid through his veins. The wind whipped him into some distant gutter.

When daylight came he lay grimly rehearsing his script for the day. If order prevails all things are possible and even tolerable. The key of course is to be in control. His shoulder was stiff from hauling the wood. He had raised his window to sleep in the cold, and now he heard the sound of a distant axe breaking, breaking the early day.

He had the turkey in the oven, the pilaff thawing, and the salad prepared before she appeared for her morning coffee. The patches of dark were still under her eyes, but her face was rested. She seemed to have taken great care with her dress. Her sand-colored hair was combed back from her face, and now he decided the color was hers. He could see the gray. She was wearing a wine-colored jumper with a gray-green, high-necked blouse beneath. They might be a nod at the Christmas colors. There was something childlike about her dress and her slender figure, and touching about her desire to please.

He drank a third cup of coffee with her, and some of the grayness drained out of his soul. She pronounced the smell of his cooking agreeable. In the glance of her eyes around the room there was something of readiness, almost he might say of anticipation. And suddenly the day began to be possible.

"Were you warm enough in the night?" he asked.

"Oh, yes. Oh, yes."

"You're not coughing today."

"Oh, no. I'm well."

After he had coaxed the stove into shimmer and the comfortable song it could sing in the morning after a night of lying fallow, he drew the curtains away from the windows, a tender curve of them like a sickle moon, the way he had planned them in the beginning. The mist was milk in the pines and the hollows.

Before she arose he had laid his gifts for her around the tree. She looked at them with a troubled face. "I didn't know."

"How could you know? It would spoil the surprise."

But she left him quickly and returned with an unwrapped heavy tin. "I was saving it for dinner." She handed it to him, then took it away and put it with the other things beside the tree. His heart misgave him. It was fruitcake of course. He had never liked it. But what else came in round tins painted with holly and weighed enough to crush the bones of your foot?

He put on some music. He made her sit in state on the sofa. Then he found his glasses on the sink in the kitchen and put them on her. "I want you to see. Can you see?" he asked.

She looked around her and down at her hands. "Oh, yes, I can."

"Are you sure you can?"

"Oh, yes. Oh, yes."

"Well, at least you will see things the way I do." He had to laugh. She looked like a small, obedient child who was given permission to try her father's glasses. They diminished her face and gave her an owlish air of wisdom. Then he handed her the packages one by one — first, the teakwood tray, then a fragile porcelain cup and saucer with a Christmas scene. For Christmases to come. And to remind her, he said, of this very day. Then a small, lacquered music box that played a carol. While it finished its song he opened the tie he had bought for himself and exclaimed at the colors. He declared that a friend had secretly left it on the seat of his car. She held her things on the tray in her lap and watched him with pale and troubled eyes, their trouble magnified by his glasses. "Do you like them?" he asked.

"Oh, yes. They're lovely."

Then he watched while she opened the tall ribboned box with the figurine, a bit of Lladro that came from Spain. She drew out the blue-and-gray girl with the pure, grave face and the goose in her arms. She held it silently. Then she touched the smooth, child's head with her hand. "Do you like it?" he asked.

"Oh, yes. I do."

"I knew you would like it." She looked at him, puzzled. "Oh, yes, I knew it . . . It reminds me," he said, "a little of you."

What he meant, he realized, was that Florence would like it . . . and that it also reminded him a little of her. But there was one box more, the largest of all. "But you've given too much." She was reluctant to open it, almost distracted. He could tell she was thinking of the whole of her cost, the somber transaction with the seedy purveyor.

"What is too much? This Christmas has never happened before." And he added gaily, "Whatever you don't like will have been too much. We can toss it into the stove and burn it."

She smiled at that and opened the box. She lifted the dark green, floor-length woolen robe, severe, elegant, very formal. "Try it on," he commanded. She did so obediently. He crossed the room to appraise it from a distance and pronounced it too long. He saw with dismay he had bought it for Florence, her height, her coloring. But it seemed to do now surprisingly well. It coaxed her colorless eyes into green. "I like it on you. You must leave it on till the room is warm."

But she took it off at once. "It's much too fine." She folded it carefully and put it back in its box.

The dinner went well, and she seemed to enjoy it. He insisted she wear his glasses while eating. It was prudent, he said, to consume nothing on faith. At his urging she took a second helping of pie. He allowed himself a generous slice of her cake and declared it superior. He toasted her fruitcake, herself, and the day. Her face was flushed to a pink with the wine. Her hair fell softly against her cheek. She brushed it away with the back of her hand, which was worn and expressive, with a tracery of veins. He had seen such a hand on a painting in Prague.

He allowed her to rest for a while after eating. Then he told her about the lake below the house, hidden from view because of the trees. "Would you like to walk down?"

"Oh, yes," she said.

At his bidding she put on a sweater he had packed for himself and then her coat. She drew a flimsy scarf over her head. He looked with doubt at her fragile shoes. But she said they were all she had brought along. "No matter," he said. "I'll keep you from falling."

Outside it was sunless and clear and cold. The mist had vanished. The path was hardly a path at all. He had to steady her over the rocks. She was light and insubstantial against him. In the trees around them festive with moss the squirrels were stammering, cracking their nuts and spitting the shells. Under their feet the acorns of water oaks crackled like flames. And then the lake was down below like a rent in the fabric of moss and leaves. Strange birds were skimming it looking for fish, with haunting cries that poured through the trees and summoned them to the water's edge.

He guided her down. Once she slipped but he caught her and held her safe. She was shivering a little. "Are you cold?"

"Oh, no."

He held her arm tightly to reassure her. The lake was polished and gray as steel. Across it a line of young bamboo was green, as if it were spring on the other side.

"It's very deep. And somewhere in the middle is a splendid boat that sank beneath me without any warning."

He watched her eyes look up and smile. "Were you fishing?" she asked.

"Yes, that I was. And the fish I had caught went down with the boat. When I came up for air they were swimming around me laughing like crazy."

He had made her laugh, in the way he could always make Florence laugh when he sounded foolish. Her laughter warmed him in some deep place that had long been sunless. Not the laughter itself, but the way he could pluck it out of her throat, summon it out of whatever she was.

He ventured, regretting the small deception: "You remind me of someone I used to know whose name was Beth. Do you think you would mind if I called you that?"

"Oh, no."

He was more than relieved to be rid of the name which he could not bring himself to repeat. He was holding her firmly. The edge of her scarf fell against his face as if she had touched him. It released him into the cold, still air. The birds were circling, ringing them with their plangent calls, weaving them into the water and trees. She coughed a little and the shudder of her body against his own was mirrored down in the polished lake. Her image in water joined to his was clearer to him than the woman he held.

As if it had lain in wait for him there, he remembered a time before the boat had vanished. It was in the summer they were building the house, the only one then for miles around. The workmen had all gone home for the day. He rowed himself to the middle of the lake and waited. He never knew why it was he had waited. And suddenly along the line of the shore a woman was walking who seemed to be Florence: the shape of her body, the way she moved, as she was in the years before her illness. Her head was bent. She was looking for something at the water's edge. He could see her reflection just below moving with her like a walking companion. Abruptly she knelt and, leaning over the slight embankment, she plunged one arm deep into the water. In the waning light he could see the gleam of her bare white arm as it disappeared. For a terrible moment he was sure she would fall and join the woman in the water below. The whole of the lake was moving in ripples, around him, past him to where she knelt. He could not call. He simply willed her, willed her to rise. And she rose and looked at him across the water. And then she turned and walked into the trees. He had never known who the woman was . . . or if she was.

The woman beside him coughed. "Do you swim?" he asked.

"Oh, no," she said.

He waited a little. "Would you like to go back?"

"Whatever you say."

They climbed the hill slowly, clinging together, pausing at intervals to catch their breath and release it in mingling clouds to the air. A rising wind sprayed their faces with leaves. He felt they were plunging deep into winter. The rock supporting the house above them loomed pearl gray in the evening light. Below them the lake had been sucked into shadow.

In the night he awoke with a cold, clear sense that Florence had called him. He lay still listening. But of course not Florence. Then he heard the sharp cough, but it did not come from the room next to his. It came from another part of his world, and it seemed on the move like the call of a bird, caged in the circle he had made of a house. It shattered his dark. Finally he put on a robe and found her in the living room with her hands and her body pressed to the stove. She stood in darkness. But she had pulled the drapery back from the window, and in the moonlight he could see her clearly, motionless as if she were carved in marble.

He switched on a lamp. She turned to him quickly a face that was stricken with grief and shame. "I'm sorry, I'm sorry."

"Were you cold?" he asked.

"A little cold. But the cough is worse when I'm lying down. I was afraid of waking you."

He saw that she had thrown over her own dressing gown the robe he had given her. "You're not to worry. I'm here to help." He noted her trembling and built up the fire.

"I'm sorry," she repeated. "I've spoiled it all."

"You haven't spoiled a thing." He fetched her a chair.

He found a jar of honey in the kitchen and a lemon he had packed; and he fed her spoonfuls of the mixture as if she were a child . . . as if he were giving Florence her medicine when she woke in the night.

"Thank you," she said. "I'm so sorry."

"You mustn't talk."

She sat by the stove, her body subdued, in an attitude of profound despair. He pulled the robe close about her shoulders and waited silently beside her chair. He felt he was on the edge of something, a depth, a life he did not want to explore. A lonely woman who had waited for years for a door to open and now was in terror of seeing it close? He drew away. Nothing is simple, he said to himself. Nothing is ever, ever simple. Though what he meant by it he could not say. He saw his own life as an endless struggle to make the complex simple.

Commanding her silence, he turned out the lamp. He drew up a chair for himself and sat near her, and waited as he had waited in the night with Florence after the stroke had forbidden her speech. The moonlight was cold on her trembling form. The circle of light at the base of the stove drew him down and ringed him with glimmering warmth. He sat half dozing in a strange sort of peace, because it was good to be with a woman on a Christmas night. And because he had bound her voice and its power to give him more.

After a time, when her trembling had stopped, he gave her another spoonful of syrup and sent her to bed with the rest of it.

In the night through the wall he could hear her weeping. He lay with some reservoir within him filling with tears. The walk through the wood had brought a memory of Florence, the sharpest one. She had been moving ahead through the trees of another wood. He had heard the rustle of her shoes in the leaves, then nothing. He thought she had stopped to peel moss from the bark of a fallen trunk for her garden at home. And so he had come on her fallen body. Then the long limbo of her stroke and death, when slowly,

slowly she had withdrawn. As he thought of it now, and had scarcely let himself think it before, there had been a period before that day when she had withdrawn herself ever so lightly. In fact for some years: "Whatever you think . . . whatever you like . . . if it's what you want." His will was hers, his desires her own. It was almost as if her helpless years were a further step in a long dependence. He had liked the deference of her will to his. He liked to arrange the life for them both. Perhaps it was true — he saw now it was — he had struck her down in her vital self and summoned compliance out of her soul. And in compliance was bred withdrawal. Yet surely, surely it was what he wanted. Making a house or making a marriage, always he had to be in control. Her death had ended his long dominion. He must admit he had reigned with spirit . . . and a certain flair.

Genial husband, genial host. And now in the dark he knew himself as the social arranger. That seedy figure in the heart of his files he had conjured out of his own deep need. The woman weeping behind the wall — weeping for a reason he could not explain — was made to his order. He remembered with shame how he had denied her a past or a name. As if he would grant her permission to be . . . what he wished, when he wished.

Sometime before dawn he made peace with himself, as a man must do.

He awoke with a start. The windows were opalescent with ice. The needles of the pines were threads of crystal. Their boughs lay heavy along the roof. He rose to shake up the fire in the stove with a thunderous clamor, for the final time. He built the flame on the hearth again. And when she emerged, her eyes faintly rimmed, the lines gone deep at the corners of her mouth, he stood before her in new humility. Today he allowed her to help him with breakfast, a good one to last them for the drive into town. Then while the kitchen was alive and steaming with the cleaning up, he asked: "If you hadn't come . . ." He began again. "If you had spent Christmas in the usual way, where would it be?"

She was washing dishes and did not answer. He heard her silence, again with relief. He said with good humor, "But the rule is you have to take half the leftovers back to wherever it is you would be if you weren't here now." He was restored as the genial host.

After a little he went into the living room and stood at the crescent line of the windows. He could see the frozen forest below, shimmering with amber light in the sun. Beside him the warmth of flame on the hearth. It seemed to him that this was enough forever — the ice-filled trees, the flame-filled room in the midst of ice, all this ice with a heart of fire. He was conscious that she had entered the room. For a moment he asked for the trees along the mountain road to break beneath their burden of ice and cut them off for another day.

He turned to see her. She was pressing her hands to the tiles of the stove — worn hands the color of the ancient tiles. "I'll show you a secret," he said to ease her. "There's a tile that was cracked, and no one knows where it is but me. And I've never told."

She seemed not to hear. It was almost time to put her back in the box, like the blue-and-gray girl with the goose in her arms. And so he told her, "I shall always remember this time . . . these days."

She sucked in her breath and turned away. He stopped and waited. She began to cry. "What is it?" he asked.

But she turned again and walked to the fire. "You're so good," she said in a stifled voice. "You're so kind."

He was moved. "But that shouldn't . . ."

"Oh, yes. Oh, yes."

He said something he had not intended to say then, perhaps never to say: "But it doesn't really have to end with this . . . But I can't go on picking you up at a bus stop."

She faced him, weeping, shaking her head.

"You've not enjoyed it?"

"Oh, yes. Oh, yes. It's the loveliest time I've ever had."

"Then why . . .? I assumed . . . Why would you be in his files . . . why would you be willing to come at all unless . . ." Then a kind of light seemed to dawn in his mind, as if he had known it all along. "You work for him," he said. "You're the secretary who was out with the flu."

She did not deny it. She wept on into her handkerchief, coughing as if he had called up her illness. "Are you?" he asked. She nodded her head. She could not speak. "But it's all right . . . it's all right. Why should I care? I really don't care if you work for the charlatan. He made this weekend possible, didn't he?"

She gave him a final, stricken look. "I'm his wife too."

"His wife!"

She wept.

He was stunned. "But why?"

Through her tears she told him. "There was no one else. And we needed the money. You don't know. The bills."

"But his files . . . the files."

"They're full of other things, not names: cleaning aids . . . other things. We have nothing at all. I bought these clothes with the money you gave." Her voice sank to a hopeless whisper. "He said I should do it. It would be all right. He said you were safe."

"Safe!"

"He said you were . . ."

"Safe?"

She did not answer.

"No one is safe! How could he send you out like this? How could he know I was safe, walking in out of the street like that?" His anger released him from hurt and chagrin. He paced the length of the curving room. He said to himself: I've been taken . . . had.

He turned to her from the end of the room. The stove beyond him was deep in whispers. The ice outside slipped and fell from the trees. "Can you approve of this . . . man? Can you love this man?"

"He's my husband," she wept.

He was forced to see with what grace she suffered them both.

And so he did indeed put her back in the box. He drove her to the bus stop and waited in the car, talking lightly of the winter ahead and the spring when perhaps he would take a trip to the West. When the bus arrived he helped her on with her packages. The music box gave a stifled cry. He saw her safely seated at the rear. Then he watched while her bus moved off and away, picking up speed with a grinding of gears, moving faster and farther away past the winter and into spring and on through a shower of summer leaves, and never reaching her destination.

BOBBIE ANN MASON

Drawing Names

n Christmas Day, Carolyn Sisson went early to her parents' house to help her mother with the dinner. Carolyn had been divorced two years before, and last Christmas, coming alone, she felt uncomfortable. This year she had invited her lover, Kent Ballard, to join the family gathering. She had even brought him a present to put under the tree, so he wouldn't feel left out. Kent was planning to drive over from Kentucky Lake by noon. He had gone there to inspect his boat because of an ice storm earlier in the week. He felt compelled to visit his boat on the holiday, Carolyn thought, as if it were a sad old relative in a retirement home.

"We're having baked ham instead of turkey," Mom said. "Your daddy never did like ham baked, but whoever heard of fried ham on Christmas? We have that all year round and I'm burnt out on it."

"I love baked ham," said Carolyn.

"Does Kent like it baked?"

"I'm sure he does." Carolyn placed her gifts under the tree. The number of packages seemed unusually small.

"It don't seem like Christmas with drawed names," said Mom.

"Your star's about to fall off." Carolyn straightened the silver ornament at the tip of the tree.

"I didn't decorate as much as I wanted to. I'm slowing down. Getting old, I guess." Mom had not combed her hair and she was wearing a workshirt and tennis shoes.

"You always try to do too much on Christmas, Mom."

Carolyn knew the agreement to draw names had bothered her mother. But the four daughters were grown, and two had children. Sixteen people were expected today. Carolyn herself could not afford to buy fifteen presents on her salary as a clerk at J. C. Penney's, and her parents' small farm had not been profitable in years.

Carolyn's father appeared in the kitchen and he hugged her so tightly she squealed in protest.

"That's all I can afford this year," he said, laughing.

As he took a piece of candy from a dish on the counter, Carolyn teased him. "You'd better watch your calories today."

"Oh, not on Christmas!"

It made Carolyn sad to see her handsome father getting older. He was a shy man, awkward with his daughters, and Carolyn knew he had been deeply disappointed over her failed marriage, although he had never said so. Now he asked, "Who bought these 'toes'?"

He would no longer say "nigger toes," the old name for the chocolate-covered creams.

"Hattie Smoot brought those over," said Mom. "I made a pants suit for her last week," she said to Carolyn. "The one that had stomach bypass?"

"When Pee Wee McClain had that, it didn't work and they had to fix him back like he was," said Dad. He offered Carolyn a piece of candy, but she shook her head no.

Mom said, "I made Hattie a dress back last spring for her boy's graduation, and she couldn't even find a pattern big enough. I had to 'low a foot. But after that bypass, she's down to a size twenty."

"I think we'll all need a stomach bypass after we eat this feast you're fixing," said Carolyn.

"Where's Kent?" Dad asked abruptly.

"He went to see about his boat. He said he'd be here."

Carolyn looked at the clock. She felt uneasy about inviting Kent. Everyone would be scrutinizing him, as if he were some new character on a soap opera. Kent, who drove a truck for the Kentucky Loose-Leaf Floor, was a part-time student at Murray State. He was majoring in accounting. When Carolyn started going with him early in the summer, they went sailing on his boat, which had "Joyce" painted on it. Later he painted over the name, insisting he didn't love Joyce anymore — she was a dietician who was always criticizing what he ate — but he had never said he loved Carolyn. She did not know if she loved him. Each seemed to be waiting for the other to say it first.

While Carolyn helped her mother in the kitchen, Dad went to get her grandfather, her mother's father. Pappy, who had been disabled by a stroke, was cared for by a live-in housekeeper who had gone home to her own family for the day. Carolyn diced apples and pears for fruit salad while her mother shaped sweet potato balls with marshmallow centers and rolled them in crushed cornflakes. On TV in the living room, *Days of Our Lives* was beginning, but the Christmas tree blocked their view of the television set.

"Whose name did you draw, Mom?" Carolyn asked, as she began seeding the grapes.

"Jim's."

"You put Jim's name in the hat?"

Mom nodded. Jim Walsh was the man Carolyn's youngest sister, Laura Jean, was living with in St. Louis. Laura Jean was going to an interior decorating school, and Jim was a textiles salesman she had met in a class. "I made him a shirt," Mom said.

"I'm surprised at you."

"Well, what was I to do?"

"I'm just surprised." Carolyn ate a grape and spit out the seeds. "Emily Post says the couple should be offered the same room when they visit."

"You know we'd never stand for that. I don't think your dad's ever got over her stacking up with that guy."

"You mean shacking up."

"Same thing." Mom dropped the potato masher, and the metal rattled on the floor. "Oh, I'm in such a tizzy," she said.

As the family began to arrive, the noise of the TV played against the greetings, the slam of the storm door, the outside wind rushing in. Carolyn's older sisters, Peggy and Iris, with their husbands and children, were arriving all at once, and suddenly the house seemed small. Peggy's children, Stevie and Cheryl, without even removing their jackets, became involved in a basketball game on TV. In his lap, Stevie had a Merlin electronic toy, which beeped randomly. Iris and Ray's children, Deedee and Jonathan, went outside to look for cats.

In the living room, Peggy jiggled her baby, Lisa, on her hip and said, "You need you one of these, Carolyn."

"Where can I get one?" said Carolyn, rather sharply.

Peggy grinned. "At the gittin' place, I reckon."

Peggy's critical tone was familiar. She was the only sister who had had a real wedding. Her husband, Cecil, had a Gulf franchise, and they owned a motor cruiser, a pickup truck, a camper, a station wagon, and a new brick colonial home. Whenever Carolyn went to visit Peggy, she felt apologetic for not having a man who would buy her all these things, but she never seemed to be attracted to anyone steady or ambitious. She had been wondering how Kent would get along with the men of the family. Cecil and Ray were standing in a corner talking about gas mileage. Cecil, who was shorter than Peggy and was going bald, always worked on Dad's truck for free, and Ray usually agreed with Dad on politics to avoid an argument. Ray had an impressive government job in Frankfort. He had coordinated a ribbon-cutting ceremony when the toll road opened. What would Kent have to say to them? She could imagine him insisting that everyone go outside later to watch the sunset. Her father would think that was ridiculous. No one ever did that on a farm, but it was the sort of thing Kent would think of. Yet she knew that spontaneity was what she liked in him.

Deedee and Jonathan, who were ten and six, came inside then and immediately began shaking the presents under the tree. All the children were wearing new jeans and cowboy shirts, Carolyn noticed.

"Why are y'all so quiet?" she asked. "I thought kids whooped and hollered on Christmas."

"They've been up since *four,*" said Iris. She took a cigarette from her purse and accepted a light from Cecil. Exhaling smoke, she said to Carolyn, "We heard Kent was coming." Before Carolyn could reply, Iris scolded the children for shaking the packages. She seemed nervous.

"He's supposed to be here by noon," said Carolyn.

"There's somebody now. I hear a car."

"It might be Dad, with Pappy."

It was Laura Jean, showing off Jim Walsh as though he were a splendid Christmas gift she had just received.

"Let me kiss everybody!" she cried, as the women rushed toward her. Laura Jean had not been home in four months.

"Merry Christmas!" Jim said in a booming, official-sounding voice, something like a TV announcer, Carolyn thought. He embraced all the women and then, with a theatrical gesture, he handed Mom a bottle of Rebel Yell bourbon and a carton of boiled custard which he took from a shopping bag. The bourbon was in a decorative Christmas box.

Mom threw up her hands. "Oh, no, I'm afraid I'll be a alky-holic."

"Oh, that's ridiculous, Mom," said Laura Jean, taking Jim's coat. "A couple of drinks a day are good for your heart."

Jim insisted on getting coffee cups from a kitchen cabinet and mixing some boiled custard and bourbon. When he handed a cup to Mom she puckered up her face.

"Law, don't let the preacher in," she said, taking a sip. "Boy, that sends my blood pressure up."

Carolyn waved away the drink Jim offered her. "I don't start this early in the day," she said, feeling confused.

Jim was a large, dark-haired man with a neat little beard, like a bird's nest cupped on his chin. He had a Northern accent. When he hugged her, Carolyn caught a whiff of cologne, something sweet, like chocolate syrup. Last summer, when Laura Jean brought him home for the first time, she had made a point of kissing and hugging him in front of everyone. Dad had virtually ignored him. Now Carolyn saw that Jim was telling Cecil that he always bought Gulf gas. Red-faced, Ray accepted a cup of boiled custard. Carolyn fled to the kitchen and began grating cheese for potatoes au gratin. She dreaded Kent's arrival.

When Dad arrived with Pappy, Cecil and Jim helped set up the wheelchair in a corner. Afterward, Dad and Jim shook hands, and Dad refused Jim's offer of bourbon. From the kitchen, Carolyn could see Dad hugging Laura Jean, not letting go. She went into the living room to greet her grandfather.

"They roll me in this buggy too fast," he said when she kissed his forehead.

Carolyn hoped he wouldn't notice the bottle of bourbon, but she knew he never missed anything. He was so deaf people had given up talking to him. Now the children tiptoed around him, looking at him with awe. Somehow, Carolyn expected the children to notice that she was alone, like Pappy.

At ten minutes of one, the telephone rang. Peggy answered and handed the receiver to Carolyn. "It's Kent," she said.

Kent had not left the lake yet. "I just got here an hour ago," he told Carolyn. "I had to take my sister over to my mother's."

"Is the boat O.K.?"

"Yeah. Just a little scraped paint. I'll be ready to go in a little while." He hesitated, as though waiting for assurance that the invitation was real.

"This whole gang's ready to eat," Carolyn said. "Can't you hurry?" She should have remembered the way he tended to get sidetracked. Once it took them three hours to get to Paducah, because he kept stopping at antique shops.

After she hung up the telephone, her mother asked, "Should I put the rolls in to brown yet?"

"Wait just a little. He's just now leaving the lake."

"When's this Kent feller coming?" asked Dad impatiently, as he peered into the kitchen. "It's time to eat."

"He's on his way," said Carolyn.

"Did you tell him we don't wait for stragglers?"

"No."

"When the plate rattles, we eat."

"I know."

"Did you tell him that?"

"No, I didn't!" cried Carolyn, irritated.

When they were alone in the kitchen, Carolyn's mother said to her, "Your dad's not his self today. He's fit to be tied about Laura Jean bringing that guy down here again. And him bringing that whiskey."

"That was uncalled for," Carolyn agreed. She had noticed that Mom had set her cup of boiled custard in the refrigerator.

"Besides, he's not too happy about that Kent Ballard you're running around with."

"What's it to him?"

"You know how he always was. He don't think anybody's good enough for one of his little girls, and he's afraid you'll get mistreated again. He don't think Kent's very dependable."

"I guess Kent's proving Dad's point."

Carolyn's sister Iris had dark brown eyes, unique in the family. When Carolyn was small, she tried to say "Iris's eyes" once and called them "Irish eyes," confusing them with a song their mother sometimes sang, "When Irish Eyes Are Smiling." Thereafter, they always teased Iris about her smiling Irish eyes. Today Iris was not smiling. Carolyn found her in a bedroom smoking, holding an ashtray in her hand.

"I drew your name," Carolyn told her. "I got you something I wanted myself."

"Well, if I don't want it, I guess I'll have to give it to you."

"What's wrong with you today?"

"Ray and me's getting a separation," said Iris.

"Really?" Carolyn was startled by the note of glee in her response. Actually, she told herself later, it was because she was glad her sister, whom she saw infrequently, had confided in her.

"The thing of it is, I had to beg him to come today, for Mom and Dad's sake. It'll kill them. Don't let on, will you?"

"I won't. What are you going to do?"

"I don't know. He's already moved out."

"Are you going to stay in Frankfort?"

"I don't know. I have to work things out."

Mom stuck her head in the door. "Well, is Kent coming or not?"

"He *said* he'd be here," said Carolyn.

"Your dad's about to have a duck with a rubber tail. He can't stand to wait on a meal."

"Well, let's go ahead, then. Kent can eat when he gets here."

When Mom left, Iris said, "Aren't you and Kent getting along?"

"I don't know. He said he'd come today, but I have a feeling he doesn't really want to."

"To hell with men." Iris laughed and stubbed out her cigarette. "Just look at us — didn't we turn out awful? First your divorce. Now me. And Laura Jean bringing that guy down. Daddy can't stand him. Did you see the look he gave him?"

"Laura Jean's got a lot a more nerve than I've got," said Carolyn, nodding. "I could wring Kent's neck for being late. Well, none of us can do anything right — except Peggy."

"Daddy's precious little angel," said Iris mockingly. "Come on, we'd better get in there and help."

While Mom went to change her blouse and put on lipstick, the sisters brought the food into the dining room. Two tables had been put together. Peggy cut the ham with an electric knife, and Carolyn filled the iced tea glasses.

"Pappy gets buttermilk and Stevie gets Coke," Peggy directed her.

"I know," said Carolyn, almost snapping.

As the family sat down, Carolyn realized that no one ever asked Pappy to "turn thanks" anymore at holiday dinners. He was sitting there expectantly, as if waiting to be asked. Mom cut up his ham into small bits. Carolyn waited for a car to drive up, the phone to ring. The TV was still on.

"Y'all dig in," said Mom. "Jim? Make sure you try some of these dressed eggs like I fix."

"I thought your new boyfriend was coming," said Cecil to Carolyn.

"So did I!" said Laura Jean. "That's what you wrote me."

Everyone looked at Carolyn as she explained. She looked away.

"You're looking at that pitiful tree," Mom said to her. "I just know it don't show up good from the road."

"No, it looks fine." No one had really noticed the tree. Carolyn seemed to be seeing it for the first time in years — broken red plastic reindeer, Styrofoam snowmen with crumbling top hats, silver walnuts which she remembered painting when she was about twelve.

Dad began telling a joke about some monks who had taken a vow of silence. At each Christmas dinner, he said, one monk was allowed to speak.

"Looks like your vocal cords would rust out," said Cheryl.

"Shut up, Cheryl. Granddaddy's trying to tell something," said Cecil.

"So the first year it was the first monk's turn to talk, and you know what he said? He said, 'These taters is lumpy.'"

When several people laughed, Stevie asked, "Is that the joke?"

Carolyn was baffled. Her father had never told a joke at the table in his life. He sat at the head of the table, looking out past the family at the cornfield through the picture window.

"Pay attention now," he said. "The second year Christmas rolled around again and it was the second monk's turn to say something. He said, 'You know, I think you're right. The taters *is* lumpy.'"

Laura Jean and Jim laughed loudly.

"Reach me some light-bread," said Pappy. Mom passed the dish around the table to him.

"And so the third year," Dad continued, "the third monk got to say something. What he said" — Dad was suddenly overcome with mirth — "what he said was, 'If y'all don't shut up arguing about them taters, I'm going to leave this place!'"

After the laughter died, Mom said, "Can you imagine anybody not a-talking all year long?"

"That's the way monks are, Mom," said Laura Jean. "Monks are economical with everything. They're not wasteful, not even with words."

"The Trappist Monks are really an outstanding group," said Jim. "And they make excellent bread. No preservatives."

Cecil and Peggy stared at Jim.

"You're not eating, Dad," said Carolyn. She was sitting between him and the place set for Kent. The effort at telling the joke seemed to have taken her father's appetite.

"He ruined his dinner on nigger toes," said Mom.

"Dottie Barlow got a Barbie doll for Christmas and it's black," Cheryl said.

"Dottie Barlow ain't black, is she?" asked Cecil.

"No."

"That's funny," said Peggy. "Why would they give her a black Barbie doll?"

"She just wanted it."

Abruptly, Dad left the table, pushing back his plate. He sat down in the recliner chair in front of the TV. The Blue-

Gray game was beginning, and Cecil and Ray were hurriedly finishing in order to join him. Carolyn took out second helpings of ham and jello salad, feeling as though she were eating for Kent in his absence. Jim was taking seconds of everything, complimenting Mom. Mom apologized for not having fancy napkins. Then Laura Jean described a photography course she had taken. She had been photographing close-ups of car parts — fenders, headlights, mud flaps.

"That sounds goofy," said one of the children, Deedee.

Suddenly Pappy spoke. "Use to, the menfolks would eat first, and the children separate. The womenfolks would eat last, in the kitchen."

"You know what I could do with you all, don't you?" said Mom, shaking her fist at him. "I could set up a plank out in the field for y'all to eat on." She laughed.

"Times are different now, Pappy," said Iris loudly. "We're just as good as the men."

"She gets that from television," said Ray, with an apologetic laugh.

Carolyn noticed Ray's glance at Iris. Just then Iris matter-of-factly plucked an eyelash from Ray's cheek. It was as though she had momentarily forgotten about the separation.

Later, after the gifts were opened, Jim helped clear the tables. Kent still had not come. The baby slept, and Laura Jean, Jim, Peggy, and Mom played a Star Trek board game at the dining room table, while Carolyn and Iris played Battlestar Galactica with Cheryl and Deedee. The other men were quietly engrossed in the football game, a blur of sounds. No one had mentioned Kent's absence, but after the children had distributed the gifts, Carolyn refused to tell them what was in the lone package left under the tree. It was the most extravagantly wrapped of all the presents, with an immense ribbon, not a stick-on bow. An icicle had dropped on it, and it reminded Carolyn of an abandoned float, like something from a parade.

At a quarter to three, Kent telephoned. He was still at the lake. "The gas stations are all closed," he said. "I couldn't get any gas."

"We already ate and opened the presents," said Carolyn.

"Here I am, stranded. Not a thing I can do about it."

Kent's voice was shaky and muffled, and Carolyn suspected he had been drinking. She did not know what to say, in front of the family. She chattered idly, while she played with a ribbon from a package. The baby was awake, turning dials and knobs on a Busy Box. On TV, the Blues picked up six yards on an end sweep. Carolyn fixed her eyes on the tilted star at the top of the tree. Kent was saying something about Santa Claus.

"They wanted me to play Santy at Mama's house for the littluns. I said — you know what I said? 'Bah, humbug!' Did I ever tell you what I've got against Christmas?"

"Maybe not." Carolyn's back stiffened against the wall.

"When I was little bitty, Santa Claus came to town. I was about five. I was all fired up to go see Santy, and Mama took me, but we were late, and he was about to leave. I had to run across the courthouse square to get to him. He was giving away suckers, so I ran as hard as I could. He was climbing up on the fire engine — are you listening?"

"Unh-huh." Carolyn was watching her mother, who was folding Christmas paper to save for next year.

Kent said, "I reached up and pulled at his old red pants leg, and he looked down at me, and you know what he said?"

"No — what?"

"He said, 'Piss off, kid.'"

"Really?"

"Would I lie to you?"

"I don't know."

"Do you want to hear the rest of my hard-luck story?"

"Not now."

"Oh, I forgot this was long distance. I'll call you tomorrow. Maybe I'll go paint the boat. That's what I'll do! I'll go paint it right this minute."

After Carolyn hung up the telephone, her mother said, "I think my Oriental casserole was a failure. I used the wrong kind of mushroom soup. It called for cream of mushroom and I used golden mushroom."

"Won't you *ever* learn, Mom?" cried Carolyn. "You always cook too much. You make *such* a big deal —"

Mom said, "What happened with Kent this time?"

"He couldn't get gas. He forgot the gas stations were closed."

"Jim and Laura Jean didn't have any trouble getting gas," said Peggy, looking up from the game.

"We tanked up yesterday," said Laura Jean.

"Of course you did," said Carolyn distractedly. "You always think ahead."

"It's your time," Cheryl said, handing Carolyn the Battlestar Galactica toy. "I did lousy."

"Not as lousy as I did," said Iris.

Carolyn tried to concentrate on shooting enemy missiles, raining through space. Her sisters seemed far away, like the spaceships. She was aware of the men watching football, their hands in action as they followed an exciting play. Even though Pappy had fallen asleep, with his blanket in his lap he looked like a king on a throne. Carolyn thought of the quiet accommodation her father had made to his father-in-law, just as Cecil and Ray had done with Dad, and her ex-husband had tried to do once. But Cecil had bought his way in, and now Ray was getting out. Kent had stayed away. Jim, the newcomer, was with the women, playing Star Trek as if his life depended upon it. Carolyn was glad now that Kent had not come. The story he told made her angry, and his pity for his childhood made her think of something Pappy had often said: "Christmas is for children." Earlier, she had listened in amazement while Cheryl listed on her fingers the gifts she had received that morning: a watch, a stereo, a nightgown, hot curls, perfume, candles, a sweater, a calculator, a jewelry box, a ring. Now Carolyn saw Kent's boat as his toy, more important than the family obligations of the holiday.

Mom was saying, "I wanted to make a Christmas tablecloth out of red checks with green fringe. You wouldn't think knit would do for a tablecloth, but Hattie Smoot has the prettiest one."

"You can do incredible things with knit," said Jim with sudden enthusiasm. The shirt Mom had made him was bonded knit.

"Who's Hattie Smoot?" asked Laura Jean. She was caressing the back of Jim's neck, as though soothing his nerves.

Carolyn laughed when her mother began telling Jim and Laura Jean about Hattie Smoot's operation. Jim listened attentively, leaning forward with his elbows on the table, and asked eager questions, his eyes as alert as Pappy's.

"Is she telling a joke?" Cheryl asked Carolyn.

"No. I'm not laughing at you, Mom," Carolyn said, touching her mother's hand. She felt relieved that the anticipation of Christmas had ended. Still laughing, she said, "Pour me some of that Rebel Yell, Jim. It's about time."

"I'm with you," Jim said, jumping up.

In the kitchen, Carolyn located a clean spoon while Jim washed some cups. Carolyn couldn't find the cup Mom had left in the refrigerator. As she took out the carton of boiled custard, Jim said, "It must be a very difficult day for you."

Carolyn was startled. His tone was unexpectedly kind, genuine. She was struck suddenly by what he must know about her, because of his intimacy with her sister. She knew nothing about him. When he smiled, she saw a gold cap on a molar, shining like a Christmas ornament. She managed to say, "It can't be any picnic for you either. Kent didn't want to put up with us."

"Too bad he couldn't get gas."

"I don't think he wanted to get gas."

"Then you're better off without him." When Jim looked at her, Carolyn felt that he must be examining her resemblances to Laura Jean. He said, "I think your family's great."

Carolyn laughed nervously. "We're hard on you. God, you're brave to come down here like this."

"Well, Laura Jean's worth it."

They took the boiled custard and cups into the dining room. As Carolyn sat down, her nephew Jonathan begged her to tell what was in the gift left under the tree.

"I can't tell," she said.

"Why not?"

"I'm saving it till next year, in case I draw some man's name."

"I hope it's mine," said Jonathan.

Jim stirred bourbon into three cups of boiled custard, then gave one to Carolyn and one to Laura Jean. The others had declined. Then he leaned back in his chair — more relaxed now — and squeezed Laura Jean's hand. Carolyn wondered what they said to each other when they were alone in St. Louis. She knew with certainty that they would not be economical with words, like the monks in the story. She longed to be with them, to hear what they would say. She noticed her mother picking at a hangnail, quietly ignoring the bourbon. Looking at the bottle's gift box, which showed an old-fashioned scene, children on sleds in the snow, Carolyn thought of Kent's boat again. She felt she was in that snowy scene now with Laura Jean and Jim, sailing in Kent's boat into the winter breeze, into falling snow. She thought of how silent it was out on the lake, as though the whiteness of the snow were the absence of sound.

"Cheers!" she said to Jim, lifting her cup.

DON RUSS

The Winter Heart

hen the autumn
afternoons have blown away
and, lavender and blue and silver and gray

with sleep, a cold December's evenings ease
toward night, we wait. When crystallizing trees

and hills have paled to vapor and the dreaming world
could vanish in a final breath of whorled

and frozen white, we hope. If what we know
of love is summer's coming just to go,

we wait and hope and — trembling — hold a start
of embers in a deeper hollow of the winter heart.

CONTRIBUTORS

JULIA ALVAREZ began her writing career as a poet and turned to fiction after the publication of a book of poems, *Homecoming*. Her short stories have appeared in many magazines and journals. Now teaching at the University of Illinois, she is at work on a collection of stories, many of which deal with growing up in the Dominican Republic and emigrating to the U.S.

DAVID BOTTOMS, who teaches at Georgia State University, is the author of *In a U-Haul North of Damascus* and *Shooting Rats at the Bibb County Dump*, for which he won the Walt Whitman prize.

MARGERY FINN BROWN lives in Berkeley, California. Her stories have appeared in numerous national magazines.

C. TERRY CLINE, JR., lives in Fairhope, Alabama, with his wife, novelist Judith Richards. His novels include *Damon*, *Death Knell*, *Cross Current*, *Mind Reader*, *The Attorney Conspiracy*, *Missing Persons*, and *Prey*.

CHARLIE DANIELS is known to many as a country-music superstar. His story-telling ability is also evident in *The Devil Went Down to Georgia*, his first collection of stories.

ANNIE DILLARD is a poet, essayist, and fiction writer. Her *Pilgrim at Tinker Creek*, winner of the Pulitzer Prize, is one of the most highly acclaimed and frequently anthologized works of the seventies.

STEPHEN DIXON, one of America's most prolific short-story writers, has published three novels, the most recent *Fall and Rise*, and five collections of stories. He teaches in the writing program at Johns Hopkins. His awards include fellowships from the Guggenheim Foundation and the National Endowment for the Arts, and a Literature Award from the American Academy and Institute for Arts and Letters.

DONALD HALL writes poetry, prose, plays, children's books, and criticism. He has also edited more than a dozen anthologies and served as poetry editor or consultant for *Paris Review*, Wesleyan University Press, and Harper and Row. His awards include the Lamont and Edna St. Vincent Millay prizes and two Guggenheims.

LINDA GRACE HOYER publishes regularly in various national magazines. Her character Ada appears in another Christmas story, "The Papier-Mâché Santa Claus," first published in the December 27, 1976 issue of *The New Yorker*.

GARRISON KEILLOR, a native of Minnesota, is the founder of the national movement for shy rights. He now lives in St. Paul, from where his radio show, "A Prairie Home Companion," originates on Saturday evenings. His books, *Happy to Be Here* and *Lake Wobegon Days*, have both been bestsellers.

BOBBIE ANN MASON is the author of *Shiloh and Other Stories*, winner of the Ernest Hemingway Foundation Award for the most distinguished first-published work of fiction in 1982. In 1984 she received an award to encourage new writers from the American Academy and Institute for Arts and Letters. Her first novel, *In Country*, was published in 1985.

HELEN NORRIS, a resident of Montgomery, Alabama, has written three novels. *The Christmas Wife*, her first collection of stories, was nominated for the Pen/Faulkner Award for Fiction in 1986.

TILLIE OLSEN is one of two American women featured in a *New Masses* cartoon of prominent authors attending the American Writers Conference in 1935. Throughout her long and distinguished career she has made literature out of the lives of working-class people. Robert Coles observed that "Everything Tillie Olsen has written has become almost immediately a classic."

DON RUSS teaches at Kennesaw College in Marietta, Georgia. His poems have appeared in numerous literary magazines, including *Poem*, *The Lyric*, *The Chattahoochee Review*, and *The Plains Poetry Journal*, as well as in the anthology *Men Talk*.

EVE SHELNUTT is the author of *The Love Child* and *The Formal Voice*, both story collections, and a book of poems, *Air and Salt*.

Her third book of short stories, *The Musician*, will be published in 1986. She teaches at the University of Pittsburgh.

LOUISE SHIVERS, author of the highly acclaimed novel *Here to Get My Baby Out of Jail*, is writer-in-residence at Augusta College. In 1986 she received a fellowship from the National Endowment for the Arts.

WILL STANTON, a World War II glider pilot, has been a full-time freelance writer for thirty-five years, contributing to magazines ranging from *Reader's Digest* to *McCall's* to *Sports Illustrated*. He is also the author of three books and a Walt Disney film.

MARK STEADMAN, writer-in-residence at Clemson University, is the author of *McAfee County* and *A Lion's Share*. He has twice been a Fulbright lecturer and has received a fellowship from the National Endowment for the Arts.

TOM TURNER published his first short story, "Sore-Tail Cats," in the fall 1969 *Georgia Review*. Since then he has written for *Intro, Rolling Stone, Sandlapper*, and *Southern Living*, among others. He also collaborated with Edward Albee on the play *Scenes from a Non-Marriage*.

JOHN UPDIKE, whom John Cheever called "the most brilliant and versatile writer of his generation," publishes fiction, poetry, and essays. Among his numerous awards are a Guggenheim, the Rosenthal Award, a National Book Award, and an O. Henry Prize.

ROBERT PENN WARREN was named America's first poet laureate in 1986. One of our most distinguished men of letters, he is the only author to have won the Pulitzer Prize in both poetry and fiction. The list of his other awards, his honorary degrees, and his major works runs pages in any literary reference book. Since his first publication in 1929, he has steadily built a body of work that makes him perhaps our greatest living author.

JOAN WILLIAMS began her literary career as a winner of the *Mademoiselle* College Fiction Contest in 1949. Her first novel, *The*

Morning and the Evening, won the John P. Marquand First Novel Award. Her fiction often deals with isolated and alienated characters in rural Mississippi. Her other works include *The Wintering* and *Pariah and Other Stories*.

ACKNOWLEDGMENTS

"The Boy Shepherds' Simile" from *In a U-Haul North of Damascus* (1983) by David Bottoms. Copyright © 1981, 1982 by Modern Poetry Association. By permission of William Morrow & Company.

Excerpt from *Lake Wobegon Days* by Garrison Keillor. Copyright © Garrison Keillor, 1985. Reprinted by permission of Viking Penguin, Inc.

"A Privileged Character" by Louise Shivers. Copyright © 1983 by Louise Shivers. Reprinted by permission.

"An American Surprise" by Julia Alvarez. Copyright © 1985 by Julia Alvarez. Reprinted by permission.

"A Carolina Christmas Carol" from *The Devil Went Down to Georgia* by Charlie Daniels. Copyright © 1985 by Charlie Daniels. Reprinted by permission of Peachtree Publishers, Ltd.

"Blue Bethlehem" by Tom Turner. Copyright © 1983 by Tom Turner. Reprinted by permission.

"New Acquaintances" by Margery Finn Brown. Copyright © 1983 by Meredith Publications, Inc. Reprinted by permission of the author and *Ladies' Home Journal*.

"A Christmas Story" by Stephen Dixon. Copyright © 1986 by Stephen Dixon. Reprinted by permission.

"Going Ahead" from *Pariah and Other Stories* by Joan Williams. Copyright © 1983 by Joan Williams. Reprinted by permission of Little, Brown and Company in association with The Atlantic Monthly Press.

"The Carol Sing" from *Museums and Women and Other Stories* by John Updike. Copyright © 1970 by John Updike. Reprinted by permission of Alfred A. Knopf, Inc.

"I Am Dreaming of a White Christmas: The Natural History of a Vision" from *Selected Poems 1923-1975* by Robert Penn Warren.

Copyright © 1973 by Robert Penn Warren. Reprinted by permission of Random House, Inc.

"Partridges, 1950" by Eve Shelnutt. Copyright © 1986 by Eve Shelnutt. Reprinted by permission.

Excerpt from *The Broken Door: An Autobiographical Fiction* by Mark Steadman. Copyright © 1976 by Mark Steadman. Originally appeared in slightly altered form in the November, 1976, *South Carolina Review.* Reprinted by permission.

Donald Hall's "Christmas Snow" reprinted by permission. Copyright © 1964, *The New Yorker* Magazine, Inc.

Linda Grace Hoyer's "Solace" reprinted by permission. Copyright © 1983 by Linda Grace Hoyer. Originally in *The New Yorker.*

"The Trail of Ernestine" by Will Stanton. Copyright © 1975 by Meredith Publications, Inc. Reprinted by permission of the author and *Ladies' Home Journal*.

"Feast Days: Christmas" from *Tickets for a Prayer Wheel* by Annie Dillard. Copyright © 1974 by Annie Dillard. Reprinted by permission of the University of Missouri Press.

"Epiphany" by C. Terry Cline, Jr. Copyright © 1986. Reprinted by permission.

"Dream-Vision" from *Mother to Daughter, Daughter to Mother: A Daybook and Reader* selected and shaped by Tillie Olsen. Copyright © 1984 by Tillie Olsen. Reprinted by permission of the author and The Feminist Press at The City University of New York.

"The Christmas Wife" from *The Christmas Wife* by Helen Norris. Copyright © 1985 by Helen Norris. Reprinted by permission of the author and the University of Illinois Press.

"Drawing Names" from *Shiloh: And Other Stories* by Bobbie Ann Mason. Copyright © 1982 by Bobbie Ann Mason. Reprinted by permission of Harper & Row, Publishers, Inc.

"The Winter Heart" by Don Russ. Copyright © 1986 by Don Russ. Reprinted by permission.